Jews, Myth and History

A critical exploration of contemporary Jewish belief and its origins

Jews, Myth and History

A critical exploration of contemporary Jewish belief and its origins

Alan Silver

Matador
9 De Montfort Mews
Leicester LE1 7FW, UK
Tel: (+44) 116 255 9311 / 9312
Email: books@troubador.co.uk
Web: www.troubador.co.uk/matador

ISBN 978-1848760-646

Email: JewsMythandHistory@gmail.com

Printed by TJ International Ltd, Padstow, Cornwall, UK

Matador is an imprint of Troubador Publishing Ltd

In memory of

Anthony Elchanan (Tony) Chuwen

אנטוני אלחנן חובן ז"ל

1924-2004

Contents

Acknowledgements

The first people that must be thanked are those that have travelled this road, or parts of it, before. Cumulatively they have become my teachers, stimulating my curiosity in the subjects I discuss. Those (sadly too many) who are no longer with us, live on. The ideas they have planted in the brains of their students have rooted and taken on new life, cross breeding with ideas planted by others.

On a personal level, I must start by thanking my wife, Gloria, not only for her support and indulgence as I disappeared into my study for extended periods but also her clarity of thought when discussing these topics with me. She too was responsible for my meeting her special father, Tony Chuwen. Tony, to whose memory this book is dedicated, is mentioned in the introduction so I will just note here that he would recognise much of the content from discussions we had down the years.

Three friends in particular deserve special thanks, as without their knowledge and professional skills there would be no book. Aviva Hay has been a constant encouragement throughout this project, and a continuous ray of sunshine. This sunshine and her hard work have helped the book finally to see the light of day. Despite her heavy work schedule, she somehow always made time available. Anthya Sadeh was kind enough to proofread the manuscript, going well beyond her professional duty in suggesting improvements. The errors that remain are entirely mine. My childhood friend, Rodney Falk, who is alluded to in the introduction was kind enough to read a late draft of the manuscript, aware that our opinions on matters religious had long since diverged. His knowledge of the Orthodox Jewish world was invaluable. He was extremely helpful in putting the other side of arguments and, in several cases, the text has been amended to take account of his ideas. I must stress that he bears no responsibility for the opinions that remain.

This book has really been an international effort. A favourite writing spot was the seclusion of Jenny and Jonny Nelson's garden in Jerusalem, so thanks to them for their hospitality and to everyone else who has helped this project, whether in Llandewi Brefi, Evn Yehuda, Boston, New York or London.

Introduction

*You have your way. I have my way. As for the right way, the correct way,
and the only way, it does not exist*

Nietzsche

J ews, Myth and History is the provisional result of a long personal
journey. For Jews today, who were born in the shadow of the
Holocaust, it may be hard to reconcile issues such as ethics, morality
and truth with the role of religion in history. Many of us have also
struggled with some of the doctrines we were given when growing up.
In this book, I aim to provide an overview of Judaism today. I will
examine critically some of the core beliefs and traditional practices. To
make sense of this information a background and context is necessary,
so first I will look afresh at the origins of both the Jews and their most
important sacred text, the Hebrew Bible or *Tanach*. As will become
clear, the early history of both is quite different to the traditional view.
A better understanding of how the religion developed should help the
reader to re-evaluate Jewish concepts and to compare them with the
many different ideas circulating in today's multi-cultural world.

The conception of this book can be traced to the 1960's, when as a
teenager brought up in a small community in England among
traditional nominally orthodox Jews, I visited Jerusalem and spent a
short time in the world of the ultra-orthodox. Rather than being
seduced by their lifestyle, I was troubled by aspects of it and had a
growing list of unanswered questions. On my return, I debated these in

letters exchanged with a close friend who remained in Israel and took the more observant path. Thus began a life long journey towards understanding the issues that are presented in these pages.

After qualifying as a dentist, I spent a year in Israel. Returning during the Yom Kippur War of 1973, I met Gloria and fell in love. This led to me meeting her father, Tony Chuwen, a most remarkable man who, like his daughter, has been hugely influential in my life and also in the thinking that has led to this book. He too was Jewish to his core, but had no place in his life for dogma.

Tony was a Holocaust survivor who, having been in two Nazi camps, bravely escaped. He jumped from a moving train transporting him to an unknown destination. He then 'hid' on false Catholic papers, taking the high risk strategy of joining the German army. He deserted as soon as he had the chance, making a daring escape by sea to Finland, where he was interned. He escaped once more, beating the odds and skiing across the frozen Gulf of Bothnia to Sweden where, at last, he was able to join up to fight on the right side.

These few sentences only skim the surface of his remarkable early life, but what made him stand out from all the other survivors of my acquaintance was his enormous inner strength. Despite the murder of his entire family (43 individuals) and following experiences beyond anything we can imagine both in the camps and after, he retained his humanity and integrity throughout his life. He also never lost his interest and curiosity in everything the world had to offer. Over the years, we had many fascinating discussions on almost all of the issues covered by this book.

I think it is both curiosity and scepticism that have fed my own interest in religion through the years. I have always been interested in travelling off the beaten track, first visiting the Far East in 1972, when I travelled alone overland along the famous 'hippie trail'. This linked Turkey, Iran, Afghanistan, Pakistan, India and the highlight of Kathmandu in the then almost secret Kingdom of Nepal. On this trip, I had my first real exposure to eastern religion and also to Zoroastrianism and Islam. Since then it has been a constant when travelling (now with Gloria who shares my curiosity) to try and find out about the local customs and religions and to visit holy sites and places of worship.

Observing the similarities and differences between religions led me to reading widely, trying always to relate new knowledge to my own Jewish roots. I was fascinated by the integration of the gods into daily life in the East and by the spirituality of some of those my upbringing had labelled pagan. I became interested in the origins of religion in general and naturally of Judaism in particular, and so began to follow developments in biblical archæology. When I retired from dental practice, I had more time available to pursue these interests. Not finding any book that tied together all the related themes that interest me (which include history, theology, mythology, archæology, philosophy, sociology, anthropology and psychology) and which combine to build the picture of how Judaism became what it is today, I found myself putting pen to paper.

The teachers and authors whom I admire most and seek out are those who can make connections across the different disciplines. Some academics are much too compartmentalised for my taste. I claim only the expertise of an interested layman in any of these fields of study and apologise to specialists who feel that I am trampling ignorantly into their fiefdoms. They will no doubt find my survey of their personal field superficial as it is my intention here to give an overview of the relevant areas of these disparate subjects and to point any reader who is interested in deeper exploration of a particular topic to my selection from the voluminous literature and academic works. My justification for taking such a multi-disciplinary approach is that all these subjects actually concern themselves with different aspects of our human story, and it is the entire story which continues to fascinate me.

The life of most Jews today bears little resemblance to the traditional pattern of their ancestors a mere century ago, and a century is a short period in the history of the Jews. Our knowledge and understanding of Jewish history has also increased dramatically during this time. This is particularly true of the early period before the arrival of the Greeks, for which we formerly had no context at all outside of the Bible's accounts and for which archæologists, historians and philologists[1] have now given us a wealth of new information. We now also understand so much more about the Bible and the process by which it reached the form we have today.

---

[1] *Philologists are those who study language, texts and inscriptions and who by their decoding of ancient languages have done so much to enhance our understanding of the ancient near east.*

This recent knowledge is taken for granted both in academic circles and among those with an interest in these matters, who seek it out. It is much less known among the majority of Jews whose main sources of information are the synagogue and sacred texts. Some topics surface from time to time in controversies between the different Jewish communities but this generally leads to a point scoring type of debate rather than a more objective examination of the evidence.

In part one of this book I offer an overview of this updated understanding of Jewish history and look at both the role of myth and the importance of reading a sacred text appropriately. The chapters discuss:

1. **Origin of religion:** I begin by looking back into prehistory to examine how our species' religious impulse translated itself into the development of religions worldwide. I also consider how religion differs from spirituality.

2. **Myth, history and the sacred; How to read a sacred text:** I discuss how myth and history have combined over time with ideas of the sacred. One result of this process is our principal sacred text, the Hebrew Bible. I consider the difference in approach necessary for understanding such a text in comparison to its profane or everyday, equivalents and contend that the misreading of sacred texts can be a key driver of fundamentalism within all of the monotheistic religions.

3. **Jewish origins:** Accounts of the history of the Jewish people have traditionally been taken straight from the pages of the Bible. This however is not, and never was, a history book in the modern sense. This chapter takes a historical, evidence-based approach to the origin of the Jews in order to try and tell this intriguing story as it may have actually happened. It is a very different story from the one most Jews are familiar with, but one that is no less fascinating.

4. **Myth and its functions:** A key theme of this book is myth, and how the use of myth is important to help us deal with our everyday human needs. Myth acts as a support package validating our place in society, our psychological and spiritual well-being and provides us with a model for how the universe operates (known

as a cosmology). Worldwide, the most widely used source of such a support package is religion.

I look at the various cosmologies on which different human societies have depended. Perhaps surprisingly, throughout history there only appear to have been five essentially different ones. One is the Jewish view, and this and the four alternative ideas are described for the reader to compare.

With this appreciation of how human belief in the divine developed, and how humanity's search for a relationship with the divine world evolved, the book now moves on to address the result of these ideas as filtered through Jewish history into contemporary Jewish beliefs and practice.

The second part of the book concentrates on beliefs and considers some topics that are basic to the Jewish belief system. This can be thought of as the theory of Judaism, which although important has traditionally been considered less so than observance and practice which will be looked at in part three. These issues of belief are often ones for which a set of answers is 'taken in with the mother's milk' and then seldom questioned later in life. My aim is to point out that these matters are not actually set in stone and that non-traditional responses may also be worth evaluating. These are the issues to be considered in each chapter:

5. **Who wrote the Torah?** Traditionally this was God in heaven who dictated it verbatim to Moses, a concept known as *Torah min hashamayim,* but today it has become clear that much help was given here on Earth. We look at the evidence and make an approach to understand the real history of this hugely important text. The contents of this chapter may still be controversial in the fastnesses of Orthodox Judaism, but evidence that the Torah is actually the result of the work of several human authors is overwhelming and no longer even controversial to anyone amenable to evidence. Of course, the belief that these authors were writing under Divine influence still remains a valid personal choice.

Divine Revelation: The whole concept that some humans receive direct instruction from supernatural beings is controversial. The problems that this raises are considered here.

6. **One God or many:** Is monotheism really a superior belief system in every way as Jews are brought up to believe, or could polytheistic belief deal with some issues better? Monotheists with open minds may be challenged by this chapter.

   Idol worship: What is an idol, and what does idol worship really entail? Can Jews be guilty of it too? A look at symbols, how to interpret them and the dangers of getting this wrong.

7. **Chosen people:** The whole idea of one group being a chosen people is fraught with philosophical problems. These issues are considered and then an attempt is made to assess the concept by putting it in context. This is done by taking an overview of the amazing universe we inhabit and at the Jews' allocated place within it. A universe, we must remember, held to have been created by the same God who chose the Jews. The description may challenge the reader's faith in this whole idea.

8. **Divine justice and the presence of evil in the world:** The age old problem of reconciling Divine justice and evil has defeated the wisest sages of the monotheistic religions. I look at the responses of Judaism to the theological challenge of the Shoah (the Nazi Holocaust) and also survey the responses to evil and suffering by other religions and philosophies. This is a brief overview from a Jewish perspective of a fascinating subject on which libraries of books have been written.

As already mentioned, for Judaism, in contrast to many religions, practice is held to be far more important than dogma or belief. With this in mind, in part three of the book I move on to look at some of the difficulties I have with how some people actually practise their Judaism. Here I am looking at traditional unreformed practice within the orthodox and ultra-orthodox sectors of the religion.

To some extent twenty-first century Judaism has become polarised. To the surprise of many people who thought that 'old fashioned religion' was in terminal decline and that secularism would win the day, the traditional orthodox segment is actually alive and well and probably the only Jewish group that is growing. This may be due to its very conservative nature, its high birth rate and to some extent its outreach work. It may also be, in some way, a reaction to the Shoah. The orthodox sector actually covers a wide range of views including the mediæval, the messianic and the modern. Although many among the modern orthodox will engage to some degree with the issues I discuss, others will not, and so for simplicity I will consider the orthodox and ultra-orthodox as a single group.

At the opposite pole in the Jewish world are secular Jews who cannot accept revealed religious dogma or the monarchical Jewish God, but retain a strong affinity - even faithfulness - towards Jewish culture and ethical values, along with shared historical memories and traditions. I count myself among this group.

Inhabiting the middle ground are a complete spectrum of Jewish groups that seek to reconcile the Jewish belief system with the facts of history and science and the realities of the modern world. These include Conservative, Reform, Liberal, Masorti, Reconstructionist, and a plethora of smaller groups. To varying degrees, these groups continue the evolution of Judaism but their weakness is that they also fragment it. One of the strongest Jewish traditions is that of difference of opinion. These groups embody this with their many opinions on how fast and deep Judaism's evolution should be. Nevertheless, despite their differences, they have generally responded effectively to the issues discussed here.

Even so, it remains valuable to examine orthodox practice, for remnants of some of these problems still retain influence and even in more liberal circles can lurk beneath the surface. These matters are also important because when non Jews think of Jewish practice, it is often that of the orthodox which comes to mind. Additionally, it is typically from those influenced by this group that dangerous fundamentalists spring.

As the word fundamentalist will come up time and again, I will define what I mean by it. I apply this term to describe those people who are closed-minded and not amenable to rational argument. Essentially these are people who know the 'truth' both for themselves and for all of us. This is discussed in more detail in Chapters 5 and 6 and a simple test is described there to determine if someone's views are indeed fundamentalist.

Returning to section three and the question of Orthodox Jewish practice, chapter by chapter, I will consider:

9. **Ethics, tolerance, and compassion:** We expect these attributes from followers of a religion, especially from those who make practice of religion central to their lives. All too often, they are hard to find among the strictly observant. In their place we sometimes discover excessive pietism and the use and abuse of the emotion of guilt to keep others in line.

10. **Torah True Judaism:** Orthodox Jews generally say that the religious law they follow is based on that of the Torah. They also claim to be very much against moral relativism, which allows laws to be modified along with changing circumstances and ideas. In practice, the situation is somewhat different and an understanding of this may produce some surprises. This chapter poses a key question for the reader: 'Should morality be based on ethics or on an ancient law code?'

11. **Treatment of women:** How women are, still today, discriminated against in many Orthodox Jewish communities. The ultra-orthodox, in particular, continue to live in a patriarchal society.

12. **Superstition and magic:** A look at superstition and belief in magic, which is still strongly entrenched within the orthodox community.

    Kabbalah has become very fashionable even among non-believers. To understand its origins and what it stands for, I look briefly at its history and give an overview of some of its main ideas. Again, libraries have been written on this topic, although many of the books describe things far removed from the Jewish roots of kabbalistic ideas.

The themes of ***myth*** and ***truth*** are either explicit or implicit in much of this book, and both merit close attention. Myth is much misunderstood and sometimes wrongly denigrated in modern thought. It is in fact an essential part of the human experience and so fundamental that it features in the title of this book.

Myth often comes 'packaged' in the form of a religion but non-believers can and do make up their own mythic package (see Chapter 4). Historically the vast majority of human beings have simply taken on the mythic package of their parents and handed it, essentially unchanged, to their children. We all appear to need such a set of ground rules in order to function properly in the world. For an individual, their personal mythic structure may remain constant throughout life or be in a state of continuous change or development.

Many people consider the meaning of myth and truth along the lines of:

'Myth is other people's religion, truth is what I believe.'

The underlying reality shows that myth is universal – and that we all rely on it to a greater extent than some of us wish to acknowledge. The concept of myth is discussed in some detail in Chapter 2. As for 'truth', Chapter 6 discusses how it becomes a danger when individuals know they possess it, not just for themselves but for everyone else. These are people that I defined earlier as fundamentalist. However closed-minded they are, I contend that they must still be allowed the freedom to choose to wear blinkers and live in a world of banned books and rigid ideas.

What I feel is essential, however, is that all who do question should have access to the fruits of human knowledge in the same way that they need access to air, water and food. This does create problems in educating the children of fundamentalists and governments need to be strong in safeguarding the rights of these children to receive at least a minimum level of secular education.

While my focus is on Judaism, I also try and look at religion in general, primarily from a philosophical point of view. Religion and philosophy differ not so much in scope as in method. A successful religion develops dogma and traditions which are upheld by followers who can feel threatened by any attempt to make radical changes in them.

By contrast, philosophy has free enquiry as its lifeblood and the greatest philosophers have typically felt it necessary to build their ideas anew from first principles. While admitting that there are some conservative philosophers and a few radical theologians, it is still fair to say that for religion, salvation lies in unexamined faith, for philosophy, in examined truth. Religion has, with some justification, been described as fossilised philosophy or philosophy with the questions left out.[2]

A good philosopher is one who is constantly seeking to get closer to the truth with regard to such issues as how it is best to live and what morality is. A good Orthodox Jew is one who has already found that truth, as revealed by God and interpreted by man. Religion is seductive in appearing to have the answers and in offering an unambiguous code by which to live. In many cases, for a believer all moral questions have already been resolved, often down to the smallest detail.

Those who question more are usually wary of accepting a religious 'package'. Indeed, they think it unlikely that they will ever arrive at a final conclusion on certain issues or that a definitive truth even exists. They have found few, if any, rules that are fixed for all times, places and circumstances, and no ready-made set of answers that is easy to accept. Sets of answers, however, are not difficult to come by – each religion has one - but none of them seems to stand up to the further questions that the truth seeker then asks. This writing ultimately concerns itself with the difficulties I find with the set of answers provided by Orthodox Judaism, and will, I hope, be of interest to open-minded Jews prepared to question these issues.

This difference in approach between religion and philosophy has been aptly, if somewhat tritely, summarised:[3]

> *Philosophy is questions that may never be answered.*
> *Religion is answers which may never be questioned.*

It is, in my opinion, the inquiry and the continuing search that opens our minds. Today, rather than religion, it can often be the arts which continue to pose the eternal questions in original ways, and by so doing sometimes give us deeper insights.

---

[2] *Simon Blackburn. 'Plato's Republic – A Biography.' Atlantic Books 2006*
[3] *A traditional quotation; anonymous.*

Study of archæology and world history shows that religion has been an inseparable part of human society from the earliest times for which we have evidence. We know of no society in which it has not been present in one form or another, and so it appears to answer a fundamental need of our human psyche. Atheists, although they may not have always called themselves that, also have a long history – but they have never held the centre ground. For most people there seems to have always been a need to believe in or to create gods, as was demonstrated amusingly by Lucretius in the first century BCE.[4] As an admirer of Epicurus, he congratulated him on emancipating humanity from fear of the gods, and then proceeded to erect a statue to the 'Divine Epicurus'.

Buddhism shows this conflict too. Although Buddhist philosophy has no place for god(s), the popular Buddhist temples contain huge statues of the Buddha, who is treated as a god, along with statues of many minor and personal deities. Only the intellectual elite seem able to maintain the Buddha's teaching. On a popular level, it appears that people need their god(s). It can be argued that for very many people supernatural beings are the only plausible source of certain benefits they earnestly desire and also the only way of making sense of their place in the world.

Dogmatic atheists, such as Richard Dawkins, make many good and valid points in their arguments against gods and religion, but they do seem to have a blind spot concerning the psychological and spiritual needs of many people. Possibly this aspect of religion does not interest them. Their case is indisputable on scientific issues such as the theory of evolution and the arguments put forward by creationists to obfuscate this are simply laughable. Nevertheless, I consider such questions to be essentially side issues for, as Wittgenstein said, all scientific issues could be resolved, yet there would still be unanswered questions for religion to propose answers to.

Science is not designed or equipped to answer metaphysical questions - that is not its role. Our psyches appear to be programmed to try and find meanings which can explain events and to seek to understand the actions of the causative agent we believe to be underlying them. This seems to be true even for events that can actually be demonstrated to be quite random. Most of us appear to have a need to feel a part of

---

[4]*This book uses the religiously neutral abbreviations BCE (Before the Common Era) and CE (Common Era)*

some wider cosmic plan, and religion is to some extent an expression of that need.

Dawkins goes on to make more extreme claims, such as a religious upbringing being a form of child-abuse. These claims may indeed have a degree of validity among religious fundamentalists who do not allow their children a general education or access to the riches of the world's knowledge. They are unfair, however, on the very many practitioners of liberal forms of religion. For all sorts of reasons many people have reached different conclusions about fundamental issues, including belief in God or faithfulness to a religious tradition, from both Dawkins and myself. As long as they do not seek to impose these views on others then they must be allowed freedom to exercise their choice. If, through free enquiry, they are persuaded by our arguments or we by theirs then I contend that all is well. Dawkins seems reluctant to allow this freedom – pressuring all to follow the dogma of atheism.

There is, without doubt, an aspect of human life that science alone cannot address. It is called variously the spiritual, the transcendent, or the numinous. Certainly, these are airy-fairy terms for complex concepts which are hard to define but they refer to a significant aspect of many people's time on Earth. We may only experience the spiritual, the transcendent or the numinous fleetingly and infrequently during our lifetime, but there is no doubt that such experiences occur, and they are often considered to be key moments in people's lives. They need not necessarily be seen as religious experiences, certainly not in the sense of organised religion. We may call them instead love, mystery, inspiration, or the human spirit. Indeed, as already mentioned, I consider that for those who reject religion the arts can often be the most helpful in interpreting this aspect of our inner life. As examples, good fiction can pose eternal questions in original ways and beautiful music can transport many to another place.

Good religious literature, like good secular literature and other works of art, is true in a mythic sense. What this means is that such works resonate within us and open us up to the spiritual and the humanitarian aspects of our life. This search for spirituality accounts for the success of eastern philosophies, such as Buddhism, in filling the void for many refugees from the monotheistic religions.

While eastern thought, like Judaism, contains much of value, it too can suffer from the danger of all religious doctrines, that of telling the initiate what to believe and how to live. I would contend that the really wise gurus of the East are those who teach that there are no answers that can be taught, we must all work it out for ourselves. There are such people although they are few and far between.

Arguably, it is the sense of the numinous that has led to the more human, more caring, more truly religious events of history. It is not just coincidence that places a version of the Golden Rule in the writings of most religions and philosophical systems.[5] However, historically there have been only a few exceptional individuals in positions of power who have put the Golden Rule into practice, and acted as role models for us all.

Many of the issues I discuss, while addressed from a Jewish perspective, are equally pertinent to other religions, in particular the monotheistic ones. The misreading of myth and metaphor and the lack of tolerance and compassion for anyone of different opinion is just as evident among Jewish settlers on the West Bank, Christian creationists and Islamic fundamentalists.

I feel it important to give evidence for the claims I make, but this more detailed information will not interest everyone. Where a simple clarification, a reference or extra detail is appropriate I use footnotes on the same page. Where lists or charts are more helpful in summarizing information, I have generally removed them to the appendix.

I will try and deal rationally with that modern problem of the English language, the sexual bias of pronouns. This is additionally complex where gods are involved, as deities are often predominantly one gender or the other. Where a god is traditionally male I will retain the male form; for a goddess the female. Where there is ambiguity I will try and show it even if it leads to an inevitable clumsiness. The Jewish God of tradition is, in this context, undoubtedly male.

When quoting from the *Tanach* or Talmud I usually include the original Hebrew for the benefit of those who are able to avoid the perils of

---

[5] *Expressed at its simplest the Golden Rule says, 'love your neighbour as yourself'. See the Appendix p.223 for details of the Golden Rule in various religions and philosophies.*

translation, the English is my own version of the classic Jewish Publication Society 1917 translation, updated for clarity. Foreign words that are not commonly used in English appear in *italics* and are explained either in the text or a footnote on first appearance. Those that recur are also listed in a glossary at the end, along with some technical words that could not be avoided.

Dates are another problem. I try to include sufficient of them for the reader to keep abreast of the passage of time. For anyone lost, there is a more detailed timeline to refer to in the appendix. I use the designators BCE and CE to distinguish events before and during the Common Era in preference to the traditional Christian BC and AD.

Part one

The background of religion, myth and Judaism

1

The Origins of Religion

Religions are different roads converging to the same point. What does it matter that we take different roads, as long as we reach the same goal? In reality there are as many religions as there are individuals. Mankind is one.

Mahatma Ghandi

Religion of one sort or another appears to be integral to humanity; indeed there is evidence of religion among early members of the genus *Homo* even long before the evolution of *Homo sapiens*. The consensus of opinion is that the development of consciousness brought with it an awareness of the transience, fragility and dangers of life and of the inevitability of one's death. The human psyche had to be able to cope with this knowledge, which could otherwise be disabling and so, perhaps, religion began as a coping mechanism.

The earliest sign found so far that can be interpreted as religious activity was among our ancestor *Homo erectus*[1] and dates from about 500,000 BCE. Stone tools have been found that were made in sizes too large to be of any practical use. These must have been produced either for beauty, decoration or ritual purposes and are the earliest evidence so far found of the 'human spirit'.

---

[1] *Homo erectus lived between 1,600,000 and 75,000 BCE. Homo neanderthalensis (Neanderthal man) lived from about 500,000 to 30,000 BCE.*

Neanderthal man was next to evolve. The first proper worship site so far discovered was among late Neanderthals and has been dated to around 60,000 BCE. It is a cave in which bear skulls were worshipped.[2] From the same period, we have the first evidence of ceremonial human burial, a further sign of developing ritual and spirituality.[3]

In about 40,000 BCE modern humans, *Homo sapiens* evolved. Dating from 30,000 BCE, figurines have been found in central Europe which appear to represent fertility goddesses. By 16,000 BCE, there is evidence of the existence of a rich culture, evidenced by the great decorated caves near the Pyrenees.

As human beings developed, major changes in their lifestyle significantly affected their mythology. This is illustrated for us by the artefacts they left behind. In the cave paintings the mythology of the hunter predominates. This period of the hunter gatherer seems to be the time when people were in awe of the elements, especially the sky, and possibly first developed a sense of the numinous. They came up with the idea of a remote sky god or high god who created everything single-handedly. Such gods are still found by anthropologists among today's aboriginal people. A sky god seems to have been too remote to be approached by people on day to day basis, but was turned to by people in crisis situations. Modern tribal elders concur, saying this god cannot be contacted and can have no direct dealings with the world of human beings.

In later mythology the sky god is often said to have gone away or disappeared. The sky gods of the ancient Mesopotamians, Vedic Indians, Greeks and Canaanites all dwindled in the mythology of their people, and were replaced by more accessible deities such as Indra, Enlil and Baal. Stories have even come down to us about how the sky god was deposed.[4] Although the sky god itself disappeared until its return with the advent of monotheism, the sky and high places never lost their power as symbols of the sacred. Myths of holy mountains and of the ascent of holy men were (and are) almost universal.

---

[2] *Found in Switzerland. The Ainu in Japan still worship the bear.*
[3] *Earliest ceremonial burial was found on Mount Carmel, Israel. The cadaver was buried in the foetal position.*
[4] *For example, Ouranos the Greek sky god was castrated by his son Kronos.*

Among hunting people shamans developed who were considered able (when in their trances) to ascend to heaven and communicate with the gods. The hunters retained great reverence for the animals they killed, and the shaman was also considered to be able to communicate with the animals and to help them be reconciled to their deaths.

A major change to impact human life, and thus religion, was the beginning of agriculture from around 8,000 BCE.[5] Just as hunting had been regarded as a sacred pursuit, this role was now taken on by farming. Fertility was a gift of the gods and concepts of Mother Earth abound. The Earth seemed to sustain all life, whether plant, animal or human, as in a living womb. Rituals such as sacrifice developed as a means of giving something back to the Earth and to recycle the sacred energies.

Offerings of plants, animals and even, in some societies, humans were made. Human sexuality was regarded as another example of divinely given fertility and so human intercourse was often considered to be a divine act that would aid the fertility of the crops. The harvest was seen as the fruit of a sacred marriage between the female soil and the seeds' divine semen, with rain a sign of the sexual congress between heaven and Earth. Ritual sex, on planting crops would therefore help improve the chance of a good harvest. In many societies Mother Earth was transformed into a mother goddess. Where she had a male consort, at this stage, the goddess was almost always the senior partner.

Around 4,000 BCE another significant development in human lifestyle occurred with the beginning of cities.[6] Fresh myths were needed to help people cope with this change to an urban lifestyle. A new fear was the return of the old barbarism, as cities that had been slowly developed with much hard work were sometimes destroyed almost overnight by violence of one kind or another. These new myths meditated on the endless struggle between order and chaos. There was a pantheon of gods, who (in the image of humans) lived in their divine societies and always had to struggle against evil divine forces that tried to bring chaos to their order. These gods, although they were the creators of humans, did not interact with them and were seen as remote.

---

[5] We mark this by changing at 8000 BCE from the Palaeolithic to the Neolithic Period.
[6] Again this is marked with a change of archaeological age at 4000 BCE from the Neolithic to the Chalcolithic.

China was an exception to this general pattern. In China, the sky god, known as Di or Tian, persisted even though there too the people found the god remote and felt the need for intermediaries. Rather than a pantheon of lesser gods, their early religion adopted ancestor worship. Individuals worshipped their own ancestors who, they believed, had gone to the sky after death and from there could act as intercessors on behalf of their descendents left behind on Earth.

Then in a significant development, from the Shang dynasty (c. 1600-1100 BCE) onwards a new myth developed. This explained that the king's legitimacy derived from the 'fact' that he alone had access to the sky god Di/Tian, and so he was the earthly counterpart of god. He was the intermediary to the remote god on high. This belief became established and, having been integrated into later philosophies, persisted in China until as recently as a century ago when it was nullified by the revolution of 1911.[7]

This brief survey can only deal with general trends; along the way, there were many fascinating local variations. As an example, ancient Egypt had a pantheon of gods but the ruler, Pharaoh, rather than being an intermediary to them, was himself divine and so a full member of the pantheon.

As societies developed and became more organised and stable, city dwellers appear to have become disillusioned with these distant deities, and yet another transformation occurred. This seems to have happened more or less simultaneously in many parts of the world during what has been called the axial age (c. 800-200 BCE). This marks the beginning of religion as we know it. New religious and philosophical systems developed: Confucianism and Taoism in China, Buddhism and Hinduism in India, dualism and monotheism in the Middle East and Greek rationalism in Europe.

Human concerns, such as suffering, are much more to the fore in these new systems which all developed in relatively advanced parts of the world and all of them contain an ethical component. They also introduced such concepts as questioning, of not accepting old ideas on trust.

---

[7] *Its echo, in Japan, the divine Emperor, continued in power until the end of the Second World War.*

The death of gods

As we have seen with the early sky gods, the existence of individual gods is finite. Like humans, they are transient and can be considered as having a life cycle. Their existence is contingent on having advocates here on Earth. An innumerable number of gods have been at the centre of cult and religion and then subsequently disappeared from the pantheon. Some, once powerful with rich temples, many priests and worshippers, and complex rituals devoted solely to them have gone 'the way of all flesh'. They have faded into the obscurity of a footnote in some scholarly work. Others are so completely extinct that no trace of their name or image remains. The argument has been made that gods exist solely within the psyche of those that believe in them and so cease to have an existence when no followers remain. H.L. Mencken made a list of the names of several hundred 'dead gods' such as *Nerbal, Anubis, Addu, Dagon, Manawyddan, Ubilulu, Uhargisi* and many, many more. He then famously asked:

> *Where is the graveyard for the dead gods?*
> *What lingering mourner waters their mounds?*

Life after death – origins of this belief

Moving from gods to humans, the belief in some form of existence beyond death is widespread. It is interesting to trace the development of this idea. The origins of belief in an afterlife are lost in prehistory. The knowledge of one's own impending death created a psychological need for a coping mechanism. Neanderthal remains have been found that were buried with supplies (suggesting a belief in another life beyond the grave) from as early as 60,000 BCE.

Wherever in the world we have evidence of early mythic history, ancestor worship and the concept of the soul are already in evidence. We have little knowledge of actual ritual practice further back than the 4th and 3rd millennia BCE, and at this time there was a division. Megalithic builders from Ireland to the Aegean had confidence in the soul's survival and in its power to protect the living. Their religious practice centred on communing with and sacrificing to their ancestors, whom they believed could provide them with fertility and success. For other peoples of antiquity, such as the Mesopotamians, Hittites and Greeks, the dead were seen as pitiable shades, unhappy and powerless.

With the rise of Egyptian civilisation from about 3,000 BCE, the cult of the dead was developed much more. Already in the Neolithic period,[8] there was a predominant belief in a subterranean underworld for the dead (along with a minority tradition of them dwelling among the stars). The new cult of Osiris, which arose by 2,500 BCE, developed this further. The Osiris story itself was a development of the, by then widespread and wonderful mythology of a murdered god who is resurrected. This mythology was common to Tammuz, Adonis and Dionysus among others at that time, and was much later integrated into the story of Jesus. However, in Egypt around 1,500 BCE, Osiris became the judge of the dead. After death each person had to undergo two acts before judgement, a trial and the weighing of their heart.[9]

Essentially all that later religions have to say about the soul, heaven, hell and the afterlife is based on the development of these ideas, a process known as syncretism. Their route into Judaism can be traced through Zoroastrianism and even Christianity. That they arrived late into Judaism is evidenced by the absence of any mention of the subject in the Torah, and very little mention or allusion to it in the *Tanach*.[10]

Incidentally, in his rejection of the notion that reward and punishment in the world to come was a proper incentive for ethical behaviour during life, Spinoza said that a person believing this:

> '..is like one of those who would follow after his own lusts, if he were not restrained by the fear of hell. He abstains from evil actions and fulfils God's commands like a slave against his will, and for his bondage he expects to be rewarded.'

Heaven and hell have a lesser role in eastern thought, as they are only considered as a staging post before the soul is reincarnated back on Earth (for the vast majority of people who have not managed to achieve release from this endless cycle).

The hero

Many of the religions that developed subsequently had a central hero figure like Osiris. Initially these were fully divine figures but in later

---

[8] *8000 – 4000 BCE*
[9] *This is described in Chapter 25 of the Egyptian Book of the Dead.*
[10] *The episode of Ezekiel and the dry bones is sometimes cited, but if this is read allegorically the allusion here is to the lost Northern tribes.*

religions, the hero appears variously in the guise of a prophet, a partially divine being, a redeemer or a miracle worker. When looked at in terms of myth, all of these heroes follow a certain lifestyle which can be divided into stages. Not all of them go through every stage, but anyone familiar with the life stories of Buddha, Zeus (Mithras and other analogues), Zoroaster, Mahavira, Mani, Moses, Jesus, and Mohammed (plus countless other heroes of now dead religions) will recognise the 'script' and find that the majority of the following apply.

These are the stages in the typical life story of a religious hero.[11]

1. Supernatural or mysterious origins
2. Birth portents
3. Perils in infancy
4. Initiation
5. Revelation from the divine
6. Journey in search of wisdom
7. Contest with demonic powers
8. Miracle-working such as cures, revival of the dead
9. Extreme ethical virtue, and/or wise sayings
10. Conflict with conservative/repressive/civil/religious authorities
11. Dramatic final scene
12. Violent, mysterious death
13. Resurrection, ascension, post-resurrection appearances and judgment of the dead
14. Myth develops relating to their life story, which is the last stage in the development of a hero

Divination and healing

The now commonly understood idea that some events occur purely at random is a modern one. For early humans, and indeed even today for many people with a religious outlook, all things happen for a reason. What is more, this reason is fully known to the god(s). This led to two important aspects of early religions both of which retain echoes in most religions today. These are divination and healing.

Divination (note the etymology - *divinare* (Latin) to be inspired by god) As the god(s) were fully aware of all things, including what would happen in the future, people naturally tried to find ways to obtain this

---

[11] *As discussed by Eliade, Campbell and Hopkins – see Bibliography*

valuable information from them. These methods are known as *divination*. Many cultures developed their own weird and wonderful methods to try and achieve it. It seems that there were certain types of individuals in all societies who claimed abilities in this field. Whether charlatans or genuine, they were able to convince their contemporaries of their prowess. Their techniques are incredibly varied, and a tribute to the ingenuity (and arguably also the gullibility) of the human species.

These techniques include numerology, astrology, use of omens (eclipses, shooting stars etc.), augury (such as examining and interpreting the livers of sacrificed animals), the use of religious texts (such as the interpretation of hidden Bible codes), reading of palms or tea leaves or other random phenomena, the use of esoteric or secret knowledge and contacting the spirits of the dead. Whichever way it was practiced, divination was an important aspect of religion and although the theology of religions such as Judaism discourages such practices, they continue at a grassroots level.

Healing: In a similar way the health of an individual and concepts such as disability, illness and infertility were considered to be a result of decisions made by divine beings. Accordingly, good health could possibly be restored if the right practices or penances were carried out and calamities could be prevented by following the rules of the local religion. Those who claimed to have access to this knowledge became healers; sometimes they were the same individuals who could divine the future.

Some healers specialised in removing curses thought to be the cause of afflictions, others gave herbs or medications which indeed sometimes helped. Yet others would require that certain religious rituals be performed. Most probably, all of them achieved some success owing to the power of the placebo response in humans. When an individual had faith in the power of the healer, then in a reasonable percentage of cases a cure would result. Once again, the later religions incorporated some of these beliefs.

Political aspect of religion

With a belief by the population that gods were in control of all human events, those able to commune with these higher beings naturally acquired authority and power within their own society. Later as society became ever more complex and groups and cultures interacted with each other, patriotism developed as each culture held a loyalty to its own wise men and a distrust of those outsiders who had other ideas.

From the earliest time of the shaman, religion started to develop a political component. The shaman was a powerful figure in the community and human nature is such that power is not easily given up. This made the development of hereditary shamans or priests a common feature of religions. It was soon followed by kings and emperors who were appointed by the gods and were their agents or were even gods themselves. Religion was too powerful a tool for the leaders not to make use of it, as Aristotle observed in the fourth century BCE:

A tyrant must put on the appearance of uncommon devotion to religion. Subjects are less apprehensive of illegal treatment from a ruler they consider god-fearing and pious. On the other hand they do less easily move against him, believing he has the gods on his side.

In similar vein, four centuries later Seneca said:

Religion is regarded by the common people as true, by the wise as false, and by the rulers as useful.

In more recent times, Napoleon put it even more cynically, saying:

Religion is what keeps the poor from murdering the rich.

It is, arguably, with the political component of religion that most issues leading to conflict and dispute arise. Many religions became linked with certain political leaders and with land, an inevitable recipe for trouble.

Religion and Spirituality

At this point, we must consider the difference between religion and spirituality. Spirituality is much more personal than religion and can be expressed as **the direct encounter with the numinous.** No dogma or political beliefs are involved. To a greater or lesser degree all human beings have a spiritual side and it seems likely that this too was one of the key reasons for the universal development of religion in all cultures.

History shows that the freedom to express spiritual, humanitarian and individual thoughts has frequently led to conflict with both the religious and political powers of the day. One need only look at the history of heresy to see examples of this. Religion is the activity of the group; spirituality is personal – part of the inner search. Sadly, the results of such a search often seem to threaten those with a vested interest in the status quo.

It appears that today, for many people, western religion fails to answer this spiritual need. Eastern religion does focus the search inwards, but can sometimes be too prescriptive as to the technique to be used to achieve this. As mentioned in the introduction, some wise gurus of the East, sadly relatively few in number, do encourage individuals to seek and then follow their own path. In the western world, the results of this struggle for spirituality are seen as far apart as the psychiatrist's couch and among the New Age cults. The psychologist C J Jung observed:

> *Among all my patients in the second half of life – that is to say over thirty-five – there has not been one whose problem in the last resort was not that of finding a religious outlook on life.*

That Jung did not mean organised religion by his words 'religious outlook' was made clear when he also wrote:

> *Religion is a defence against the religious experience.*

The discovery of personal spirituality can be a transforming experience which has the power to alter the direction of people's lives. Spirituality has been considered the poetry of life, compared to the prose of religion. It has been pointed out that the routine of daily life has to be experienced in prose, as society could not operate any other way. The important thing, though, in this author's opinion is to keep a place for the poetry too. D H Lawrence had something to say on this, and we will leave it to him to close this chapter:[12]

> *It is a fine thing to establish one's own religion in one's heart, not to be dependent on tradition and second-hand ideals. Life will seem to you, later, not a lesser, but a greater thing.*

---

[12] *The quote comes from Lady Chatterley's Lover, and is, of course, in prose. This idea is expressed widely in Lawrence's poetry too, more subtly and beautifully, but less suitably for the 'sound-bite' quote needed here.*

2

Myth, History and the Sacred

How to Read a Sacred Text

Truth is stranger than fiction, but fiction is often truer
Frederick Raphael

J ewish religious practice is very much text based, and Jews are rightly known as a people of the Book.[1] The Book in question is the Hebrew Bible, the *Tanach*. This is more accurately a collection of books, comprising of the five books of Moses – the Torah, the books of the prophets – *Neve'im*, and assorted other writings – *Ketuvim*. These books make up the canon of the *Tanach*; they are the prime Jewish sacred texts, but how should we read them?

This may seem a strange question, but we do read texts in different ways. Think how differently one approaches reading a history book, a novel, a legal contract, a poem, a Greek myth or a philosophy book. The *Tanach* contains elements of all these different genres and sometimes seems to switch from one to another without notice.

However, the crucial difference with the *Tanach* is that it is a **sacred** text. The word sacred derives from the Latin *sacrare* – to set apart as

---

1 *People of the Book (Arabic اهل الكتاب - Ahl al-Kitab), was originally a Moslem term for their fellow monotheists. Orthodox Jews traditionally extend the meaning of the word 'book' to also include the Talmud.*

holy. People of the ancient world, long before the advent of Judaism, divided their world into two separate spheres of the sacred and the profane. The sacred is the realm of the gods, of ritual and of symbolism. The profane is the everyday rational world.[2] Items introduced into the sacred realm are often given a ceremony or 'rite of passage' to mark their transition to their new holy status.

This idea of the separation of the sacred and profane is expressed simply and clearly in the prayer recited on lighting the *Hanukah*[3] candles:

אין לנו רשות להשתמש בהם אלו ליראותם בלבד

We are not allowed to make use of them, but only to look at them

It is ritual that transforms an object from being simply the product of an artisan's workshop into something sacred - an object that can no longer be used for mundane purposes and is subsequently accorded special respect as holy. A believer also treats a sacred text differently from a much loved book from the secular or profane world. For devout Jews and Moslems there is even a custom of kissing a sacred text after reading it.

The sacred realm consists not only of place but also of time. Both can be sanctified. For Jews, *Shabbat*[4] very clearly separates the week between sacred and profane time with ritual acts being performed to demarcate the transition when it begins and ends.

In ancient times, the world was further subdivided into cosmos and chaos. Cosmos was known territory where one could live in relative safety while chaos was the world beyond. Cosmos was protected by the deities that were known; chaos was the realm of unknown gods or devils.

Within the known world or cosmos, certain holy places were set aside and became sacred. Initially they could have been chosen because of

---

[2] *Émile Durkheim (1858-1917) was the first to write of this distinction. He was descended from three generations of Rabbis but led a completely secular life. He spent much time demonstrating that religious phenomena stemmed from social rather than divine factors. His book, 'The Elementary Forms of Religious Life' discusses this topic. Rudolf Otto (1869-1937) later explored similar ideas in 'The Idea of the Holy'.*
[3] *Hanukah – 8 day winter Jewish festival*
[4] *Shabbat – the Jewish Sabbath (Friday sunset until Saturday evening)*

their appearance (mountains such as Mount Fuji [*illustrated*] require little imagination for this) or alternatively because a miracle or an appearance of a god is believed to have occurred there. Once a location has been assigned the status of sacred, this is very long lasting. Many sacred places have retained their holy status even when the local people's religion has changed radically. The new religion's symbols are simply incorporated into the architecture.

As for a newly built religious building, it becomes a sacred space once it is sanctified by the rituals performed within it.

Sacred time was defined by Eliade[5] as a sort of eternal mythical present that is periodically revalidated by means of rites. It is a circular version of time within which, for example, religious men and women may celebrate an annual festival by reliving a sacred event that took place long ago, possibly even in the mythical past. Such events can recur unchanged again and again in this non-linear time. Within the sacred realm, then, a religious person can experience a valuable sanctuary from the profane world - a sanctuary both of time and place.

Bearing all this in mind, if we now pick up our Jewish sacred text and start to read the two creation stories with which the first book, Genesis, begins, we immediately find that we have to make decisions. Should we read the text literally or metaphorically? A critical mind soon discovers that an exact literal reading presents many problems owing (among other things) to the contradictions contained within the text itself.[6] This problem was already discussed over eight hundred years ago by Maimonides, who put it as follows:[7]

> He [God] ... *found it necessary to communicate to us in allegorical, figurative and metaphorical language. ... It has been treated in metaphors*

---

[5] *Mircea Eliade (1909-1986) in his book 'The Sacred and the Profane' (This was written without acknowledging Durkheim's ideas, although it does acknowledge Otto).*

[6] *One early example is the differences of detail between the separate creation stories of Genesis 1 & 2. See Chapter 11 – Torah min hashamayim and the appendix for many more examples.*

[7] *From the introduction to the 'Guide for the Perplexed' (1186). I quote from Friedlander's translation of the original Arabic Dalalat al-Hairin.*

in order that the uneducated may comprehend it according to the measure of their faculties and the feebleness of their apprehension, while educated persons may take it in a different sense.

While this sounds patronising to our modern ear the point is well made. This text is not always to be taken literally. In fact what Maimonides called 'allegorical, figurative and metaphorical language' could actually more succinctly be called 'myth'.

Unfortunately, in modern times a semantic problem has developed, and the words *myth* and *mythology* have become widely misunderstood. Many use and understand them to mean made up and untrue. However, the word mythology used in relation to sacred texts (both Jewish and of other religions) should be considered neither to be derogatory, nor to be calling these texts untrue. These texts are only untrue if they are misread as something they never set out to be.

A **myth** should be regarded as a way of expressing more simply concepts too elusive for ordinary logical explanation. A simple example from the early part of the Bible is the story of Cain. When God accepts Abel's offering while rejecting Cain's, we can all relate to Cain's feelings towards his brother. All who have a sibling have, in some sense, been Cain. We can live through and learn from this myth, and unlike Cain, we do not have to commit murder. That this is a story, and that these specific events may never have actually occurred is completely irrelevant. A myth does not impart factual information, but is primarily a guide to behaviour and so is helpful to many who find themselves in similar circumstances, and such circumstances occur repeatedly down the generations.

Indeed, some myths are found so widely (though dressed in different garments when they appear in different cultures) and describe such universal human experiences that we know them as archetypal myths.[8] Religious literature is usually mythic, that is to say it makes use of myth, symbols and metaphors. If such writing is treated literally rather than symbolically (as religious fundamentalists who misunderstand

---

[8] *After Carl Jung. The opposite type of myths, which are specific to a particular people are known as tribal myths. These tend to highlight the good points of the group they relate to, and emphasise the drawbacks of either everyone else or the opponents of the group.*

this whole concept often do) it can indeed become untrue, remote, absurd and even dangerous.

To put this another way, myth can be considered as an account of an event that in some sense happened once, either in reality or imagination, it does not matter which. However, this account is in fact being used as a metaphor for similar events that happen repeatedly in human experience. Myth can show us how to behave when we face this type of situation ourselves and we validate these myths in a practical way when we follow their example.

We all understand how helpful a metaphor is as a means of clarifying complex ideas and routinely use metaphors ourselves without a second thought. We understand that a metaphor is true in every sense except the literal one. If I call someone a rock, the person would understand immediately that I am referring to their characteristics, their strength and steadfastness, not their physical make-up. If we read that a woman turned a blind eye to something we all know, without thinking about it, that we are not being given information about her eyesight. Why then do some people find it so difficult to understand that myth operates in exactly the same way? Both myth and metaphor make connections from our inner world to the world outside, the conscious to the unconscious. Writing without either would be both dull and lacking in depth.

This difficulty with myth seems to be primarily a modern problem. In classical times it was accepted that there were two ways of arriving at truth and understanding. Plato called these *mythos* and *logos* (reason). Both were essential to make sense of the world and both were of equal importance as they complemented each other.[9]

Reading our accounts of creation, we should soon realise that a literal, analytical approach (*logos*) that is appropriate to texts such as a legal contract or a scientific work, is inappropriate for (at least this part of) our sacred text. Here we need to use our romantic or imaginative mind as we would for a poem or literary novel. This way of reading allows the reader to be open to both myth and metaphor. It lets the

---

[9] *Interestingly, in Hesiod and Homer logos is characterised as an untrustworthy even crafty form of speech, while mythos is 'something to be believed and obeyed'. (Bruce Lincoln, Theorising Myth. University of Chicago Press, 1999)*

symbolism and nuances contained in the text resonate within the reader's mind.

Prior to the Enlightenment, this approach would have been perfectly natural. It was with the rise of science and rationality that *logos* came to the fore. However, even today, when one confronts the suffering and tragedy which are an inseparable part of human existence myth(*os*) can still be the more helpful approach. As Isaiah Berlin said:

It is myth that gives us the sense of reality.

As soon as one accepts that sacred texts use myth and that these myths are a way of imparting insights that are communicated more easily that way, then the text is genuinely more likely to speak to us and reveal these extra layers of meaning. This way of reading depends more on intuition than rationality, just as one can often appreciate the meaning of a piece of music or work of art better by bypassing rational thought.

It is very important to bear in mind that originally the biblical texts were written for their contemporary audience. They were intended to reflect contemporary issues from a theological point of view in order to get messages across. However, as the texts in many cases were written in an allegorical or mythic form, the way they dealt with the contemporary issues often presented the reader with eternal truths. This meant that the allegories could be reinterpreted and still be relevant in changed circumstances during subsequent historical periods.

The biblical sacred text carries, especially for the religious, a heavy burden from the accumulated layers of these subsequent interpretations which have expanded the text's meanings down the centuries. Even though many of these meanings are not directly present in the text, they have developed the authority of age and tradition and an informed reader brings them to mind when reading a sacred work that they are familiar with. For example, it is hard for a Christian who has been to Sunday school (and even a western educated Jew[10]) to read the story of Eve and the serpent in the garden

---

[10] *Or a Jew with knowledge of Kabbalah, which borrowed the idea of original sin from Christianity, and incorporated it into its belief system.*

of Eden without being conscious, at some level, of the concept of original sin. It does not matter that this idea does not actually appear in the text itself.

The biblical text itself is often very spare. Many narratives unfold with minimum detail, giving hardly any characterisation to the participants. For example, the whole dramatic story of the *Akedah* (the near sacrifice of Isaac) takes place in just nineteen sentences. It is left for the interpreters to fill in the detail. The interpretations of the Talmudists in particular have effectively been incorporated into the Bible's story. When young children are told these stories they are taught an amalgam of both what is in the text and details added by both classical and contemporary interpreters.

By mediæval times, in both Christian and Jewish exegesis there were traditionally considered to be four methods to interpret the biblical text. In theory at least, every verse of the Bible can be interpreted by each of these four methods.

For Christians by the 13th century these methods were defined as:
- *Littera* - the literal - to teach the reader the 'facts'
- *Allegoria* - the allegorical - to teach what should be believed
- *Moralis* - the moral - to teach how to behave (much used in preaching sermons)
- *Anagogia* - the anagogical (spiritual or mystical) interpretation

In Judaism, these same four ways of interpreting biblical texts are known as:[11]
- *Peshat* - the literal
- *Remez* - the allegorical
- *Drash* - the moral or homiletical - the explanatory stories are known as *midrash*.
- *Sod* - the secret or hidden meaning - this is the one most sought by mystics (especially kabbalists).

For both Christians and Jews only one method uses *logos*, the other three use *mythos*. In both cases, the literal meaning of the text was seen as just the starting point for interpretation. What can sometimes make

---

[11] *A mnemonic used to remember these four methods is the Hebrew word 'pardes' (paradise).*

things difficult for us when reading the *Tanach* so long after its composition, is that the text is underpinned by an outdated cosmology. For its contemporary readers this cosmology was taken for granted and fully understood. For today's readers, brought up with different ideas, it can interfere with understanding. In a similar way, some of the symbols used have gone out of date and so cease to resonate (or set up associations and connections for the reader) in the way they would have done when they were first written. This can be a problem in reading classic literature too, for dead myths and metaphors no longer speak clearly to us and so we may lose a layer of meaning that the text once contained.

It is worth a small digression here to mention that a *miracle* in a sacred text is fully intended to be a *super*natural event. It was intended as a symbol of the power of the Deity to carry out an 'impossible' act if He so chooses. Those who seek to find a rational explanation for miracles mistake their function; miracles are symbols and should not be taken literally. If such events can be explained logically then they cease to be miracles.

Hopkins[12] defines a miracle as 'reported and wondrous events, whose explanation involves supernatural intervention.' He goes on to state that sceptics might initially think that miracles don't happen, but they are wrong. They do happen but only in this special sense. Miracles occur, not when someone reportedly sees them, but only when we hear or read about them – and believe the story in a literal way. The miracle takes place in the believer's mind. In this manner, miracles can exert their influence on religious history.

It is not just religious fundamentalists who misread sacred texts. The reason I called Dawkins dogmatic in the introduction is that he too reads sacred texts with a literal, scientific mind (purely as *logos, littera or peshat*) and he is also sometimes aggressively self assertive in his presentation. Unlike many religious fundamentalists however, Dawkins does not draw dangerous conclusions from his literal readings of sacred texts and then proceed to act on them in the sure knowledge that he possesses the 'Truth'. Dawkins makes use of logical contradictions and other problems within the texts to debunk them all, sometimes throwing out the baby with the bath water. In this way

---

[12] *Keith Hopkins. 'A World full of Gods.'*

he, like so many of the religious individuals he criticises, misreads the texts.

In fairness, unlike religious fundamentalists, Dawkins is fully amenable to rational argument and so one cannot take this comparison too far. My sympathies are with him, for in order to debate these matters with fundamentalists it is necessary (as I will do, particularly in Chapter 5 and the appendix) to look at the small details of the text. This is in order to show up the many logical errors that one is faced with if trying to read these texts literally. What Dawkins fails to do, is to recognise the mythic value of this literature for non-fundamentalist religious adherents. Even for the secular, these texts have mythic value and in any case, they also contain an essential background for the understanding of western history, art and culture.

Returning to the *Tanach*, we have read the creation stories and of the Garden of Eden and hopefully understood these events in mythic terms. At some point in our continued reading, we reach what appears to be real historical narrative. Whether one considers this to start with Noah, Abraham or not until the Book of Kings is unimportant. When one reaches the point of reading what seems to be history, how should it be understood?

To begin with, we must realise that the concept we moderns understand as **history** would have been completely foreign both to the biblical authors[13] and their contemporary readers. History, in today's sense, simply had not yet been invented. For the ancients, history was a repository of eternal truths and of collective memories. The agenda of the 'historical narratives' of the *Tanach* was quite different from that of a modern history book. These accounts were intended to tell founding (or aetiological) stories of the Children of Israel and of their relationship with their God. Those stories that were set in the past were intended primarily to explain the present circumstances to contemporary readers.

It is simply wrong to read sacred writings such as the *Tanach* as anything that resembles our modern idea of historical narrative. The scholar Frank Moore Cross helped to clarify this for us. He described

---

[13] *Anyone surprised at the mention of Biblical 'authors' will find an explanation in Chapter 5.*

biblical history from the patriarchal period onwards as epic narrative. He explained as follows:[14]

> *The epic form, designed to recreate and give meaning to the historical experiences of a people or nation, is not merely or simply historical. In epic narrative, a people and their god or gods interact in the temporal course of events. In historical narrative only human actors have parts. Appeal to divine agency is illegitimate.*

The Bible contains writing full of metaphor and symbolism; writing that is often true in a mythological sense, and so may be more aptly described as a mythological history of a people. Again, it must be stressed that this is not a derogatory remark, quite the opposite; we obtain some of our greatest insights through mythology. The problem can actually be with some readers who understand without difficulty when they read ordinary books that metaphors and symbols are devices designed to help deepen understanding, rather than literal truths. When reading the *Tanach*, however, they treat metaphors and symbols as facts. By so doing they often not only miss other levels of meaning, but may sometimes pursue these metaphors down blind (and potentially dangerous) alleys. They completely mistake the symbol for its reference.

Mythology is an essential part of any culture or religion, and indeed an integral part of the way all human beings deal with the past. One needs only to listen to a bereaved person describing the one who recently died to understand how quickly a mythologizing process can set in. Memory is selective, collective memory even more so. Even modern historians often fail to give an objective account of recent events, if such objectivity is indeed possible. For the biblical writers, objectivity and historical accuracy were never priorities. Their aim was to give a theological explanation of history rather than an accurate record of events.

One should also consider the concept of time. Sacred texts are often written in 'sacred time', which is a completely different notion to historic time. Karen Armstrong calls sacred time 'everywhen', as it can simultaneously represent the past, present and future. Many cultures have stories of a golden age, a mythological period in their past when

---

[14] In 'Canaanite Myth and Hebrew Epic'. Frank Moore Cross, Harvard U.P.1973

god(s) and superheroes roamed the Earth. The idea of placing events sequentially in a historical time frame is a relatively modern one. Indeed, the Hebrew language has no word of its own for *history*.[15] Bertrand Russell comments on this difference when writing about pre-modern history:[16]

> *All history until the eighteenth century is full of prodigies and wonders which modern historians ignore, not because they are less well attested than facts which historians accept, but because modern taste among the learned prefers what science regards as probable.*

When considering the history of our region, the ancient Near East, there is even more of a contrast between the eighteenth century view and that of today. If one had tried to get an account of the history of our region from the most knowledgeable eighteenth century historians, the only source they would have had available to provide this was the Bible. There was nothing to compare its 'historical' accounts with; we had absolutely no context in which to evaluate the Bible's accounts.

This situation has changed radically. The turning point was 1798 when Napoleon campaigned in Egypt and what was known as the Holy Land. Seeing himself as a latter day Alexander, he took with him scholars and explorers who were to investigate the history and culture of the lands he conquered. Once interesting artefacts started to be discovered, piece by piece a context was constructed. We began to be able to give an account of past events in this important region where such human breakthroughs as the first cities and the first alphabet took place. We learned of forgotten cultures and of inscriptions in unknown languages which eventually were deciphered. This allowed us to read these texts and learn even more about life in the region during ancient times.

There were, of course, false starts. Only in relatively recent years have archæologists, historians and philologists helped us to develop a coherent early history of our region and people. In the 19th century, the early days of biblical archæology, those involved usually had an

---

[15] *Apart from the modern loan word 'historia –* הסטוריה*' the Oxford Hebrew-English Dictionary only lists* תולדות *and* עבר*, meaning genealogy and past. In Israeli schools history lessons are called* תע"י *which is an acronym for* תולדות עם ישראל *literally, the generations of the people of Israel.*

[16] *Bertrand Russell. 'An Outline of Intellectual Rubbish'*

agenda. In many cases, they were looking for evidence to prove that the Bible narratives recorded true history.

As scientific research scandals have shown, setting out to prove something true, rather than taking an open minded approach, can be dangerous. One tends only to 'find' the evidence one wants and to ignore anything else. Furthermore, if, as is often the case, the evidence can be interpreted in several ways, one chooses the way that best helps make one's case.

In recent times, there has been a more objective approach by many archæologists who try to allow the evidence to speak for itself. They consider that their brief is to discover as much as they can about what really happened in the past and whether it confirms or contradicts the biblical account is not their prime concern. There have also been some very valuable archæological surveys of the region which have filled in much background detail. The days of archæologists with a spade in one hand and a Bible in the other are coming to an end.

This study of real history need not destroy the credibility of the Bible if we have learned how to read our sacred text. The Bible is a theological work, giving us often very beautiful insights into what it is to be human. It is full of metaphor, symbolism and poetry, and it needs to be read in that spirit. To look objectively at its historicity is in no way to impugn its literary greatness or theological profundity. Lest I get carried away, I must add that it also contains many passages of turgid prose along with no shortage of outdated Iron Age[17] ideas.

What we must not do is look to the Bible for an account of history in the way that we understand it today. Those who collected the stories and wrote the biblical text never intended it to be so. They were writing a founding story and epic of Old Israel, from which theological and philosophical lessons could be learnt, and overall they succeeded magnificently. They gave an account of the events of tradition which inevitably differ from the events of history. Problems only arise when the story's metaphors and symbols are misread as facts.[18]

---

[17] *Iron Age – 1200 BCE to the beginning of the Classical Age in 332 BCE*
[18] *Joseph Campbell says these symbols are the keys to spiritual understanding and mystical revelation. Reading the Tanach as metaphor is also supported by both Maimonides (in the 'Guide for the Perplexed') and*

As should now be clear, the whole concept of history that is based on rational scientific *logos* is a modern construct. *Mythos* was still respectable until the Enlightenment which led to a glorification of reason and a systematic attempt to explain away mythology. The zeitgeist of that time was that humanity had successfully transcended the need for mythological forms of thought. It has taken the passage of time for us to understand that both forms, *mythos* and *logos*, are still needed as they complement each other. To make sense of the confusing biblical historical stories one needs to bear in mind that history told as *mythos* is only untrue if taken literally. It can still be true poetically or symbolically. Remember that *mythos* is an essential part of every culture or religion and an integral part of the way we human beings deal with the past. It is not to be denigrated. Objectivity was never a concern of the biblical writers. Their priority was that events should be interpreted consistently theologically by their contemporaries for whom they were writing, rather than to give future generations an accurate chronological account.

Interestingly, this does mean that it is sometimes possible to recover real history from the text by examining, not the events of the story, but the way it is told. In other words, the study of the theological message being conveyed can to help inform us both about the history of the time it was written and about the interests of the group that wrote it. To demonstrate this, I have drawn up a chart in the appendix showing the 'spin' applied by the different schools of biblical writers.[19]

To better understand this traditional approach to history, and as a reminder of how cultures who have not been exposed to modern ideas think about past events, consider the following two examples. François Garnier, a French explorer of 1860's Indochina, wrote:

> *'A sense of history is absolutely absent in the [people of] Lao[s], their imagination is fired by fables and extraordinary legends, with no precise date, making it impossible to appreciate their historical value.'*

Nachmanides (i.e. both the Rambam and the Ramban). Reading the Tanach in this manner also solves many textual problems. For example, the text appears, on plain reading, to call for genocide against Amalek – very troubling (see Deuteronomy 25:19 and 1 Samuel 15). If Amelek is read, as I believe it should be, as a metaphor for evil in general, then the meaning is much more palatable both theologically and morally.
[19] *See 'J E D and P – the biblical spin doctors' –p227*

A century later Dervla Murphy, who was travelling among the highlanders of Ethiopia's Simien mountains tells of shepherds on watch by the campfire at night chanting a saga of the history of their brave ancestors and their exploits. She wrote:[20]

> *'For highlanders, history is not of the past, seen down an orderly vista of dates and events, it lives within them, as inspiring memories of courageous or cunning individuals who may have lived, for all they know, a hundred or a thousand years ago.'*

This was exactly how it was for the early readers of what have now become our sacred texts. Texts which were also often based on collective or folk memories, or on oral stories that had been retold over a long period and had naturally been modified along the way with the emphasis changed to suit new circumstances.

Joseph Campbell[21] cites an example of the correct way of understanding sacred stories. This is how the Sioux Indian, Black Elk, related a vision:

> *'I saw myself on the central mountain of the world, the highest place..... (It was) Harney Peak in South Dakota. But the central mountain is everywhere.'*

In other words the holy mountain or most holy site of one's religion, whether Harney Peak, Mount Kylash, Mount Fuji, Mount Sinai, Mount Horeb, Mount Ararat, Mount Sapan[22] or Mount Olympus, is not a small geographical location but is everywhere. The mountain can be (metaphorically) accessed wherever the one who holds it sacred happens to be. A holy mountain or a holy land receives its sacredness within the psyche of the believer.

If only the literalists who would fight and kill for their holy lands could understand this. As Campbell also wrote:[23]

> *'Every religion is true in one way or another if understood metaphorically. But if it gets stuck inside its own metaphors and interprets them as facts, then it is in trouble.'*

---

[20] *Dervla Murphy. 'In Ethiopia with a Mule'. Flamingo, 1994*
[21] *Joseph Campbell (1904-1987) worked and lectured extensively on Comparative Mythology. See Bibliography for a selection of his works. This quote is from, The Power of Myth. Doubleday 1988. p89*
[22] *Mount Sapan (now in Syria) was the home of Ba'al and the pantheon of Canaanite gods.*
[23] *Ibid p56*

To read the *Tanach* metaphorically is not heretical. As quoted earlier, Maimonides himself, in the introduction to his *Guide for the Perplexed* stressed that these writings necessarily use, 'allegorical, figurative and metaphorical language.' He added:

> *'Every time that you find in our books a tale the reality of which seems impossible, a story which is repugnant to both reason and common sense, then be sure that the tale contains a profound allegory veiling a deeply mysterious truth; and the greater the absurdity of the letter, the deeper the wisdom of the spirit.'*[24]

By contrast, if one reads the *Tanach* as straight history one faces insoluble problems of logic caused by the anachronisms, contradictions, logical impossibilities, and clear evidence of political spin and folklore contained within the text. As a single example, the text contains three separate and very different stories of the historical Israelite conquest of Jerusalem.[25] Even the most ardent believer in the Bible as history must concede that at least two of these stories are untrue or they defy the rules of logic. Read the text metaphorically, however, and it tells a more consistent story.

Literalists seem to close their eyes to this type of evidence, which is so strong as to be fully accepted by virtually all scholars. The exceptions are those in orthodox and fundamentalist circles where it is seldom even addressed, much less engaged with. For those wanting to consider such evidence, more detail is found in Chapter 5 and in the appendix. This evidence is fascinating also for what it reveals about the process of the composition of the text and of the motives of those involved.

Going into detail to show flaws in the *Tanach*, if read as a work of history, is primarily intended to demonstrate to literalists, who in my opinion completely misunderstand the work, how untenable their position is. Those who read it as a sacred text, in the way its intended readership naturally did early on, will continue to gain understanding from many parts of the *Tanach*, and will not be in any way concerned about the fact that that they are reading a mythic work.

---

[24] *Admittedly, these views of Maimonides were considered heretical by other rabbis at the time. (1186)*

[25] *1. Before Joshua's death – see Joshua 12:8 and Joshua 12:10*

2. After Joshua's death – see Joshua 15:63 and Judges 1:8

3. By King David – see 2 Samuel 5:5-7 - see appendix p.229 for some other contradictions in the text

Literalists, who devote their lives to analysing the text word by word and even letter by letter will continue to obtain much data, but their approach sometimes has little or nothing to do with the work itself. In the same way that an over-detailed analysis of a work of literature in a university class can sometimes ruin the artistic essence of it and leave even its original author bemused when hearing of meanings that were never intended, this Talmudic *pilpul*[26] sometimes obscures both the plain and the mythic meaning, and seeks to impose rigidity on the text. It is fascinating to see how, when the clear meaning of a text is considered theologically inappropriate, the Talmudists' ingenuity in finding a 'more suitable' interpretation is unrivalled.

As will become apparent in Chapter 6, religious literalists' behaviour in trying to determine and fix God's will, and in having a rigid fixed idea of what God is and what He demands from each individual has dangers. It can make them act in such an inflexible way, that they may even find themselves in serious danger of committing a form of idolatry.

Secular rationalists likewise can fail to benefit from their reading, if they see only the contradictions, anachronisms and the Iron Age cosmology and philosophy. By doing so, they miss out on the eternal mythic truths and the wisdom in the text, attributes which have helped so many people in their daily lives.

For the biblical text to remain valuable and continue to speak to current and future generations it is, in my opinion, necessary to rediscover the pre-enlightenment approach of reading it as *mythos*. At the same time we must keep our modern rationality functioning so that we realise we are not reading the literal 'Truth' for all humanity.

---

[26] *Pilpul – the Talmudic system of analysing a text by continuous questioning and analysis, discussing the smallest detail at great length.*

3

Jewish origins

Where did the Jewish people come from?

Israel is a country with a great deal of history and very little geography
Isaiah Berlin

Anyone whose understanding of the origins of Judaism derives from a traditional Jewish education may have at some point asked themselves, 'What really happened in early Jewish history, and how did the Jewish religion actually develop?' While it is unlikely that we will ever be able to answer these questions fully, a much clearer picture of Jewish origins has emerged over the last two centuries due to the work of modern historians who take an evidence based approach. This account of current thinking contains some surprises for those who have been brought up on the Bible as history and have not kept in touch with these developments.

We must start by understanding that, as discussed in the previous chapter, we cannot apply our modern idea of what history consists of to the Bible's stories of the past. So how should we proceed if we wish to know more of the real historical origins of the Jewish people? When trying to find information on the early history of Judaism one needs to be clear about the relative value of different sources. Ideally, one uses primary sources to write history in the sense that we understand it today. A primary source is either an artefact, usually found by an archæologist, or even better, a written source that originates from the period being studied. These items still require critical interpretation, but only contemporary political bias will affect what they tell us, not subsequent events and interpretations.

Secondary sources, such as ancient texts written in a later period, can also be valuable, but must be interpreted with greater caution. In the context of Israelite and Jewish origins, the *Tanach* must be treated as a secondary source at least until the time of the Exile. This is because we have clear evidence that, even though some parts of the *Tanach* are considerably older than this, their text remained subject to editing. For the Torah, editing continued until it was canonised around the 5th century BCE. *Neve'im* (prophets) was open for a further four centuries and *Ketuvim* (writings) was finalised only in the first century of this era.[1]

When looking for the historical origins of Judaism, one must take note both of the discoveries of archæology and of the meaning that can be gleaned from the 'archæological' layers within our sacred texts. These interwoven narratives were written over a considerable period, and traces of the contemporary interests of the writers can frequently be recovered and taken account of. The interaction between history and theology is of the utmost importance. So too are the significant occasions in early Jewish history when theological reaction to political events helped maintain the people, by intelligently adapting the religion to cope with these changes of circumstance.

The Bible's opening book, Genesis, begins with two different creation myths, which echo earlier traditions from Mesopotamia. After further mythic material, such as the two interwoven flood stories that also have earlier parallels in the region, it moves on to what appears to be the real history of the patriarchs.

According to tradition, the religion's origin is with the 'monotheistic' ideas of Abraham. However, the gods (the plural is deliberate) of the patriarchs are versions of pre-existing gods. Abraham's El was a well

---

[1] *Minor changes did continue to the text of the Tanach. The vowels were not added, sentence and paragraph breaks finalised and some minor detail finally fixed until the Masoretic text of the 10th century CE. This then became the standard text for Jews to use. See appendix p.239 for more details on the texts of the Tanach*

established Canaanite deity, Isaac had his own god called *Pachad* (פחד, fear or awe), as did Jacob with *Avir* (אביר, mighty one).[2]

Historians believe that Abraham was originally the chief patriarch in the tradition of the Southern Kingdom (Judea), while Jacob fulfilled that role for the Northern Kingdom (Israel). In the Bible, Isaac is a less developed character who links them together and creates the family relationship between them. It is notable that Isaac almost disappears from the narrative after the *Akedah* when he is not even mentioned as descending the mountain with Abraham.[3] He subsequently makes only cameo appearances to marry (at 40), have children (at 60) and on his deathbed (at an old age).

The God of early Jewish biblical narrative is a tribal god, leading His people in holy battles. He lacks two essential attributes for a universal God - transcendence and compassion. At a later stage, with the prophets, this God is transformed into a truly monotheistic God, a solitary, universal God with a higher morality.[4]

In the books of the Bible that deal with early 'history', there are many references to Yahweh as being chief among gods or the most powerful god. There are almost no monotheistic references nor, surprisingly, anything in the text to show Abraham to be a true monotheist. There are also many other occasions where monotheism is questionable.[5] God at this stage was not omniscient nor omnipotent nor even universal. We are dealing here with the practice of *monolatry*, which is the worship of and exclusive loyalty to one chief god, while acknowledging the existence of other gods.

This still seems to be the case with the story of the revelation at Sinai. For example, the first of the Ten Commandments is given in a form that actually demands that people practice monolatry rather than

---

[2] *El Elyon was the old Canaanite chief deity and El Shaddai the god of the mountain top. Pachad appears in Genesis 31:42; Avir in Genesis 49:24.*

[3] *There has been a long hidden tradition that Isaac was indeed sacrificed in an earlier version of the story.*

[4] *Is the God that appears to Abraham as one of three men, the same God as the mountain top power that appeared to Moses? Later still God, in His final speech in the Tanach, speaks to Job 'out of the storm'. Is this the same God? The development of the concept of God merits a close examination.*

[5] *Some examples: Who....can compare with YHWH among the divine beings. Psalm 89:7*
And God said, 'Let us make man...' Genesis 1:26 (why use the plural?)
The Nephilim (Divine beings) who had sex with human women Genesis 6:4 (a remnant of early mythology)

monotheism. It accepts the existence of other gods, while forbidding the Children of Israel to worship them. It states:[6]

לא יהיה לך אלהים אחרים על פני

You will not have other gods besides Me

Returning to the account of the patriarchs, there is much in them that is reminiscent of founding legends of peoples and places worldwide. Whether these stories represent mythologized versions of real events or are pure mythology is impossible to determine and in any case is of little importance.

Moving on to the story of the Exodus, in addition to the biblical account, we now can look for evidence (and so far find only silence) in the Egyptian records. The historical question of whether Israelites were enslaved in Egypt remains open, but what has become clear is that the Exodus could not have occurred historically in the manner described by our tradition. There are three powerful sources of evidence to support this statement.

Firstly, despite the considerable amount of archæological work that has been carried out, no evidence has yet been found either of the presence of Israelites in Egypt[7] or of their Exodus. Even bearing in mind the truism that absence of evidence is not evidence of absence, we should remember that we are dealing with a literate Egyptian culture from which we have detailed written records. Accordingly, absence of evidence at this particular place and time must be considered at the very least, surprising.

Secondly, there is no time frame during which the Torah's story is compatible with the known history of Egypt and the Levant. All dates that have been suggested have to be ruled out due to significant historical problems.[8] This statement refers only to the natural, not the supernatural events of the traditional story. The latter are always a matter of belief, and therefore outside the scope of a historical

---

[6] *Exodus 20:1 (also Deuteronomy 5:6)*

[7] *There certainly were Semites present, however.*

[8] *For a more detailed discussion see 'The Date of the Exodus, The historical study of scripture' by Dennis Bratcher 2004, available at http://www.cresourcei.org/exodusdate.html. There are many other historical approaches available, which generally reach the same conclusion. This one, written by a questioning believer, shows simply explains why no date fits.*

account. Nevertheless, bear in mind the discussion on miracles in the previous chapter, which explained that when miracles are believed to have occurred then this belief can itself influence later events.

As an example of why the Bible's account does not fit the history of the region, consider that we now know that Canaan (the Promised Land) was under Egyptian control between roughly 1480 and 1150 BCE. This period covers all possible dates during which the exodus could have taken place. Did the Children of Israel escape from the Pharaoh's army in Egypt simply in order to fight them again in Canaan? If so, why is such an important fact not referred to in the Torah? Why do Egyptian records have no mention of this invasion of the territory they occupied in Canaan?

Moses and the Exodus - wall painting in the synagogue at Dura Europos

Thirdly, archæological examination of sites mentioned in the Bible as being along the route of the Exodus or subject to conquest has produced evidence that actually contradicts the biblical account.[9]

So where did this magnificent story of the Exodus come from? Unlike the creation and flood stories, so far as we know it is not based on a

---

[9] *Archæology has shown several such sites to have been unoccupied at the relevant period. For details see the chart in the appendix, p.238.*

pre-existing myth from a previous civilisation of the area. It seems to be a unique story that is very deeply rooted in Jewish tradition. While it clearly contains some purely mythological elements, it *may* be based on collective memory of some real historical event.

There is no doubt that the author(s) were familiar with Egypt and its culture. An example of this can be seen in the story of the ten plagues, which can be interpreted as successive Egyptian gods being symbolically defeated. Seen through Egyptian eyes, this sequence of plagues leads up to the sun god, Amon-Ra, being disabled, causing three days of total darkness. They then climax with a direct attack on the man-god Pharaoh himself, when his firstborn son and successor is killed along with the other Egyptian firstborn.[10]

One hypothesis is that some Israelites did indeed go down to Egypt, or perhaps may have originated there,[11] while the rest of the people were originally Canaanite. If so, it is most likely that some or all of the tribe of Levi were in Egypt.[12] The reasoning behind this assertion goes as follows. If one studies the names of the many individuals mentioned in the *Tanach*, each and every person whose name shows Egyptian influence is a Levite.[13] There is not a single such name in the *Tanach* among members of any other tribe. This technique of studying names is a well established technique for tracing movement among peoples. If one studies immigrants today, and indeed throughout history, one sees that the second and subsequent generations often take on personal names which are local to the family's new home.

This idea is strengthened by Levi being the only tribe not to have its own tribal area, and so they were perhaps the only tribe originally without roots in the land. Further evidence supporting Canaanite origins for the majority of the people includes:

---

[10] *In Egypt, as generally in the region, the firstborn was considered to belong to the gods, and often served in the temple. This concept later came into Judaism, but a ceremony was decreed to 'redeem' them from this obligation. For more on this possible interpretation of the 10 plagues see* http://www.ancientdays.net/plagues.htm

[11] *It is possible that the tribe of Levi had been influenced by Pharaoh Akhenaton's form of monotheism. His followers had to leave Egypt after his death when his theology was eradicated from Egyptian culture. I have come across no conclusive evidence to refute this rather neat explanation, but it must also be borne in mind that Akhenaton also believed himself to be a god, so was hardly a true monotheist.*

[12] *Meek. Hebrew Origins: p32 et seq.*

[13] *Examples are Moses, Assir, Pashhur, Hophni, Phinehas, Merari and Puti-el. Two Levites have the name Assir, three have Phinehas and four Pashhur.*

- the strong coincidence between the areas ruled by early Canaanite city states and those 'allocated' to the different tribes of Israel
- the similarities in earlier Canaanite cultic practice relating to sacrifice to that given in the Torah
- the similarity between the design for Solomon's temple given in the Bible and that of pagan temples of the period in the region such as the one excavated at Eyn Dara in Syria.[14]

The pagan temple at Eyn Dara in Syria, dating from 10th to 8th centuries BCE, which was built to the same plan as the one 'given by God' for Solomon's temple.

Alternatively, a second hypothesis suggests that the Exodus story derives from a folk memory of the Hyksos kings, who originated in Canaan and went to Egypt where they ruled for over 100 years. Around 1540 BCE,[15] the Egyptians threw them out and pursued them back to Canaan. The Hyksos were Canaanites, not Israelites, but it is quite possible that some of them and their descendents took to the hill country to avoid the Egyptians, who stayed on and occupied Canaan. If so, they were likely to have become part of the *habiru* (Egyptian for

[14] *The Eyn Dara temple in the Afrin valley, not far from Aleppo, is also notable for the hybrid creatures eagle, lion, ox and human found there, exactly the creatures seen by Ezekiel in his famous vision. This cannot be coincidence; rather it is more evidence of syncretism from Canaanite religion.*

[15] *For easier reading, dates are only given selectively in the text. To follow the history chronologically there is a timeline in the appendix pp. 236-238.*

displaced people)[16] who in turn may have become the Hebrews and Israelites. Possible support for this theory is found in the *Tanach's* 'memory' of David's early life as a bandit leader in the hill country.[17]

Ideas such as these, with varying degrees of plausibility, attempting to explain how the Israelites came into existence, will no doubt continue to be proposed to try and deal with the difficulties the historical record creates. From primary source evidence, however, one can only conclude that neither an exodus from Egypt nor a conquest of Canaan occurred historically in any manner similar to the biblical account.

If, instead of reading it as history, the Exodus story is read as myth, readers may find themselves following an account of the symbolic death and rebirth of a people. In Judaism, unlike other religious traditions of the region, it is not god who dies and is resurrected, but the people who descend into Egypt to be reborn at Sinai as God's chosen. That, speaking symbolically, could be the reason why none of those who were in Egypt, not even Moses, were allowed to enter the Promised Land. It may also be a factor in explaining the date selected to celebrate the festival of Passover. When first introduced in 621 BCE,[18] the date chosen for the festival was one the people of the Levant already associated with death and rebirth. The 14th of Nisan was the date of the pre-existing pagan festival of the resurrection of Adonis.

There are many other valid ways of reading this story mythologically. Some may read it as a rite of passage of the people. For others, the timeless story of oppression and freedom may produce resonances that are more personal. Given the many persecutions of Jewish history, it will have served this function time and again. The Baal Shem Tov understood this, saying:

> *Every person has his own Moses, his own Egypt and his own Pharaoh, and every Exodus is a personal journey.*

---

[16] *Habiru or hapiru – this was considered by some scholars to be the etymology of ivri – Hebrew, but the academic consensus has moved increasingly against this idea.*

[17] *1 Samuel 22:1-2; 27:2-9; 25:13*

[18] *According to 2 Kings 23:23. The text also says that Passover had previously been celebrated in the time of the Judges (though not the reigns of previous Kings). This is almost certainly an ætiological legend. The Torah's instruction to celebrate Passover (Numbers 9:1-14) is part of the P source (see Chapter 5), and so likely to date from the 7th century.*

The great value of reading the story as myth is that it is continuously revalidated, as it is understood in a form relevant to its readers and in a certain way lived through again by them.

In the Joshua stories describing the conquest of the Canaanite cities,[19] Yahweh behaves like an Iron Age tribal God. It has been commented that the morality of a god is often not much in advance of that of his worshippers, and sometimes considerably behind. With regard to the cities ransacked in the name of Yahweh, Baring and Cashford incontrovertibly argue:[20]

A truly transcendent and universal deity cannot, ontologically, take sides, least of all order the slaughtering of one race by another.

We also note that Yahweh seems to have limited powers at this stage since iron chariots proved too much for him to overcome.[21] The story of the settlement of Canaan in the Book of Judges, by complete contrast to the Book of Joshua, tells of much more gradual and less violent events. This version also fits the archæological findings better, as these findings imply that Yahweh's religious conquest of Canaan was indeed gradual and involved significant elements of conversion of the indigenous people.

The technique of uniting different tribal patriarchs as 'brothers' in a founding legend was well established in antiquity as a means of forging alliances between neighbouring groups, and this could well be behind the stories of Joseph and his brothers. It is likely that each of the tribes in Canaan originally worshipped its own deity, several of which had the same name as the tribe.[22] As the tribes were gradually converted to the worship of Yahweh, it became expedient to make their patriarchs 'brothers'.

Moving forward in time, there is no historical evidence either from the archæology of Israel, or from the writings of the surrounding area, to

---

[19] *Numbers 33:52-56, Deuteronomy 20:10-17, Joshua 8:18-29 and passim*

[20] *Baring & Cashford. 'The Myth of the Goddess'. Arkana 1991*

[21] *Judges 1:19; 'Yahweh was with the men of Judah. They took possession of the hill country, but they were unable to drive the people from the plains, because they had iron chariots'.*

[22] *Dan, Gad, and Asher are all names of Canaanite deities. The same technique may also account for the linking of Abraham (Judah's patriarch) with Jacob (patriarch of the Northern Kingdom of Israel) through the less developed character of Isaac. Similarly, Jacob and Esau link the tribes of Israel and Edom.*

show that David and Solomon ruled from Jerusalem.[23] If they did so, the wealth of their kingdoms, especially that of Solomon, has been grossly overstated in the Bible. Archæology demonstrates that Jerusalem was very small in their time. We only start to find evidence of the building work and artefacts of a more advanced society, along with a significant expansion of the city, from the late eighth century. This is two centuries too late for David and Solomon.

It must also be considered significant that not a single reference to trade with Solomon has yet been found among the considerable contemporary records we now have available from neighbouring civilisations. Bear in mind the Bible's account of Solomon's extensive empire and trading links in the region. Likewise, we have not found any confirmatory records from states we are told sent him their royal daughters to marry, despite the clear diplomatic motives behind such alliances in the ancient world.

It seems likely that in reality David and Solomon were local military leaders, or founders of dynasties whose names were passed down in the collective memory of the people, and about whom stories developed.[24] A comparison could be made with Gilgamesh, who appears to have been a real king of Uruk[25] a millennium and a half earlier, and around whose memory the famous mythological 'Epic of Gilgamesh' later developed.

A trace of how this process of building up David's memory may have happened remains in the *Tanach*. A single verse records how the otherwise unknown Elchanan slew Goliath. In the much better known version of this story, Elchanan has been displaced by David.[26] This version is told dramatically over 58 verses and is now one part of the larger than life account of the 'history' of David.

The Bible lists twelve 'bridging kings' linking Solomon to Hezekiah. These divide rather too neatly into six who 'did what was evil in the sight of the Lord' and six who 'did what was right in the sight of the

---

[23] *The Tel Dan inscription which seems to contain the words* בית דוד *- House of David' dates from the 8th century, 200 years later, and was of course found a long way from Jerusalem to which there is no clear link*

[24] *For a detailed discussion of the place of David & Solomon in history, see 'David and Solomon' by Israel Finkelstein and Neil Asher Silberman, Free Press 2006*

[25] *Gilgamesh is recorded as the 5th king of Uruk (Southern Mesopotamia). He reigned around 2600 BCE.*

[26] *The Elchanan story is at 2 Samuel 21:19. The David version takes the entire chapter of 1 Samuel 17.*

Lord'. These individuals may well have existed and been tribal leaders, but it is unlikely that they were full kings. From the literary point of view, their stories are clearly typological, that is they were made to fit within a pattern.

When the Bible was composed, these oral traditions were recorded as 'history' and they gave the people a sense of pride that their ancestors had once lived in a golden age. That this empire was mythical was completely irrelevant. Remember, history in today's sense had not yet been invented.

Archæology shows us that Jerusalem was only about 12 acres in size at the time of Solomon and so could have supported a population of only about a thousand. Not a likely capital for an empire stretching from Egypt to the Euphrates. It is interesting to consider that a thousand equals the total number of wives and concubines the Bible attributes to Solomon, so the city would have been seriously lacking in men. In reality, as the writing of the Bible's 'history' took place several centuries after the events, its authors would have most likely been unaware of such details. Even had they been aware of them, they would not have been concerned by such errors of fact.

These stories seem to originate from sources writing a 'history' of Judah. It seems likely that these Jerusalemites would not have wanted their national history to originate with Omri[27] who had his capital in the north. The writers utilised memories of the former Egyptian empire in Canaan, which they combined with elements from the lives of Kings Omri and Hammurabi,[28] to create a beautiful story of a golden age centred on Jerusalem.

It is with King Omri and his son Ahab that the biblical account starts to move towards evidence-based history. From Omri's time on, we have sufficient primary and secondary source evidence to start building a general picture of events. The *Tanach* portrays Omri negatively as he did not follow Yahweh. Omri's historical record,

---

[27] *Many historians consider Omri to be the first proper 'historic' king in Israel's history. He reigned from c. 885-874 BCE (sources still disagree about dating of this early period of history, but there is general agreement to within 5 years). Incidentally, Omri's territory probably extended south to include the future Judah so in one sense this was a United Monarchy.*

[28] *Hammurabi c.1810-1750 BCE, was perhaps the most important King of Babylon. Echoes of his famous law code can be found in the Tanach.*

however, is impressive. He founded Samaria as the Israelite capital[29] and established peaceful ties both with Judah to the south and Sidon and Tyre to the north. He also conquered Moab in the east, to bring economic prosperity to the Northern Kingdom.[30]

In Israel however, it was not the kings but the prophets who were responsible for the early development of the religion. We can now start to follow both political and theological developments, which ultimately will combine to produce the form of Jewish religion we have today. Gradually, via the prophets, the image and concept of God was transformed. As this occurred and a personal and ethical God developed, the moral consciousness of the people evolved.

The first prophets of the 'Yahweh-alone' movement, as this early move towards monotheism has been called, were Amos and Hosea. They seem to have been active in the Northern Kingdom during the reign of Jeroboam II (c. 786-746 BCE). They preached against the materialism and decadence in Israel, which then was at its most prosperous - a position achieved by paying tribute to Assyria. Hosea claimed that the greater the tribulation of the people, the greater the power of Yahweh. He records a polytheistic land. He speaks of Israel as an unfaithful wife, even as a prostitute. The prophets seem to have been the catalyst that began the changes towards the beginnings of Judaism.

In 722 BCE Assyria conquered and ended the existence of the Northern Kingdom of Israel. The development of the Yahweh-alone movement now relocated to the Southern Kingdom of Judah, whose population was increased by refugees arriving from the north. Seven years later in Judah, Hezekiah came to the throne and his twenty-eight year reign was a time of dramatic events. Our early history was always intimately bound up with the fortunes of our more powerful neighbours - the Egyptians, Hittites, Philistines, Assyrians, Arameans, Babylonians, Persians, Greeks and Romans. Unfortunately, this history has a major recurring theme of rebellion against the current superpower, and sadly almost every one of these rebellions ended badly.[31]

---

[29] *Previously the capital was at Tirzah.*

[30] *This was recorded on the Moabite stele, now in the Louvre. This is interesting also for the way it describes the Moabite god, Chemosh, in terms that could be taken straight from the Tanach.*

[31] *The exception, arguably, are the Hasmoneans who got their timing right (when the Greeks were in decline).*

In 705 BCE, Sennacherib became king of Assyria, the contemporary regional superpower. Hezekiah rashly joined with Egypt to rebel against him, with tragic results. Inevitably, Sennacherib invaded Judah. In anticipation, Hezekiah had fortified Jerusalem and safeguarded its water supply but was unable to protect the rest of his territory. The Assyrians besieged, conquered and pillaged the land. Judah was devastated, only Jerusalem and a rump of territory remained uncaptured. Archæology has found widespread devastation at this time, bearing out the relief in Sennacherib's palace of the siege, capture, plunder and burning of Lachish.[32] Judah's territory shrank

Judean family being driven into captivity following the fall of Lachish
Relief from Sennacherib's palace at Nineveh   *(British Museum)*

drastically and Hezekiah had to pay heavy tribute. The prosperous state he had once ruled was all but destroyed at his death. King Hezekiah (c. 715-687 BCE) battled for Yahweh but lost much of his territory to Assyria.

---

[32] *Now in the British Museum - the campaign is also recorded in the Assyrian state records, which list 46 cities besieged and records Hezekiah trapped in Jerusalem 'like a bird in a cage'. It is not known why Sennacherib lifted the siege. The biblical account of a plague is suspect, and that of Sennacherib's subsequent assassination anachronistic. According to Sennacherib's records, the tribute (as well as money) included Hezekiah's daughters, concubines and musicians.*

Despite the political setbacks, or arguably because of them, the prophets continued to innovate theologically. From the late eighth century, three ideas increased in strength, ideas that have influenced Judaism until today. These were; one God, one dynasty and one city. They made central a belief in a city protected by a resident God[33] and administered by his appointed bloodline of kings.[34] During this period, the prophets created an aura of sanctity about Jerusalem. According to the Bible, this enabled Hezekiah to decree that it was only possible to worship God in Jerusalem and so all other temples and shrines had to be destroyed.[35] This destruction of shrines was aided, ironically, by the Assyrians who did much of the destroying for him.

The concept of a holy city seems to have begun in 760 BCE, when a severe earthquake devastated Judea but left Jerusalem unscathed. The prophets claimed this as a sign from on high. In 722 BCE when the Northern Kingdom was destroyed but Judah left alone, their case became stronger. Finally, in 701 BCE when Sennacherib destroyed most of Judah, but lifted the siege of Jerusalem without capturing it, the case was 'proved'.

Back in the political world, Hezekiah's successor, Manasseh astutely managed to patch things up with Assyria, and paid it only modest tribute. His long reign (c. 687-642 BCE) was peaceful, a time of recovery and expansion.[36] He restored religious pluralism; Ba'al and Asherah were allowed back, for which the *Tanach* gives him a terrible review. His theological reputation was so bad that nine centuries later the *Mishnah* even barred him (by name) from entry to the world to come! Nevertheless, during his reign the country recovered from Hezekiah's loss of territory and prospered, so politically, he must be considered a successful king.[37]

---

[33] *Strictly a God who causes his name to dwell there – Ezra 6:12; 2 Chronicles 12:13*

[34] *This is the Deuteronomistic ideology. The Deuteronomist school edited much of the Torah to remove conflicting ideas - although traces of these remain.*

[35] *Some historians consider this as Deuteronomist propaganda, citing evidence of the building of temples in Arad and Lachish during Hezekiah's reign, and continuing use of the high place in Beersheva. They consider that centralisation really occurred later with Josiah. There was also a temple at Elephantine, in Upper Egypt, where a variant of the religion was practised. The Elephantine Jews had a shrine to God (whom they called Yahu) in their temple, along with shrines to two goddesses, Asham-bethel and Anath-bethel. This temple was destroyed in the late 5th century BCE following a dispute with their neighbours over Passover sacrifices.*

[36] *Judah expanded south and east; we even have evidence of trade with south Arabia.*

[37] *Finkelstein suggests that many of the stories of David and Solomon's golden age use details appropriate to the time of Manasseh. These stories help to integrate the refugees from the former Northern Kingdom into Judah by giving Israelites and Judeans a common past.*

Manasseh was succeeded by his son Amon, who was assassinated two years later and then by his eight year old grandson, Josiah, who was to reign for 31 years. This was a period of major change. The young Josiah was influenced by the prophet Zephaniah and the high priest Hilkiah. He was back on Yahweh's side. In 622 BCE the book 'found' by Hilkiah during the restoration of the temple[38] is thought to be the core of Deuteronomy (Chapters 12-26). This was used to prompt Josiah's reforms, which were in accordance with Deuteronomist ideology; the removal of Ba'al, Asherah and other idols from the temple, the exclusive worship of one God, and the closure of the provincial shrines. He introduced the festival of Passover, centralised national observance of New Year and Tabernacles, and introduced a spectrum of laws dealing with justice, social welfare and morality. Prior to this, Yahweh's position had been that of the chief god of a people who practised monolatry. Josiah's reforms consolidated the ideology of the prophets of Hezekiah's time.[39]

During Josiah's reign, Assyria was in decline and Egypt and Babylon were on the rise.[40] In the territory of the former Northern Kingdom of Israel, there was a power vacuum after Assyria withdrew. This gave Judah the opportunity to expand northwards, while continuing to centralise the religion on Jerusalem. Then, in 609 BCE disaster struck. King Josiah, who had been Yahweh's greatest advocate, and was aged only 39, was killed by the Egyptians in battle.[41] Consequently, Egypt briefly took control of the territory of Judah.

Four years later, the Babylonian King Nebucharnezzar crushed the Egyptians at the battle of Carcamesh and Egypt left the region for good. The threat now came from the expanding Babylonians who, in 597 BCE, besieged Jerusalem which capitulated. Many leaders, priests and artisans were carried off into exile in Babylon, and the vassal king Zedekiah was put on the throne. This proved a tragic mistake. Foolishly, Zedekiah rebelled, inevitably leading to the Babylonian recapture of Jerusalem in 586 BCE. This time, as punishment for what was seen as Zedekiah's treachery, they destroyed the temple and devastated the city.

---

[38] *see II Kings 22:8*
[39] *Josiah echoes the actions attributed to Hezekiah, but Josiah is more likely the one to have actually done them, or at the very least to have done them effectively.*
[40] *In 612 BCE Nabopolassar (father of Nebuchadnezzar) of Babylon overthrew the Assyrians.*
[41] *At Megiddo, the Egyptians were led by Necho.*

That could well have been the end of the history of Judah and its people. However, depending on your beliefs, in either an accident of history or by divine intervention, about fifty years later the Babylonians were conquered in their turn by the new superpower, Persia.[42] An early act of the Persian king, Cyrus, was to free the displaced peoples of his new empire. His policy was to allow his subject people a degree of local autonomy, including freedom to worship their own gods. Some Judeans took the opportunity to return to what now became the Persian province of Yehud. The majority, however, chose to stay in Babylon, where they were becoming a rich and influential community. Those who remained supported their more idealistic compatriots with donations, especially to rebuild the temple. The province of Yehud was to continue until Alexander's conquest in 332 BCE and this period of exile in Babylon and return to Yehud was the true historical time of the emergence of the *Yehud-im* (the people of Yehud - the Jews).[43]

The successive tragedies of the destruction, first of the Northern and then the Southern Kingdoms, should have been a theological disaster for Yahweh. Paradoxically though, it led to a significant breakthrough in thought during the political decline which followed. It was the prophets, whose innovation was to produce a completely new explanation for the people's suffering (or *theodicy*). This explanation claimed that Yahweh was such a great God that he could shape the destiny of nations and He was using his power to chastise his people. The overwhelmingly powerful kings of Assyria and Babylonia did not have the support of more powerful gods (which would have been the standard understanding in the ancient world for a nation being conquered). The kings were actually instruments of Yahweh in punishing the people of Israel and Judah. Moreover, the people deserved it, and no matter what disaster was to befall them, it was to be seen as proof of Yahweh's righteousness and power.

The disaster of Josiah's early death in battle, despite him doing right in the eyes of the Lord was explained (somewhat illogically) as punishment for the great (theological) wrongs of his grandfather

---

[42] *In 539 BCE, led by Cyrus, who believed himself to be an agent of the god Marduk. The Judeans naturally saw him as an agent of Yahweh.*

[43] *The Hebrew word for Jews is* יהודים *—Yehudim. The etymology would appear to be 'Yehud – im, the occupants of Yehud', and hence date from this period.*

Manasseh, who by the normal criteria of history seems to have been a good king, and who, by contrast, died of old age after fifty-five years on the throne.

This idea was developed into a coherent theology by the Deuteronomist literature[44] which was probably written between the 7th and first half of the 6th century BCE (i.e. during Josiah's reign and the Exile). The theological ideas included the 'chosen people' concept. Judah's new relationship with God was to be interpreted by using the twin concepts of election and covenant. God had selected his chosen people and made his covenant with them. Disasters were treated as punishments and successes as rewards for renewed fidelity.

This theology gave the keeping of God's commandments a new meaning. The laws of the Deuteronomic code (Deuteronomy 12 to 26), the covenant code (Exodus 20:23 to 23:33) and the holiness code (Leviticus 17 to 26) formed a basis for an exclusive way of life, and led to the Judeans becoming a separate and exclusive people.

During the Exile, this may not have had a major impact back home in Judah itself, but it had an enormous one among the exiles in Babylon, who instituted Shabbat observance and synagogue worship. These changes were, of course, also needed in response to the loss of the temple as a basis for ritual. Zoroastrian[45] ideas on death and resurrection were later acquired from the Persian religion and started to influence the Judeans in Babylon. Ideas about angels and demons were also acquired and it is at this stage that these formerly anonymous figures of pre-exilic folklore acquired names and personalities.[46] This adoption of Persian ideas took place during the Exile and continued afterwards through those Jews who remained in this very important community.

Theologically too, a major change was required now that religious practice could no longer be centred on Jerusalem. A portable God became essential so that He could accompany his adherents wherever fate took them. This need for portability became a major stimulus towards the development of a fully universal God and true

---

[44] *The Deuteronomist literature comprises: Deuteronomy, Joshua, Judges, Samuel 1 & 2, Kings 1 & 2.*
[45] *Zoroastrianism, the religion of Persia, is an ancient religion which is fundamentally dualist.*
[46] *See the books of Zechariah and Tobit*

monotheism. Also during the Exile, it seems likely that all the disparate old texts that had been preserved were brought together. These included texts from both the former Northern and Southern Kingdoms. Each tradition had a creation story and tales of their own patriarch (Jacob and Abraham respectively). They also contained many similar stories, such as that of the flood, with some differences of detail. These were artfully combined and were supplemented by the priestly writings and by the book of Deuteronomy found by Josiah. The Torah was now taking shape.

Ezra reading the Torah.
Fresco from the synagogue
at Dura Eurobos.

Only a small number of Judeans returned from Babylon to Yehud after 539 BCE. It took until 516 BCE for a rather modest second temple to be inaugurated in Jerusalem. Ezra and Nehemiah were the key players in the next stage of the story of the early *Yehudim*. It is very difficult to date Ezra reliably, but around 458 BCE, a hugely important political development occurred.[47] Ataxerxes I, the King of Persia, most likely at Ezra's prompting, decreed the Law of Moses to be the effective civil law in Yehud. It was not unusual when running an empire to allow a colony to operate its legal system in accordance with local tradition. Provided internal order was maintained, the colonial power was not very interested in the details, and continuing local custom and practice usually led to fewer problems. This important aspect of life was to be kept unchanged by the Greeks that followed and even to a degree by the Romans.

This decree has, in the author's opinion, not been given the importance it deserves in Jewish history. It is only slight exaggeration to compare it with Constantine's acceptance of Christianity, (the effect, if not the scale, was similar). The decree meant that Yehud had

---

[47] *458 BCE is the traditional date, equating to the 7th year of the reign of Ataxerxes 1. Others suggest 428 or as late as 398 (which would make Ezra contemporary with Ataxerxes II. The later date seems scholars' current popular choice. For a clear discussion of this dating problem see 'Persia and the Bible'. Edwin M. Yamauchi pp.253-258. Ezra came to Jerusalem with a royal scroll ordering the people of Zion to obey Yahweh's commandments as if they were the King's decrees.*

become a theocracy, so that a Ba'al worshipper, for example, now had to obey Torah law in his daily life. Torah law was now backed by the state and ultimately by the Imperial power.

With great ceremony, Ezra read the Torah to the people and then it was established as both the civil and the religious law. The Torah, with its new authority, moved to the centre of the lives of all the inhabitants of Yehud. As the entire population now had to comply with Jewish law there was a much greater incentive for followers of other gods to adopt the Jewish religion. From this point onwards, we can consider the Torah as being finalised or closed. It had effectively become canonised. The new religion of the Jews and their Torah had an effective political as well as a religious base.

From a religious point of view, by accepting the Torah, individuals could now receive spiritual benefits comparable with those Zoroastrians got from their own complicated religious code and which had so influenced the exiles in Babylon. Jews now 'knew' that all would be well if they fulfilled the demands of their Torah, and if reward did not arrive during their time on Earth, it would surely await them in the world to come.

This concept of Yahweh as a God who acts in history led some adherents of the Yahweh-alone movement to break out of the old world-view that both good and evil were permanent realities of life. They began to look forward to a future when all would be perfected. This messianic view was portrayed by Ezekiel, who was exiled as a young priest.[48] He wrote from Babylon of a future when the final crisis would be overcome in Judea, the Temple would be rebuilt and the exiles gathered in. Yet again, these ideas were strongly influenced by Zoroastrianism.

From this point on, we have true monotheism. The 2nd Isaiah,[49] who prophesied during the Exile, was arguably the first true monotheist. Prior to this, it appears that monolatry was still being practiced. As examples of monolatrous belief, Micah 4:5 (8th century) wrote:

---

[48] *Ezekiel was exiled after the first Babylonian conquest of 597 BCE. As discussed elsewhere his vision of the chariot is a symbolic vision of God leaving the temple in Jerusalem before its destruction.*

[49] *The biblical book of Isaiah is a composite. The first part (Chapters 1-39) is understood as primarily the work of Isaiah of Jerusalem who prophesied from 740 BCE. The next part refers to events long after his death (post-exilic) and its anonymous author is known by scholars as deutero-Isaiah or the 2nd Isaiah.*

כי כל העמים ילכו איש בשם אלהיו; ואנחנו נלך בשם יהוה אלהינו לעולם ועד.

'For let all the peoples walk each one in the name of its god, but we will walk in the name of Yahweh for ever and ever.'

Judges 11:24 (6th century) said:

הלא את אשר יורישך, כמוש אלהיך אותו תירש; ואת כל אשר הוריש יהוה אלהינו, מפנינו אותו נירש.

'Will you not possess what Chemosh, your God gives you to possess? So whoever Yahweh, our God has dispossessed before us, we will possess.'

Isaiah will have none of this. He has Yahweh challenging the other Gods and showing them to be false and without power. He is dealing with a situation where the Israelites are scattered and powerless, and so their God can only save them (and therefore continue to exist for them) if he is omnipotent and alone in the firmament.

In Yehud, Judaism continued to evolve. After Alexander's conquest of 332 BCE, Hellenistic ideas strongly influenced and indeed polarised Jewish thought.[50] The Levant was rapidly Hellenised and many *polis* type cities arose.[51] These surrounded Jewish Samaria and Jerusalem, which the Greeks saw as rural backwaters, like other relics of the past that remained within their empire. The Jews in their turn reacted in different ways to the Greeks.

Jewish responses to Hellenism can be compared to the effect of the Enlightenment on the Jews of more modern times. In a similar way, back then, a Jewish reform movement sprang up which, in this case, wanted to embrace Hellenism. The reformists wanted to universalise the sacred texts and purge them of what they saw as provincial and parochial ideas. [52]

---

[50] *After Alexander's death, his empire was split in three by his warring generals. Antigonus took Asia Minor, Seleucus Syria (Antioch) and Mesopotamia, and Ptolemy took Egypt. From 323-200 Jews were ruled by the Ptolemies, 200 onwards by the Seleucids.*

[51] *Polis – Greek style semi-autonomous city or city state - local examples were coastal Tyre, Sidon, Gaza, Byblos, and Tripoli while inland were Shechem, Marissa, Philadelphia (Amman) and Gamal (in Jordan).*

[52] *We know relatively little about this reform movement; the truism of history being written by the victors applies. In 173 its leader, Menelaus, the Jewish high priest found an ally in Antiochus Epiphanes, the Seleucid monarch. Antiochus' motives seem purely mercenary. He was strapped for cash, having to pay enormous tribute to Rome, and he took advantage of the three men, Onias Jason and Menelaus who were vying for the position of high priest. Menelaus (as a tax farmer) made the highest offer (using also the temple treasures) and took this position of power. With this powerful backing, he attempted to impose his reforms by*

The more conservative Jews responded to this threat with the new theological idea of the apocalyptic literature. This concerned itself with human beings' last days on Earth and with the end of time. An early example was the Book of Daniel,[53] which is the last book of the *Tanach* and dates from around 150 BCE. It claims forces of cosmic evil to be loose in the world, one of which can be recognised as symbolically representing the Greek ruler, Antiochus Epiphanes. Another reason for the development of this new theology was that the Deuteronomic theodicy of just reward and punishment for faithfulness had broken down. It was clear that the faithful suffered under the Greeks, while those who assimilated often prospered.

The Jewish community was now polarised and, as is typical in such circumstances, those prepared to use violence came to the fore. In what was the first war in recorded history to be waged over religion,[54] the Hasmoneans fought to maintain Jewish practice. They led a successful revolt against these reformers and their Seleucid backers, and ultimately gained independence for the Jews. The new apocalyptic ideas, which mobilised believers into fighting against what they saw as the forces of evil, led to religious practice becoming much more extreme, especially during the period from 134 BCE under John Hyrcanus. He had a mercenary army, which in its zeal to eliminate unbelievers, would slaughter inhabitants of captured cities who would not convert to Judaism.[55] He also tried to destroy the Samaritans, besieging and demolishing their city of Samaria and destroying their temple on Mount Gerizim.

The Samaritans are a somewhat mysterious group. They seem to be descended from a remnant of the original Northern Kingdom and from converts among those resettled in Samaria by the Assyrians and Greeks. Around 424 BCE, they separated themselves from mainstream Judaism as a result of a dispute about the centrality of Jerusalem.[56] They built their own temple on their holy mountain,

---

changing temple practice. In 167 he seems to have gone too far defiling the temple by introducing Greek practices, possibly even the sacrifice of pigs.

[53] Some consider that the earlier book of Ezekiel contains apocalyptic ideas. There were many other apocalyptic works contemporary with Daniel, but only Daniel made the canon.

[54] It was also the first recorded war to have religious martyrs, dying rather than converting.

[55] For example, he pillaged and burnt Scythopolis, and in Idumea captured Adora and Marissa, slaughtering those who would not convert.

[56] This gives indirect evidence that the Northern Kingdom never had a tradition of a united monarchy under David and Solomon in Jerusalem, having roots firmly in the North.

Mount Gerizim. In 128 BCE, this was destroyed by John Hyrcanus, who was trying to exterminate those he considered heretics.[57] Nevertheless, a small number of them have survived to the present day. They believe only in Torah law,[58] rejecting the later books of the *Tanach*, rabbinical interpretation and of course the Talmud.

John Hyrcanus' son, Alexander Janneus, followed his father's example of holy intolerance with forced conversion, massacre and expulsion characterising his conquest of neighbouring territory. The Jewish nation expanded rapidly and violently. When Alexander Janneus died in 76 BCE, the Jewish world was split. The Hasmonean state had been able to expand at a time when Seleucid power was waning but before Rome had become strong enough to displace the Greeks. Now Rome was strong and waiting in the wings.[59] As always, the Jews' fate was ultimately dependent on their relationship with the regional superpower.

Not everyone had been happy with the despotic rule of the Hasmoneans. Apart from their cruelty, there were also objections that they were not kings in the Davidic line and that they had usurped the role of the high priest. There were now several varieties of Judaism, and subsequent events were to determine which was to survive.

The Sadducees[60] were mainly involved with the Temple and ritual. Because of this, and their rigid priestly law code, they could not easily adapt to change. As a group, they did not long survive the destruction of the Temple.

The more extreme Essenes saw even Jerusalem as corrupted by Hellenism, and went off into the desert to form communities like Qumran, from where they have recently become better known through the Dead Sea Scrolls (the earliest of which dates from around 250 BCE). The Essenes were a relatively small, ascetic order, who, along with their militant wing the Zealots[61] were nearly all killed during the first century CE Jewish war with Rome. Their ideas,[62]

---

[57] *He was also angered that the Samaritans had not supported them in their revolt against the Greeks*

[58] *See the appendix p240 for more information on their sacred texts.*

[59] *In 63 BCE Antipater was to make Judea a Roman client state.*

[60] *The Sadducees rejected Pharisaic ideas of the Oral Law and resurrection of the dead.*

[61] *or Kanna'im, or Sicarii.*

[62] *These included resurrection and messianism, derived from Zoroastrianism and Greek Pythagorean thought.*

however, lived on and were particularly influential on Christianity, which itself began as another branch of Judaism.

Other Jews, perhaps the majority, disliked the isolationists and fanatics. They learned Greek, probably initially for business and translated the *Tanach* into Greek (the Septuagint). They sent their children to a Greek *gymnasium* and Hellenised their names, especially in the influential and large Jewish community of Alexandria. The book of Kohelet (Ecclesiastes) which is thought to date from this period illustrates the dilemma between new foreign ideas and inherited piety.

Two catastrophic events now occurred, which were to mean either the end of Judaism or that the religion had to reinvent itself. These were the destruction of the second temple by Titus in 70 CE during the first Jewish revolt against Rome and the even more catastrophic Bar Kochba revolt sixty years later. The latter had an impact on the Jewish world that, arguably, was later only matched by the Shoah. It resulted in the majority of Judea's Jews being killed, exiled or sold into slavery.

Only two significant Jewish groups survived these twin disasters; the Jewish Christians, who were led initially by Jesus' brother James, and the Pharisees.[63] In the lead up to the Bar Kochba revolt of 135 CE, there was conflict between these two groups. Rabbi Akiva considered Bar Kochba to be the Jewish Messiah and convinced the *Sanhedrin*[64] to support the revolt under his military leadership. For Christians, of course, the Messiah had already come, and the two religions now effectively divorced. Both adapted to the new reality by producing very different new texts and changing the form of their own religion.

Christianity has the former Pharisee, Paul, primarily to thank for becoming an independent religion. The Christians produced the New Testament which referred to and reinterpreted the *Tanach*. Although they were subject to persecution early on, they received a huge political boost in 312 CE with Emperor Constantine's conversion to Christianity, which henceforth became the official religion of the Roman Empire.

---

[63] *The Pharisees had been around since at least the time of John Hyrcanus. They were originally called Hasidim. The etymology of Pharisee is to separate, and that is what they ultimately achieved.*
[64] *Sanhedrin — an assembly of judges, effectively a High or Supreme Jewish Court.*

The Pharisees took a different route. Following the defeat by Rome, they put emphasis neither on messianism and Jewish nationalism like Akiva and Bar Kochba, nor on radical new theology like the Christians, but on religious observance instead. Hillel, who had come from Babylon, became the most respected authority among the Pharisees and was the catalyst in transforming Pharisaic Judaism into what became mainstream Rabbinic Judaism. His family dynasty became the recorders of the law and Judaism today is still coloured by his influence.

The Pharisee's breakthrough, with the *Mishnah*, was to make use of a Greek idea, the unwritten or Oral Law, in order to re-interpret the written law. To validate this new law it was said to have been given by God to Moses alongside the Torah, but never previously written down. By using this new concept, many Torah laws could be modified to the changing times and circumstances, which helped Judaism survive its new situation. The traumas of the destruction of the temple and the aftermath of the revolts meant that a new relationship was required with the sacred texts. The concept that Torah study could be redemptive has no precedent in the Hebrew Bible but was strongly influenced by the ideas of Plato. Indeed, unlike the Christian New Testament, the *Mishnah* makes little reference to the *Tanach*, nor does it concern itself unduly with dogma and belief. Its authors' prime concern was how Jews behaved and how they could remain a holy people despite the loss of their temple.

Present Jewish practice is based on the Talmud that the Pharisees' spiritual heirs, the rabbis, completed over the subsequent centuries. This was finalised around 500 CE and its code of behaviour has proved very effective at keeping Jews in the Diaspora as a separate people from their host nations. It is then, through the Pharisees and the rabbis that Judaism finally emerged to become the religion that we are familiar with - but considerably later in history than many people seem to think. It is instructive to consider how important the events of history have been in shaping the Jewish religious practice of today. As we have seen, momentous events produced imaginative theological responses which several times adapted the religion so that it could survive. Their influence, and thus the echoes of this ancient history, still affects the way Judaism is practiced today.

4

Myth and its four main functions

One is a framework to live in. How does the Jewish model compare?

――――――――――

All things are metaphors
Goethe

The late Joseph Campbell, who spent his life studying and teaching about different religions and the mythologies which underlie them, considered that every individual needs to accept a mythology of one sort or another. He felt that without such a background framework to fall back on we would be psychologically unable to function normally in the world. This applies to us all, whether religious or secular. According to Campbell, this mythic background which underpins our ideas and behaviour (regardless of whether it comes from a religion or elsewhere) serves the following four main functions:

- **Cosmological function**

  The human psyche has a need for a practical framework which can explain and make sense of our experiences. We need to have a working knowledge on some level of fundamental matters such as how the solar system, Earth, moon, weather and eclipses operate; causes and cures for illness; and how to grow our food. We need this understanding in order to function practically in the world. Our understanding may be scientifically correct or completely hypothetical; the important thing is not its accuracy but the fact that we feel that we can, to some degree, rely on it. Imparting this background knowledge was originally one of the functions of oral tradition. It was then taken over by sacred texts, and has now largely been usurped by science.

- ## Social function

It has always been a fundamental habit for the leaders of human societies throughout the ages to seek to maintain the established social order. This is consistent worldwide in many diverse situations and historical times, and occurs whether the leadership is religious, political or both, and whether the established order is a fair one or not. When external factors, such as war or revolution, cause the social order to change each new incoming system in its turn quickly seeks to perpetuate itself.

Each individual needs to be able to relate to the wider community, and know her or his place in the pecking order. Religions provide clear social structures. (This is why from the earliest times of human beings living together in social groups, religion has helped establish a social order.) This aspect of life is now largely secularised in the West but a religious framework still persists strongly elsewhere. Some of what we now consider as outdated and unacceptable remnants of traditional social structures (such as the *dalits* or untouchables in India or the oppression of women in many traditional societies) remain extremely hard to eliminate.

- ## Mystical or metaphysical function

An important aspect of being human is the opening of one's mind to the dimension of mystery and the experience of a feeling of awe and wonder. This mystery and awe heightens awareness of life's 'big questions', and at least starts the process of addressing them. While some people concern themselves much more than others with questions such as 'what is the purpose of our existence?' we all need to consider such issues to some degree (either consciously or subconsciously). We must do this in order to affirm life and to be able to continue to function in this seeming indifferent world.

- **Psychological or pedagogical function**

  We all have psychological needs which are, or should be, addressed by the mythic structure we accept. We look to this myth for guidelines on how to balance our conscious life with our instinctive urges or to put it another way how to balance the life of the body with that of the spirit.

  Our mythic background is also helpful if, in one way or another, it reconciles us to the knowledge of our transience and ultimate death. Without this, we could be paralysed from acting in the world.

  Each individual obtains a centring and harmonisation by 'giving her or himself up' to one of the 'mythic authorities'. This authority could be a god (in one form or another) but does not have to be. Nietzsche suggested the following list of alternatives to gods: conscience, morality, reason, social interest, history, happiness or happiness of the majority.

Campbell correctly stated that western religion no longer addresses the cosmological and sociological functions adequately, having been overtaken by changes within society and in scientific knowledge since the religions were founded. Recent books written in favour of atheism by Dawkins and others also show up religions' shortcomings in these two important areas very effectively. However, these books are much less impressive at demonstrating atheism's ability to help people with the metaphysical and psychological aspects of their lives. The evidence would seem to show that for a large portion of mankind the traditional myths, symbols, ritual and dogma of religion still serve them well in this regard.

The following chart summarises how Campbell's four types of need can be responded to for believers (whether from the East or the West) and for atheists.

Function	Believer	Atheist
Cosmological	Sacred texts Dogma Oral tradition	Science can already give many of the answers, and understanding improves over time.
Social	Public ritual acts Community Hierarchical structure of most religions (clergy, priests or shamans)	Political structure and ethical law code (especially in a democracy) provides the framework and friends and family the community.
Metaphysical	Sacred texts Dogma Oral tradition	Philosophy, acceptance of an absence of answers to all questions and/or acceptance that an individual's life is subject to factors that are completely random
Psychological	Faith Prayer Ritual Spirituality Meditation Trust that divine forces will protect one	Some argue there is 'a God shaped hole' but atheists may have 'faith' in something else (see above for Nietzsche's list). It is also argued that the arts should now take over this role from religion. An atheist can still have a sense of the numinous or of human spirituality, without needing to believe in supernatural beings.

We have been dealing so far with religion in general. Let us now evaluate how Judaism copes with these four functions.

In relation to the **metaphysical** function, we must bear in mind that we are dealing with matters not amenable to proof, and for which we will never have definitive answers. For a person who is happy to accept a 'package' that gives a set of answers backed by the full authority of a religion, then the Jewish metaphysical 'package' can function well, and when accepted with faith it effectively resolves these issues for many people.

By contrast, for those amenable to evidence, science now offers the only realistic model to view **cosmological** questions. Our sacred texts have charming stories and notions, but we would no more rely on their accuracy today than we would use them for their medical advice should we fall sick. Their underlying cosmology of a three tiered Earth at the centre of a universe ruled by a monarchical creator God is simply outdated, as surely as the scientific explanations we have today will be in another 2000 years. However, that is the point of science; today's explanations are the best science can currently offer. They are an approach to the truth but not truth itself. Unlike sacred texts that are set in stone for all time, scientific explanations will be modified as new knowledge becomes available.

Historically, humanity has only produced five significantly different ways of dealing with cosmological questions. These are each described later in this chapter so that the reader can assess them individually.

Sociologically speaking, things have also moved on. Patriarchal power and hierarchy were very much part of the world of the *Tanach*. Currently in the West we value equality and fairness, and attempt to be much less judgemental of alternative lifestyles. Accordingly many people today cannot accept the attitudes of the *Tanach* and Talmud on lifestyle questions. In which way these matters will change again in the future is unknown and unpredictable. Unlike science, where knowledge once obtained is 'out there' and in that sense must progress, in matters of ethics and social mores history shows that repression can occur surprisingly quickly. Any progress we feel has been made must be constantly guarded.

Traditional Judaism has failed to move with the times and maintains many of the prejudices of a different age. It often actually claims this as a virtue, but this attitude does a disservice to those in its community whom it does not treat fairly: women, homosexuals, chained women, *mamzerim*[1] and others. A religious court system in which the evidence of a woman or a gentile is given less weight that of an orthodox Jewish man can no longer be acceptable. The progressive branches of Judaism are very much aware of these failings and have dealt with most of them.

On other sociological aspects, Judaism scores extremely positively. It strongly promotes a very effective community with all the advantages this brings to individuals *who are included*. Judaism's traditions, with the cycle of annual festivals and the rituals that mark life's transitions are extremely effective in providing social cohesion. The caveat is that

---

[1] *Mamzerim (singular mamzer) – bastards - outcasts from Judaism solely due to their parents' circumstances*

Jewish communities and rituals tend to be very clannish, and often exclude even other Jews with different levels of observance.

These advantages of community and the annual cycle of events also assist the **psychological** functions of the religion. Buy into the faith package and there are clear psychological benefits:

- Personal prayer can have a meditative and stress relieving function.
- Being part of a community can make life much easier with its built in support system (providing you can conform to the community's mores).
- Living in a faith community and having virtually all one's decisions – big and small – made externally makes life much simpler and less stressful, as long as one's spirit does not rebel or wish to assert its individuality.
- Faith in a benevolent divinity that takes care of believers on an individual basis must also be helpful psychologically (if one can manage it).

However, some perceive problems from a psychological point of view for Judaism (and the other monotheistic religions). One of these is the suppression of the goddess in monotheistic mythology; another is the lack of a theology of an immanent god present in all nature including humanity. Others consider it problematic for the monotheistic religions that they have lost their knowledge of the transcendental or spiritual experience.[2] In reaction to this, we see a rise of interest by Jews in esoteric practices, such as Kabbalah and even such phenomena as Jewish Buddhism.

Returning now to the **Cosmological** function of myth, there have been five main cosmologies - or models of 'the way it is', in wide circulation in different parts of the world. These explain the relationship between mankind and nature in very different ways. There are some detailed variations on these themes (such as dualism) but the five models are a useful generalisation. The first two are eastern models, the second two western (the Jewish model being the third). The final model is ancestor worship, which arose early on in many parts of the world, being widely

---

[2] e.g. Alan Watts, who lectured and wrote extensively on this. See his 'Myth and Religion'. This would not be true of Sufis or Hassidic Jews or other mystical or esoteric monotheists.

practiced in China before Confucius. It is still important to the native religions of places as far apart as Madagascar, Haiti and Australia.

In the pre-scientific age, these models answered a need that most individuals felt. This was to 'understand' a single human being's place in nature and how the individual came to be part of the world. Most religions include quite detailed cosmologies, for example, creation stories and explanations of illness and suffering. They also tell followers how to behave in order to please or appease the god(s). In the modern world, science has increasingly usurped this function of religion, in particular in relation to illness. This was once the preserve of the priests and the shamans and while even in the West there remains much superstition and quackery, most individuals faced with serious illness today choose to take advantage of scientific medicine.

Mankind's Five Main Cosmological Models

A dramatic model

In this model, god is not the creator and director of the world ruling from on high, but an 'actor' taking part in the 'play' of life here on Earth, while playing all the roles at once. Every person[3] is god in a mask. This is the Hindu formula, *tat tvam asi* – you are it. We are all a part of god, thus the world is ruled by some 'energy' that feels and is in tune with the dance of the universe. This 'god' or life energy is known to Hindus as Brahman.

'Brahman' is by no means the same as what adherents of western religions mean by the word God. If, in a Judeo-Christian society someone says that he has discovered that he is god, he could very easily find himself committed to a mental institution. In India the reaction would more likely be: 'How good that you found out for yourself what the enlightened ones already know'. Such a discovery would be considered perfectly natural; because adherents of Eastern religion consider that we are all a part of god.

The principle of organic growth

The Chinese model of *Tao* - Lao Tzu, the traditional father of Taoism, said of the Tao:

---

[3] Note the etymology: persona (Latin) – 'that through which comes sound' – a word used initially to refer to the masks actors wore in Greek theatre which identified their characters and projected their voices.

The great Tao flows everywhere, both to the left and to the right. It loves and nourishes all things, but does not lord it over them. When merits are achieved it lays no claim to them.

Essentially in this model the world just *is*. Nature is something that happens independently without a governor, in the same way that one's heart beats without being told, or the way one grows from child to adult without any conscious input telling one's bones to lengthen. The key teaching for humanity is not to disturb the balance.

It would appear that as the Tao 'explains' everything, followers of Taoism have no need to develop more concrete explanations for how the world came into being and operates. This model can be considered very passive, so much so that the Taoists were criticised by their rival Confucianists that 'they would not move themselves to pluck out a single hair, even if by doing so they could save the world'.

A political model

This is the Judeo-Christian viewpoint in which a monarchical creator God structured the world and all in it, imposing power and authority from above. God expects, and on occasions demands, respect, loyalty and devotion from his subjects. God can be described in anthropomorphic terms, man having been created in his image. God has revealed his instructions telling humanity how to behave through the revelation contained in sacred texts, which were given directly to a few selected individuals.

Daniel Harbour provides an interesting argument for rejecting this model in his book, 'An Intelligent Person's Guide to Atheism'.[4] Harbour states that theistic religions have a worldview which he describes as a **Baroque Monarchy**; that is to say that the explanation usually involves complex origin myths, dogma, ritual and supernatural being(s). This is baroque in its complexity and monarchical in its didactic advice or instruction.

---

[4] *'An Intelligent Person's Guide to Atheism.' Daniel Harbour. Duckworth 2001*

Using logic, common sense and Ockham's razor[5] Harbour argues that we should always prefer explanations in the form of a **Spartan Meritocracy**. In other words, we should make as small a set of assumptions (or hold as small a number of theories) as possible, and should be willing to discard and replace each of these on a purely meritocratic basis in the light of new evidence. (This is an exact description of the scientific model, below.)

Theistic religions are based on networks of unwarranted assumptions that are subjected to no tests of merit, but are held on the basis of scripture or tradition (baroque monarchies). This argument appears compelling as far as western religion is concerned, but it cannot be used to disprove the very different ideas of God from the east.

A further serious objection to the Jewish monarchical world view is the argument that it reduces the individual's position in this life to that of a serf or supplicant. A believer cannot fully express individuality, especially not a possibly heretical opinion for fear it may impact on crucial Jewish desires for such goals as:

- the individual's next life
- the individual's fate in 'the world to come' (heaven)
- the coming of the messiah

This objection continues by stating that individuals can only start to freely enjoy this life and to develop fully as human beings if they behave as if this life is the only life there is and do not accept unevaluated codes of behaviour. This remains true regardless of what may or may not happen after death.

A scientific model

In this model, the natural world operates according to laws and principles that are followed consistently. The goal of science is to fully understand these principles and as steps along the road ideas (hypotheses) can be suggested which are tried out and tested. These ideas, should they stand up over time, become theories which are then considered the best explanation that we have come up with thus far of the way things operate. Theories are strengthened if new knowledge is

---

[5] *Ockham's razor is a philosophical tool which states that where there are multiple explanations for something, each of which seem equally valid, we should choose the simplest one. It is named after its originator, William of Ockham (c. 1288-c.1348). Sir Isaac Newton (1643-1728) restated it 'more is vain if less will serve'.*

in accordance with what they had predicted and modified if it is not. An example of a theory being strengthened by new knowledge is evolution, whose predictions were confirmed both by the later science of genetics and the discovery and application of DNA, especially its ability to trace links between different animal species.

In this model, no supernatural forces can be admitted unless they can be demonstrated experimentally. This has (so far) excluded god(s) from the model as external actor(s) in the cosmology of the Earth. It has not excluded them however as internal actor(s) in the human psyche. Indeed some work by cognitive scientists appears to show that the human brain was genetically conceived to encourage religious beliefs,[6] and what may be considered as the home of God, (the location of mystical ecstasy), may have been located in the brain's upper rear parietal lobes.[7]

Ancestor worship - a human link to the gods

This early religious model holds that after death we pass to another world, that of the spirits and the gods. When our ancestors died they entered that world and they can now be our personal link to the gods. If we treated them well while alive and now treat their spirits well after their death, they will look out for us and help to protect us from life's dangers. The gods are too distant and powerful for an individual to approach, but our ancestors can act as intermediaries to help bridge the gap for us.

Echoes of these ideas remain even where more sophisticated theology is introduced. Among monotheists one sees shrines at graves of great rabbis, saints or holy men where the faithful visit to pray for health, fertility or business success, sometimes making long pilgrimages to do so. The rationale can only be the belief that these long dead individuals will intercede with God on behalf of the living.

---

[6] *Andrew Newberg and Eugene d'Aquili. Why God Won't Go Away: Brain Science and the Biology of Belief. Ballantine New York 2001.*

[7] *A radioactive tracer was injected into the cerebral blood supply of meditating Tibetan Buddhists and praying Franciscan Monks. Their brains were scanned to locate areas of increased activity. This was found in the left and right upper rear parietal lobes.*

Part two

Basic Jewish

beliefs

re-examined

5

Torah min hashamayim - was the Torah written in heaven or on Earth?

He who seeks the truth must listen to his opponent
Isaac Samuel Reggio

The Torah itself makes no claim as to authorship, divine or otherwise. It is an anonymous work. The first explicit attribution[1] we have of authorship to Moses (as God's scribe) appears some 1500 years after the time generally given for Moses in the pages of the Talmud:[2]

כל ישראל יש להם חלק לעולם הבא שנאמר (ישעיהו ס) ועמך כולם צדיקים לעולם יירשו ארץ נצר מטעי מעשה ידי להתפאר ואלו שאין להם חלק לעולם הבא האומר אין תחיית המתים מן התורה **ואין תורה מן השמים** ואפיקורוס.

*All Israel have a portion in the world to come, for it is written,[3] 'your people are all righteous; they shall inherit the land for ever, the branch of my planting, the work of my hands, that I may be glorified', but the following have no portion therein: he who maintains that resurrection is not a biblical doctrine, **that the Torah was not divinely revealed**, [literally 'the Torah is not from heaven'] and an apikoros.*

---

[1] *In the post-exilic books of Ezra, Nehemiah and Chronicles there are references to Torat Moshe, which is probably best translated as instructions of Moses. This may indicate the start of the tradition.*
[2] *Talmud Sanhedrin 90a (Mishnah).*
[3] *Isaiah 60:21*

This is a section of the *Mishnah* (Oral Law) dealing with heresy. At the time it was written (c. 200 CE) Rabbinic Judaism was developing out of Pharisaic Judaism but had by no means yet won the day against the competing Jewish groups. Ideas which the *Mishnah* condemned as heretical were usually ideas that were very much in circulation among these groups at the time. This is just a short extract, other types of heretics are also condemned and it is interesting to note that the rabbis had no problem deciding who was allowed to enter and who was barred from the world to come. For example, seeing neither arrogance in usurping God's role as heaven's gatekeeper, nor logical difficulty in making such a pronouncement nine centuries after his death, they denied King Manasseh[4] a place in the world to come.

Returning to the *Mishnah* quoted above, we should note that the three groups barred from heaven were each perceived as threat to the Pharisaic rabbis. Those *denying resurrection,* refers mainly to the Sadducees who held this view and like the Samaritans did not accept the Oral Law. *Apikoros* referred to those attracted by Greek ideas and philosophy, particularly the ideas of Epicurus. Those who denied the divine origin of Torah include the Gnostics, whose ideas were influential at the time. One must always bear in mind the political background of this writing.

The Talmudic rabbis themselves, however, clearly did not hold the view that every word of the Torah came directly from God. In a *Gemarra* written some centuries later, the Talmud says:[5]

ומי כתבן משה כתב ספרו ופרשת בלעם ואיוב יהושע כתב ספרו ושמונה
פסוקים שבתורה.

Who wrote the scriptures? — Moses wrote his own book and the portion of Balaam and Job. Joshua wrote the book which bears his name **and [the last] eight verses of the Pentateuch.**

This verse states the opinion that parts of the Torah were written directly by Moses along with a small portion by Joshua.[6] Clearly, it was

---

[4] See p.56 for a historical assessment of this 7th century BCE King of Judah.

[5] Talmud Baba Batra 14b (Gemarra) - the Gemarra is an early commentary on the Mishnah. The Mishnah was compiled by the Rabbis known as the Tannaim up to around 200CE. The Gemarra was the work of the Amoraim in the 3rd to 5th centuries. Mishnah and Gemarra together make up the Talmud, although further commentaries continued to be added.

[6] 'Moses' own book' is Deuteronomy. The Balaam story of Numbers 23-24 clearly stood out to the Rabbis as being in a different style to adjacent passages. The last verses of Deuteronomy concern Moses' death - odd for God to have dictated this directly to Moses.

not considered heretical in Talmudic times to state that part of the Torah was the work of man rather than the word of God, nor did it represent a threat. This situation did not change significantly until the seventeenth century, when Spinoza[7] was perhaps the first to take a secular approach to scripture. He was excommunicated by the Jewish community of Amsterdam while still in his twenties, for what were considered his heretical ideas on God and the Jewish sacred texts. With the later rise of biblical criticism, from the nineteenth century onwards, different religious authorities revisited the *Mishnah* quoted at the opening of this chapter. They now needed to decide on exactly what was meant by the phrase *Torah min hashamayim* (Torah from heaven).

The maximalist position (somewhat incredibly) is that the entire *Tanach*, Talmud and even the pronouncements of 'wise' rabbis up to today still arrive '*min hashamayim*'. A still strict orthodox interpretation is that the Torah came straight from heaven and is entirely the word of God, transcribed verbatim by Moses. More liberal orthodox thinkers argue that perhaps not all the Torah is meant; the most liberal interpretation only requires a belief that the first two of the Ten Commandments came directly from heaven.

While there are proponents of every permutation of meaning for the word *Torah*, for this discussion let us take the middle, and clearest meaning - the Pentateuch or first five books of the *Tanach*. For these books, we have strong evidence against divine authorship from two sources. Firstly, biblical scholarship and secondly, from the content and moral values expressed in the text of the Torah itself. The separate issue as to whether the text was divinely inspired will always remain unanswerable. Such a claim is not susceptible to proof and so it will not be discussed here.

One should also consider the actual process of divine revelation. By its nature, such revelation is only given to the individual who hears it. To everyone else it is just hearsay. Conceptually, it seems strange that if God wanted to reveal important instructions for humanity, He would do it by confiding in just a single individual. By revealing himself to a crowd or at least a group there would be so much less reason for

---

[7] *Baruch Spinoza 1632-1677, excommunicated 1656*

doubt.[8] Today, in the West, an individual hearing the voice of divine revelation is usually, rightly or wrongly, referred to a psychiatrist for help. Omar Khayyam made a similar point in this quatrain written almost 1000 years ago:[9]

> *'And do you think that unto such as you*
> *A maggot-minded, starved, fanatic crew,*
> *God gave the Secret, and denied it me?*
> *Well, well, what matters it! Believe that too.'*

For reasons of logic too, one needs to be suspicious of revelation. For a theory in science to be accepted experiments and observations made to test it should give results that support each other. By contrast, the instructions to humanity received in the various reported divine revelations worldwide have varied widely in their content. Had one been true, and the others false, then it would surely be reasonable to expect some confirmatory sign from on high.

There are two other serious logical problems with divine revelation. The first is that each religious group has perfect faith that their own revelation is divine, while dismissing everyone else's as either superstition or lies. No single group, however, has any evidence to validate their revelation over the competing ones. Secondly, the very idea that divine revelation is imperfect and may need correcting or revising is sufficient to demonstrate that the original revelation could not have been made by a God who is perfect and consistent. The Talmud, as will be shown, changes and overrules many Torah laws. The New Testament and the Koran claim to be new instructions for humanity. It is surely humans who err, not God who makes mistakes and later has to issue corrections. Would not a perfect God have given us moral laws from the start? God could, for example, have banned slavery rather than condoning it.

---

[8] *In this context, the Talmudic story of Rabbi Eliezer and the rabbis ignoring a voice directly from God (Baba Metzia 59a-b, see p174) is interesting. In the 'history' of revelation, from Moses to Mohammed, from Mormon Joseph Smith to Christian Scientist Mary Baker Eddy the divine voice generally speaks only to a single person. At Sinai God announced His intention to speak directly to the people, but it is not at all clear from the text that He actually did so. It is argued that He spoke the first two commandments directly, but even this is a matter of interpretation. On plain reading, the people only heard thunder and trumpets and saw lightning and smoke.*

[9] *Omar Khayyam (1048-1131) 'The Ruba'iyat of Omar Khayyam' (Richard le Gallienne's rather free verse translation)*

Returning to the question of divine authorship of the text; biblical scholarship has, over many years, presented an overwhelming case for the multi-authorship of the Torah. While there will continue to be academic arguments over details, such as whether there were four main authors or more and who the editor (redactor) was that combined the texts into the form we know, the basic debate concerning the Torah's historical origins is over. Except in what must be called fundamentalist circles, all scholars who are amenable to evidence now accept that the Torah is made up of texts from several sources, and that it was composed by various writers, not one God.

If one studies the text of the Torah, the clear differences of style, of 'spin', of language and of vocabulary between different passages are simply too striking to be ignored by anyone examining them critically and objectively. So too are the anachronisms and contradictions that these different passages contain. All this is clear evidence against only one author being responsible for their composition, regardless of whether that author was human or divine.

The reason I call those that still believe strictly in *Torah min hashamayim* fundamentalists, is that they fail a test which has been devised to distinguish the fundamentalist from the open minded. The test is to ask the holder of what seems to be a fundamentalist viewpoint the following two questions:

- *What evidence, if presented to you, would persuade you that your view is wrong?*
- *If you were to be presented with such evidence, would you then change your view?*

A fundamentalist is one who either says no such evidence is possible to the first question, or who answers no to the second question. Such people would perhaps contend that they are simply following the word of God and so there is nothing more to discuss. They are confirming that they have in fact closed their minds to rational argument. We, who do not share their vision, must understand that they have abdicated their right to take any part in further discussion of this issue. This may sound harsh, even totalitarian, but consider what it really means. Fundamentalists essentially say, 'this is our position, it is non negotiable. We do not, can not, or will not support our position with rational evidence, and certainly will not give consideration to evidence you present that contradicts it. In effect, we refuse to enter into reasonable and rational debate with you; we want you to accept our position because we say so and because we genuinely believe it to be true.'

Accordingly, these fundamentalists must be allowed to go on their way. They can maintain their position for themselves (subject to it causing no harm to others) but cannot be allowed to unduly influence the position of the rest of us, nor stop our continuing research and debate.

Bearing this in mind and returning now to the question of biblical origins, the evidence of biblical scholarship is so overwhelming that believers in *Torah min hashamayim* today hardly ever attempt to enter proper debate. One need only read both mainstream and relatively conservative works on the Bible to find that multi-authorship is taken as a given. This applies to almost all articles written by academics from non-fundamentalist institutions. Multi-authorship is no longer considered to be controversial any more than, say, the theory of evolution or of a flat-earth (and it is generally the same people who find problems with each). As discussed above, those who do not accept these ideas in most cases either will not look objectively at the evidence, or simply choose to ignore it.

They may be wise in this approach – to engage fully in the debate may prove too great a test of faith. This danger was demonstrated in the late nineteenth century within the Catholic Church. By then, contradictions in the biblical text, which had been pointed out much earlier by scholars such as Maimonides and Ibn Ezra, and subsequently examined by Hobbes and Spinoza in the 17th century, were coming to public notice. This was a result of the work of the school of biblical criticism begun in Germany by Wellhausen around 1870. To deal with this controversy, the Catholics assigned some of their best scholars to study the evidence so they could argue the church's case effectively in academic debate. To Rome's embarrassment and humiliation, this plan backfired. Once these scholars had made a detailed study of their opponents' arguments they were filled with intellectual doubt and questions. Over time more and more of them were won over by the arguments for multi-authorship. Becoming known as the Modernists, they then began to subvert the Church's position.[10]

---

[10] For example, Alfred Loisy, a most respected Modernist, asked publicly how certain doctrines could still be maintained. In 1893 he was dismissed from his teaching position, but he continued with his questioning.

In 1902, Pope Leo XIII set up a commission to supervise and monitor Catholic scholars, to ensure their conformity to the 'party line'. It was too late. The Church realised it dare not enter into the open debate, and that to allow its best students free access to scholarship was to put their loyalty under too great a test. Accordingly, the commission in 1905 (now under Pius X) declared that biblical texts were to be regarded as literally 'true history'. Works of the Catholic Modernist scholars were added to the index of forbidden works and any scholarship exploring the early history of Christianity was also banned. Rome effectively withdrew into a bunker of its own, where it remained until 1943.[11]

Orthodox Judaism has remained in denial somewhat longer. This important subject is still not much studied and certainly not openly addressed even today within this community. This is an untenable position looking forward, as once knowledge is 'out there' it won't go away. In 2007, as this book was being written, there was the first real chink of light in this failure to address biblical criticism among Orthodox Jews[12] when James Kugel, an ex-Harvard professor of Hebrew and an impeccably Orthodox Jew published a book[13] in which he acknowledged arguments for the multi-authorship of the *Tanach*. He valiantly attempted the very difficult task of both accepting modern scholarship and maintaining traditional orthodox belief (in the author's opinion with rather limited success).[14] Some among the more conservative orthodox community reacted to his book by questioning his orthodox credentials. It is now to be hoped that others from the orthodox community will follow Kugel's example and begin to engage with the evidence for, as Aldous Huxley said, 'facts do not cease to exist because they are ignored'.

---

[11] *Pope Pius XII issued the encyclical* Divino Afflante Spiritu *which allowed for modern biblical studies.*

[12] *The few Orthodox Jews who had actually looked properly at biblical criticism have generally accepted the overwhelming evidence that different styles exist in different passages. One method devised to try and stay within the tradition is the Behinot (analysis) method (originated by Rabbi Mordechai Breuer) which claims the differences do not reflect different authors, but rather different forms of expression by the divine author to transmit different types of messages (for example, stringency versus compassion). This is used in many yeshivot (seminaries) especially those of religious Zionism. While not addressing, much less answering, the full arguments of Biblical criticism, it acknowledges the problem, and so is a step forward.*

[13] *How to Read the Bible, A Guide to Scripture Then and Now. James L Kugel. Free Press 2007*

[14] *Psychologists would say someone trying to maintain these two contradictory beliefs is suffering from cognitive dissonance. Kugel admits that traditional Judaism and modern biblical scholarship are actually irreconcilable, but suggests that a Jew can recognise both the validity of modern knowledge and the sanctity of the Bible by interpreting it neither in accordance with the plain meaning of the text, nor by following the interpretation of the latest scholarship. He suggests that Jews should remain faithful to the interpretations of the early interpreters, the Talmudic rabbis. They should treat the biblical text as a manual entitled: 'To Serve God'.*

The now widely accepted documentary hypothesis holds that there were (at least) four main writers or schools of writers who composed the text we have today. They each had different priorities and political aims. They have been given shorthand names for ease of discussion. These are:

J –   who wrote in Judah (Southern Kingdom) and characteristically referred to God as Yahweh (Jahweh in German).

E -   who wrote in the Northern Kingdom and referred to God as **E**lohim.

P -   the **P**riestly school.

D -   the writer of **D**euteronomy.

In today's parlance, each of these writers could be considered to be demonstrating the art of the spin doctor. For a chart showing some of their private interests and priorities, and how these biases influenced the text we have today, see the appendix (p.227).

The sources J, E, P and D are probably better understood as 'schools' with a common standpoint, rather than individual authors. The exact dating of the writing of the Torah is controversial, but the sequence of composition is thought to be something like this:

- The process started possibly as early as the second millennium BCE with the composition of poems now embodied within the Torah.

- The composition of the E source and the covenant code (Exodus 20-23) occurred during the first half of the 8th century BCE in the Northern Kingdom of Israel. The covenant code itself is set out in the same form as contemporary treaties between Assyria and its conquered vassal states.

- In Jerusalem during the second half of the 8th century BCE, the Holiness code (Leviticus 17-26) and the J source were composed. Later, after the fall of the Northern Kingdom (722 BCE), the E source was redacted by the J circle.

- The writing of the Priestly Torah, P, possibly took place in Jerusalem between the 8th and 7th centuries BCE. It may have been composed or finalised by Jeremiah or his scribe Baruch ben Neriah around 622 BCE.[15]

- In 621 BCE the book of Deuteronomy was published in Jerusalem by Josiah, and other texts were edited by the Deuteronomists.

- After the Exile in 586 BCE, the final redaction of the Torah took place in Babylon where the texts above were combined (probably for the first time) into a single integrated work.

- The Torah was published by Ezra in Jerusalem in the mid 5th century BCE.

- The Torah was canonised (fixed) in the 5th century BCE, *Neve'im* 3 or 4 centuries later and *Ketuvim* (and hence the entire *Tanach*) towards the end of 1st century CE in Yavneh after the destruction of the second temple.

Many of these dates are controversial and scholars have plenty of fuel for argument on both dates and detail. However, this is a probable sequence and set of dates for the process and, more importantly, gives an insight into the type of process it was. The long gestation period and the many individuals involved in it is clear and beyond doubt so that even if some details of the model above prove incorrect, some similar process must still have occurred.

It is worth remembering that the books of the Torah were individual books (or more correctly scrolls) which remained open for editing at least until the Babylonian Exile. The nature of scrolls meant that they generally continued to be written as individual 'books' until Talmudic times.[16] Having multiple books contained on a single scroll makes them unwieldy and difficult to use for anything except sequential reading such as that later practiced in the synagogue. The codex, or book form that we are now familiar with, originated in the last century BCE and only became more common in the subsequent centuries.

The texts of the different writers were edited, or redacted to use the technical term, in order to produce the Hebrew text that is still in use

---

[15] *This is the most difficult source to date. Many scholars believe it was the work of priests of Aaron's line as late as 450 BCE. It is also a composite of different priestly groups, and some scholars refer to one group of priestly writers as **H**, which stands for Holiness, H was credited with writing the Holiness code of Leviticus.*
[16] *Among the large number of scrolls found at Qumran only four contained two books and none three or more.*

today.[17] We do not know who the redactor(s) was, although many consider it may have been Ezra or his scribe. When two or more sources had a version of the same story, sometimes the redactor kept each source separate, quoting one after the other, as in the two creation stories of Genesis 1 and 2.[18] The redactor's aim appears to have been to preserve as much of the ancient traditions as possible while clearly not being concerned that some of the details of these traditions conflicted. Sometimes, the traditions were cleverly interwoven, as occurs in the flood story analysed in detail below. Occasionally, a short text was inserted to smooth the flow.

For both a fascinatingly different way of reading the Torah and a level headed summary of the overwhelming evidence for the Documentary Hypothesis, I recommend: 'The Bible with Sources Revealed' by Richard Elliott Friedman. To give a flavour of the results of this intricate detective work, there follows the story of the flood which has been dramatically separated into its two original sources P and J.[19]

Before reading this story, it is worth considering the flood from a theological point of view. It soon becomes clear that such an event does not fit comfortably into the monotheistic model of a perfect creator God who cares about humanity and who judges people on an individual basis. It is, in fact, one of several stories in the Torah with origins in prehistory. The clearest example in the Torah of such a remnant that is out of keeping with what was to later to become Jewish theology is the reference to the Nephilim:[20]

הנפלים היו בארץ בימים ההם וגם אחרי כן אשר יבאו בני האלוהים אל בנות האדם וילדו להם המה הגברים אשר מעולם אנשי השם.

It was in those days, and later too, that the Nephilim appeared on Earth – when the divine beings (literally 'sons of gods') cohabited with the daughters of men, who bore them offspring. They were the heroes of old, the men of renown.

This 'memory' of divine beings having sex with women on Earth and producing the Nephilim (some species of offspring with special

---

[17] *Actually a text very close to that of today. The text accepted by Jews today is the Masoretic text which was finalised around the 10th century CE (see appendix for more information).*
[18] *Written by P and J respectively - such examples are known as doublets.*
[19] *Author's translation - separated according to Friedman's assessment of sources*
[20] *Genesis 6:4 (J text)*

powers) clearly belongs to an earlier worldview than that of the Hebrews, and belief in such divine beings is difficult to reconcile theologically with normative Judaism.[21]

Flood stories are found among the myths of many people of the region. They are so widespread that they may be an echo of some collective memory of a cataclysmic event of prehistory. A plausible hypothesis ascribes this to the inundation of the large area of well populated land north of Anatolia, when the Bosphorus opened and the resulting inundation formed the Black Sea.[22] The human losses must have been enormous and the survivors no doubt would have produced 'explanations' involving activity of the gods.

Alternatively, Mesopotamia, with its large flood plain between the Tigris and Euphrates rivers, was a place that regularly suffered from floods and was the setting of several versions of the flood story. The Levant, by contrast, has no history of serious flooding and geographically with its large areas of hill country is an unlikely location for such a story. The true origin of the flood stories will always remain a subject of speculation, but it is clear that the many different versions circulating in the region have a common source.

Theologically these accounts are more compatible with the relationship between human beings and the gods as described by the Chinese philosopher Lao Tzu:

Heaven and Earth are ruthless, and treat the myriad creatures as straw dogs.

or two thousand years later by Shakespeare: [23]

As flies to wanton boys are we to the gods
They kill us for their sport.

For a belief system which posits a perfect creation by a God who judges his creatures individually, the idea of a God prepared to wipe out the human race and start again raises many difficulties. Why was God's

---

[21] *Belief in the Nephilim (sometimes translated as giants) continued. The 2nd century BCE apocryphal 1st Book of Enoch has an interesting story in which God sent the flood in order to rid the Earth of the Nephilim.*
[22] *This occurred around the 6th millennium BCE. The area flooded by seawater included a large freshwater lake.*
[23] *King Lear iv(i) 36-37*

first creation so flawed, and was humanity after Noah really 'new and improved'?

The two flood stories that were circulating in the Hebrew world were essentially the same, but had differences of detail, and the redactor combined them so cleverly that on a superficial reading they appear to be one story. To appreciate the skill involved I have separated the two stories. First read the story as the J school told it. The capitalised word *GOD* in this text represents the Tetragrammaton (YHVH – יהוה):

And GOD saw that man's evil on Earth was great and that all of his inner thoughts were evil all the time. And GOD regretted that He had made man on Earth, and was grieved in his heart. And GOD said: 'I will blot out from the face of the Earth man whom I have created; both man, beast, creeping thing, and bird of the air; for I regret that I have made them.' But Noah found favour in the eyes of GOD. And GOD said to Noah: 'Go you and all your household into the ark; for I have seen you have been righteous before Me in this generation. From every clean beast you shall take yourself seven pairs, each with his mate; and of the unclean beasts two, a male and his mate; Also from the birds of the air, seven pairs, male and female; to keep their seed alive on the face of the Earth. For in another seven days I will make it rain on Earth for forty days and forty nights; and all that exists that I have made I will blot out from the surface of the Earth.' And Noah did according to all that GOD commanded him.

And Noah and his sons, his wife and his sons' wives, together went into the ark because of the waters of the flood. And on the seventh day the waters of the flood came upon the Earth. And the rain fell on the Earth for forty days and forty nights and GOD shut him in. And the flood was forty days upon the Earth; and the waters increased, and bore up the ark, and it was lifted up above the Earth. And the waters strengthened and increased greatly upon the Earth; and the ark drifted on the surface of the waters. And the waters flowed exceedingly over the Earth; and all the high mountains under the skies were covered. And the waters strengthened and the mountains were covered by fifteen cubits. All in whose nostrils was the slightest breath of life, whatever was on dry land, died. And He blotted out every living substance which was upon the face of the ground, both man, and cattle, and creeping thing, and bird of the sky; they were blotted out from the Earth; and Noah only was left, and those that were with him in the ark.

And the rain from the sky was stopped. And the waters receded from the Earth continually. At the end of forty days Noah opened the window of the ark which he had made. And he sent out a dove to see if the waters were abated from the surface of the ground. But the dove found no resting place for her foot, and she returned to him in the ark, for water was on the surface of all the Earth; and he put out his hand, and took her, and brought her in with him inside the ark. And he waited another seven days; and again sent out the dove from the ark. And the dove came back to him at evening time; and there in her mouth was an olive-leaf freshly plucked; so Noah knew that the waters had diminished from the Earth. And he waited another seven days; and sent out the dove; and she did not return to him ever again. And Noah removed the covering of the ark, and he saw that the surface of the Earth had dried. And Noah built an altar to GOD; and taking some of every clean beast, and some of every clean bird, he offered burnt-offerings on the altar. And GOD smelled the pleasant scent; and GOD said in his heart: 'I will not again curse the ground because of man; for the inclination of man's heart is evil from his youth; nor will I again destroy every thing living, as I have done. While the Earth endures, planting and harvest, cold and heat, summer and winter, and day and night shall not cease.'

Having read J's account, which stands as a complete story of the flood on its own, now consider the P version, and look out for the differences of detail. The word God here represents the Hebrew *Elohim* - אלוהים:

In his generation Noah was a righteous and blameless man; Noah walked with God. And Noah had three sons, Shem, Ham, and Japheth. And the Earth became corrupt before God, and the world was filled with violence. And when God saw the Earth and how corrupt it was, for all flesh had corrupted their way upon the Earth. God said to Noah: 'I will put an end to all flesh, for the Earth is filled with violence because of them, and now I will destroy them with the Earth. Make yourself an ark of gopher wood; make an ark with rooms, and cover it inside and out with pitch. And this is how you shall make it: the length of the ark will be three hundred cubits, its breadth fifty cubits, and its height thirty cubits. You shall make a window for the ark, and finish it a cubit from the top; and you shall set the door of the ark in the side and make lower, second, and third levels for it. And now I am about to bring the flood, water onto the Earth to destroy all flesh which has the breath of life under the skies; everything that is on the Earth shall perish. But I will establish My covenant with you; and you shall go into the ark, you and your sons, and your wife and your sons' wives with you. And of every living thing of all flesh, two of every sort shall you bring into the ark, to keep them alive with you; they shall be a male and a female. Of the birds after their kind, and of the cattle after their kind, of every creeping thing of the ground after its kind, two of every sort shall come to you, to be kept alive. And take with you everything that is eaten, and store it; it shall be food for you and for them.' Noah did all that God commanded him, so he did.

Of the clean beasts, and of the beasts that are not clean, and of birds, and of every thing that creeps on the ground, two by two, male and female pairs, they went to Noah and into the ark, as God had commanded Noah. In the six hundredth year of Noah's life, in the second month, on the seventeenth day of the month, on that same day all the fountains of the great deep were broken up, and the windows of heaven opened. On that very day Noah, with Shem, Ham, and Japheth the sons of Noah, and Noah's wife with the three wives of his sons together entered into the ark; they, and every beast after its kind, and all the cattle after their kind, and every creeping thing that creeps upon the Earth after its kind, and every fowl after its kind, every bird, every winged thing. And they went to Noah into the ark, two by two of all flesh which has the breath of life. And those that went in were the male and the female of all flesh, as God had commanded him. And all flesh perished that moved on the Earth, both fowl, and cattle, and beast, and every swarming thing that swarms upon the Earth, and every human. And the waters remained strong on the Earth for a hundred and fifty days.

And God remembered Noah, and all the animals and all the cattle that were with him in the ark; and God made a wind pass over the Earth, and the waters diminished; the fountains of the deep and the windows of the skies were closed, and after a hundred and fifty days the waters decreased. And the ark rested in the seventh month, on the seventeenth day of the month, on the mountains of Ararat. And the waters decreased continually until the tenth month; in the tenth month, on the first day of the month, the tops of the mountains were seen. And he sent out a raven, and it went back and forth until the waters were dried up from the Earth. And it was in the six hundred and first year, in the first month, the first day of the month, that the waters dried up from the Earth. And in the second month, on twenty seventh day of the month, the Earth was dry. And God spoke to Noah, saying: 'Go out of the ark, you and your wife, your sons, and their wives together. Take with you all the living things that are with you, of all flesh, birds, cattle, and every creeping thing that creeps upon the Earth; so they may swarm in the Earth, and be fruitful, and multiply upon the Earth.' And Noah went out, his sons, his wife, and his sons' wives with him; every beast, every creeping thing, and every bird, whatever moves on the Earth, by their families they went forth out of the ark.

Another complete flood story! The differences of detail are striking, J sends out a dove, P a raven. P's timescale is much longer than J's. J takes seven pairs of clean beasts and birds into his ark, P only two.

There are many differences of language too, the most obvious one being the different name used for God.

Separating the two stories like this allows one to appreciate the work of the redactor. Below are the two texts that you have just read combined back into the more familiar form in which they appear in the book of Genesis. To identify the sources the J source here appears in italics. There are two other short insertions[24] which are printed in a different font.

Genesis 6:5 And GOD saw that man's evil on Earth was great and that all of his inner thoughts were evil all the time. 6 And GOD regretted that He had made man on Earth, and was grieved in his heart. 7 And GOD said: 'I will blot out from the face of the Earth man whom I have created; both man, beast, creeping thing, and bird of the air; for I regret that I have made them.' 8 But Noah found favour in the eyes of GOD. 9 This is the genealogy of Noah. In his generation Noah was a righteous and blameless man; Noah walked with God. 10 And Noah had three sons, Shem, Ham, and Japheth. 11 And the Earth became corrupt before God, and the world was filled with violence. 12 And when God saw the Earth and how corrupt it was for all flesh had corrupted their way upon the Earth. 13 God said to Noah: 'I will put an end to all flesh, for the Earth is filled with violence because of them, and now I will destroy them with the Earth. 14 Make yourself an ark of gopher wood; make an ark with rooms, and cover it inside and out with pitch. 15 And this is how you shall make it: the length of the ark will be three hundred cubits, its breadth fifty cubits, and its height thirty cubits. 16 You shall make a window for the ark, and finish it a cubit from the top; and you shall set the door of the ark in the side and make lower, second, and third levels for it. 17 And now I am about to bring the flood, water onto the Earth to destroy all flesh which has the breath of life under the skies; everything that is on the Earth shall perish. 18 But I will establish My covenant with you; and you shall go into the ark, you and your sons, and your wife and your sons' wives with you. 19 And of every living thing of all flesh, two of every sort shall you bring into the ark, to keep them alive with you; they shall be a male and a female. 20 Of the birds after their kind, and of the cattle after their kind, of every creeping thing of the ground after its kind, two of every sort shall come to you, to be kept alive. 21 And take with you everything that is eaten, and store it; it shall be food

---

24 *The first is thought to be by the Redactor, the second from a different source.*

for you and for them.'   *22* Noah did all that God commanded him, so he did.

Genesis 7:1 And GOD said to Noah: 'Go you and all your household into the ark; for I have seen you have been righteous before Me in this generation.   2 From every clean beast you shall take yourself seven pairs, each with his mate; and of the unclean beasts two, a male and his mate;   3 Also from the birds of the air, seven pairs, male and female; to keep their seed alive on the face of the Earth.   4 For in another seven days I will make it rain on Earth for forty days and forty nights; and all that exists that I have made will blot out from the surface of the Earth.'   5 And Noah did according to all that GOD commanded him.   6 And Noah was six hundred years old when the floodwaters covered the Earth.   *7 And Noah and his sons, his wife and his sons' wives, together went into the ark because of the waters of the flood.*   *8* Of the clean beasts, and of the beasts that are not clean, and of birds, and of every thing that creeps on the ground,   *9* two by two, male and female pairs, they went to Noah and into the ark, as God had commanded Noah.   *10 And on the seventh day the waters of the flood came upon the Earth.*   *11* In the six hundredth year of Noah's life, in the second month, on the seventeenth day of the month, on that same day all the fountains of the great deep were broken up, and the windows of heaven opened.   *12 And the rain fell on the Earth for forty days and forty nights.*   *13* On that very day Noah, with Shem, Ham, and Japheth the sons of Noah, and Noah's wife with the three wives of his sons together entered into the ark;   *14* they, and every beast after its kind, and all the cattle after their kind, and every creeping thing that creeps upon the Earth after its kind, and every fowl after its kind, every bird, every winged thing.   *15* And they went to Noah into the ark, two by two of all flesh which has the breath of life.   *16* And those that went in were the male and the female of all flesh, as God had commanded him; *and GOD shut him in.*   *17 And the flood was forty days upon the Earth; and the waters increased, and bore up the ark, and it was lifted up above the Earth.   18 And the waters strengthened and increased greatly upon the Earth; and the ark drifted on the surface of the waters.   19 And the waters flowed exceedingly over the Earth; and all the high mountains under the skies were covered.   20 And the waters strengthened and the mountains were covered by fifteen cubits.*   *21* And all flesh perished that moved on the Earth, both fowl, and cattle, and beast, and every swarming thing that swarms upon the Earth, and every human;   *22 all in whose nostrils was the slightest breath of life, whatever was on dry land, died.   23 And He blotted out every living substance which was upon the face of the ground, both man, and cattle, and creeping thing, and bird of the sky; they were blotted out from the Earth; and Noah only was left, and those that were with him in the ark.* 24 And the waters remained strong on the Earth for a hundred and fifty days.

Genesis 8:1 And God remembered Noah, and all the animals and all the cattle that were with him in the ark; and God made a wind pass over the Earth, and the waters diminished; 2 the fountains of the deep and the windows of the skies were closed, *and the rain from the sky was stopped.* 3 *And the waters receded from the Earth continually;* and after a hundred and fifty days the waters decreased. 4 And the ark rested in the seventh month, on the seventeenth day of the month, on the mountains of Ararat. 5 And the waters decreased continually until the tenth month; in the tenth month, on the first day of the month, the tops of the mountains were seen. 6 *At the end of forty days Noah opened the window of the ark which he had made.* 7 And he sent out a raven, and it went back and forth until the waters were dried up from the Earth. 8 *And he sent out a dove to see if the waters were abated from the surface of the ground.* 9 *But the dove found no resting place for her foot, and she returned to him in the ark, for water was on the surface of all the Earth; and he put out his hand, and took her, and brought her in with him inside the ark.* 10 *And he waited another seven days; and again sent out the dove from the ark.* 11 *And the dove came back to him at evening time; and there in her mouth was an olive-leaf freshly plucked; so Noah knew that the waters had diminished from the Earth.* 12 *And he waited another seven days; and sent out the dove; and she did not return to him ever again.* 13 And it was in the six hundred and first year, in the first month, the first day of the month, that the waters dried up from the Earth; *and Noah removed the covering of the ark, and he saw that the surface of the Earth had dried.* 14 And in the second month, on twenty seventh day of the month, the Earth was dry. 15 And God spoke to Noah, saying: 16 'Go out of the ark, you and your wife, your sons, and their wives together. 17 Take with you all the living things that are with you, of all flesh, birds, cattle, and every creeping thing that creeps upon the Earth; so they may swarm in the Earth, and be fruitful, and multiply upon the Earth.' 18 And Noah went out, his sons, his wife, and his sons' wives with him; 19 every beast, every creeping thing, and every bird, whatever moves on the Earth, by their families they went forth out of the ark. 20 *And Noah built an altar to GOD; and taking some of every clean beast, and some of every clean bird, he offered burnt-offerings on the altar.* 21 *And GOD smelled the pleasant scent; and GOD said in his heart: 'I will not again curse the ground because of man; for the inclination of man's heart is evil from his youth; nor will I*

again destroy every thing living, as I have done.   22 While the Earth endures,
planting and harvest, cold and heat, summer and winter, and day and night shall
not cease.

I still remember reading Friedman's 1988 book, 'Who Wrote the Bible?'
and understanding how the flood stories had been combined. It was
one of those eureka moments, to actually see the Redactor's work in
action. It felt as if a coded message had been deciphered. For those
interested, the appendix includes a chart summarising the differences
between these two stories, and comparing them with an earlier near
Eastern flood story (p.224).

What this exercise has established beyond doubt is that the Bible does
not speak with only one voice, that of one author – Divine or
otherwise. It speaks with many, and includes many contradictory
statements. Some examples of these are also listed in the appendix.

Every statement in the Bible supplies ammunition for those literalists
who wish to debate 'God's instructions'. Such literalists are described
by Karen Armstrong as engaged in a futile biblical tennis match - one
person serves Exodus 21:2, the other returns Deuteronomy 15:13, and
so it goes. Agreement is seldom reached and all because neither of them
reads the text as it was intended, as a sacred text. The redactor clearly
found no problem with these contradictions and it is impossible to
believe he wasn't aware of them. No, these divergent traditions must
have been included deliberately.

This same literary habit of repeating alternative traditions without
feeling the need to harmonise the details can be found as recently as
medieval times in the writings of Arab chroniclers. As was discussed
earlier, we are not dealing here with the modern conception of history.
If the text is read as a sacred text should be, that is metaphorically and
as a whole, these conflicts are of no consequence. If read in this way,
the divergent traditions tell the very same symbolic story and actually
strengthen one another.

To think of this in another way, consider the story of Romeo and Juliet
and its retelling in West Side Story. Both carry the same message; both
tell the same myth and teach us the same lessons. That the characters'
names and the cultures they come from are different is ultimately

irrelevant. A modern biblical style redactor with something to say about revenge would most likely include both versions.

If biblical scholarship had not already effectively resolved the authorship question, one could reach a similar conclusion from a completely separate study. This is an examination of the morality of events in the *Tanach* which are described either without censure or as paradigms to aspire to. As Shakespeare observed:[25]

The Devil can cite scripture to suit his purpose.

The morality we generally find in the *Tanach* is that current and acceptable at the time of writing, not that of today. Clearly, the *Tanach* stories do not demonstrate any form of absolute or ideal morality. There follows a list of such issues and a chart in the appendix (p.234) gives further details and references for the examples cited.

a. Genocide, arrogance and cruelty

There are many examples of this, but the slaughter of a conquered people (such as Ai or Amalek) is, from a twenty first century viewpoint, about as bad as it could get.

b. Family law issues

In a system of just reward and punishment, the punishment of children for their antecedent's crimes is immoral. However, it is both accepted and advocated in the *Tanach*. As examples, Job's children were killed early in the book as part of Job's trials or in the book of Joshua, Achan's children were stoned to death in punishment for their father's crime of looting. It is also enshrined in the Torah that children can be punished for the crimes of their antecedents down to the third and fourth generations.

Even worse is the treatment of children born *mamzerim* (bastards). They receive this label because of irregularities in the relationship of their parents, remain disadvantaged for life (unable to take part in normal community life or marry freely) and the stigma is retained by their offspring for ten generations.[26]

---

[25] *The Merchant of Venice i(iii) (Antonio)*
[26] *Deuteronomy 23:2*

Similarly, family laws such as levirate marriage[27] (and the demeaning *halitzah* ceremony necessary to avoid it)[28] or the ban on a Cohen marrying a divorcée are relics of an outdated system. Today, a legal code that treats people in this manner must be considered to infringe human rights.

c.   Slavery

Today any form of slavery would be thought of as absolutely immoral in most societies but it is condoned in the Torah in keeping with the morality and practice of its time.

d.   Sex and marriage

Sexual mores change with time. We would not consider the 'spilling of seed on the ground' by Onan to be a capital offence, particularly one so serious that he and Er (who was wicked in the sight of the Lord, in a way that we do not know), were killed directly by God.[29] Polygamy was acceptable in Jewish law until the 11th Century CE when Rabbi Gershon, in an example of coming to terms with changed morality, outlawed it for Ashkenazi Jews.

e.   Homosexuality

Should it be forbidden and is it a capital offence? Society's views of homosexuality have certainly changed for the better since the priests of the Holiness School[30] wrote these things in Leviticus.

f.   Trial by ordeal

This is cited in the Torah as the correct way to deal with a woman suspected of adultery. Very few would support its use today (and indeed its practice was stopped by the rabbis early on).

---

[27] *Levirate marriage (Yibbum) is the practice of a woman marrying one of her husband's brothers after her husband's death, if there were no children, in order to continue his line. Other cultures practicing this include Hindus, Samaritans, Xiongnu, Mongols and Tibetans.*

[28] *See Deuteronomy 25:7-10. The woman has to spit in the face of, and remove a shoe from the man who either he or she refuses to marry, as a symbolic act of renunciation of their willingness to perform Yibbum (levirate marriage). My late father and his brother's widow, when recently bereaved, had to carry out this outdated ceremony, and were both very much upset by it.*

[29] *Other named individuals killed directly by God in the Torah for sinning or disobedience were Lot's wife (Gen. 19-26); Aaron's sons, Nadab and Abihu, for their 'crime' of making unauthorised fire (Lev. 10:1-2, Num. 3:4, 24:61;) and Korah, Dathan, and Abiram (with their families) for opposition to Moses (Num. 16:27). There were of course many, many more killed by God in collective punishments, starting with the flood.*

[30] *These priests are believed to have written the Holiness Code which runs from Lev. 17 to the end of the book. The priests had formerly maintained a strict distinction between morality and ritual. Their innovation was to emphasise the close affinity of both of these as components of holiness. See The Divine Symphony by Israel Knohl.*

g.   Attitudes to sickness, infertility and disability

The Torah's description of infertility as a punishment from God was (and in many orthodox circles still is) widely accepted. Infertility is only blamed on women. That men are sometimes responsible is never considered. There were similar attitudes to leprosy and other diseases and to physical handicap. The handicapped were barred from making sacrifices in the Temple – today this would be seen as cruel discrimination against a disadvantaged group.

h.   Women's role

The position of women has changed as society developed. If there is a single moral position concerning a woman's role, few would argue for that of the biblical period.

i.   Mistreatment of children

These are some examples of immoral treatment of children that are condoned by the *Tanach*:

1) God's acceptance of the killing of Achen's and Job's children (described in b. above)
2) Incitement to murder babies in battle by dashing them against rocks
3) God's approval of the stoning to death of brides found not to be virgins
4) Human sacrifice

   Jephthah sacrificed his daughter as a burnt offering to keep a vow to God. In contrast to Abraham with Isaac, God did not instruct him to spare his child. In another case, the King of Moab, finding he was losing a battle against Israel, sacrificed his son. He was rewarded (presumably by God) with victory.
5) Elisha cursing the young men who made fun of his baldness and so 'causing' forty-two of them to be mauled by bears
6) The punishment for a 'rebellious son' is to be stoned to death.[31]

j.   Other examples of dubious morality

Examples of what most people today find to be immoral behaviour, that is condoned by the *Tanach* include:

1) The rape of Dinah and its aftermath where Simeon and Levi murder and plunder Shechem. Is this justice or morality at work?
2) Elijah, following the contest with Baal's priests, ordered four hundred and fifty of them to be killed 'and let not one escape'.

---

[31] *This excessive punishment laid down in the Tanach was effectively overruled by the Rabbis. See Chapter 10*

Incidentally, he left the priestesses, who were worshippers of Asherah alone.

3) Saul asked David for a dowry for his daughter of one hundred Philistine foreskins (hoping for David to be killed in obtaining them) and David returned with two hundred!

4) David's cynical behaviour towards Bathsheba's husband Uriah in having him killed in battle by putting him in the front line so that David could marry Bathsheba. God's punishment for this behaviour was a slow death for David and Bathsheba's young child!

5) The threat of male rape in Sodom and Gilbeah, which was prevented by the offering of virgin daughters in their place

6) The call for the genocide of the tribe of Amalek. (I would read Amalek as a mythical people used as a metaphor for evil, but the plain reading is referred to here.)

As will be discussed further in Chapter 10, these examples also demonstrate that morality does indeed change with time. Few would disagree that most of these changes have been for the better. It would surely be reasonable to expect divine decrees to be valid or moral for all time and so this is strong evidence for the claim that the contents of the Torah and *Tanach* have origins with man rather than God.

In conclusion, we have sufficient evidence either from biblical scholarship or from a review of the morality advocated in the Bible to conclude that human, rather than divine, beings authored our sacred texts. When all this evidence is considered together then such a conclusion would appear indisputable.

6

Is one God really better than many, and can Jews be idolaters too?

God is the name we give to ideas that transcend thought.
That which can't be known is what man calls God.
Joseph Campbell

Those individuals who have been through the educational system of any of the monotheistic religions have generally been so influenced by the apparent strength of the argument for there being only one God, that they scarcely give this fundamental issue a second thought. This concept is taught didactically to the young and it is so ingrained that monotheists tend to look at religions that have other ideas as primitive. However, as we have seen, the Judeo-Christian model of a solitary monarchical creator God is just one possible model of how nature and the universe functions. This model or one of four others is used by most members of the human race to underpin their lives. The five choices were described in Chapter 4 and readers will have been able to make their own assessment as to their relative merits.

In this chapter we will consider only the role of God or gods within those models that invoke them. If we question whether one God is a superior concept to many gods, we may find the answer is not as clear-cut as we expected. We must start by trying to set our cultural bias aside and look with an open mind at how monotheistic, dualistic and polytheistic religions deal with life's big questions. In doing so we must treat religions on a theoretical level and judge them by their ideas and philosophy and not necessarily focus on how they are practiced. Followers of all religions (like people in general) seldom, if ever, live up to their ideals.

We begin by reminding ourselves of the background. Evidence of man's religious activity is found as early as the Palæolithic[1] period. Monotheism is, by contrast, less than 4000 years old. The monotheistic religions such as Judaism, Christianity and Islam with one omnipotent, omniscient, omnipresent deity who has revealed himself in historic time to a select few individuals, are well enough known.

Dualist religions may not be so familiar. Zoroastrianism, an early example of dualism, was a major religion of ancient times and is one of the oldest religions still being practised. It predates Judaism, whose development it significantly influenced. To oversimplify a complex belief system, Zoroastrians believe in the existence of one powerful god, Ahura Mazda, and a second less powerful deity, Angra Mainyu. The former is all good and ultimately will be strong enough to triumph; the latter evil and the source of both human evil and that of the imperfect world we inhabit.

Pope Innocent III

Other dualist religions include Manichæism (which flourished from the 3rd to the 8th century of this era), Gnosticism (along with various related heretical dualist Christian sects) and Catharism. The Gnostic 'heresies' and the Cathars were ruthlessly put down by the church. Catharism was effectively extinguished by the genocide of the Albigensian crusade ordered by Pope Innocent III in the early 13th century. Cathars, in common with other Gnostic sects, believed that the god of this impure and flawed world was a demiurge or lesser god. By living a pure and abstemious life one could obtain Gnosis, or secret knowledge, of the higher God who dwelt outside of this Earth. Cathars believed no clergy or priests were necessary for this process

---

[1] *Palaeolithic Age 250,000–14,000 BCE*

and held the Christian priesthood to be impure and corrupt. Unsurprisingly, the dissemination of these ideas led to their fatal conflict with the church.

Polytheism and ancestor worship are the two oldest forms of religion known. Polytheistic, pagan or nature religions sprang up apparently independently in many different parts of the world at an early stage of human development, well before recorded history. Common themes involve worship of the sun and moon, sacrifices or offerings of food to appease the gods, and the erection of shrines - often with representation of the gods (which can pejoratively be called idols). We are very familiar with the constant argument against these man made gods in the *Tanach*. However, by simplistically accepting the concept that idol worshippers believe the statue to be an actual god, rather than a symbol of divinity, we misunderstand pagan belief. We patronise polytheists by imagining that people we call primitive believed a stone[2] idol (say) to be a source of divine power, rather than a symbol of it.

A worshipper did, however, very much consider the idol as an integral part of the realm of the sacred. As already discussed, in early religion the predominant world view was that of a complete separation of the sacred from the profane. There was a total separation between sacred space, sacred time and sacred objects and their profane everyday equivalents. When a new idol was constructed, there were often quite elaborate ceremonies to mark its passage and acceptance into the realm of the sacred. An example was the *mis pi*[3] ceremony in Mesopotamia during which the often beautifully decorated idol was carried in procession alongside water and trees, and its 'mouth' offered food and drink. The idol maker then symbolically 'cut off' his own hand and denied that he had made it.

Equivalent ceremonies continue in monotheistic communities today, such as that by a Jewish community to mark their acquisition of a new *sefer Torah*.[4] This ritual introduces the new man made object into the realm of the sacred. In a similar way, artefacts that have been worshipped or venerated for a long time move more deeply into the

---

[2] To early (Palaeolithic) man stone itself probably symbolised the properties of strength, permanence, solidity and an absolute mode of being, which contrasted with the transient, vulnerable human state.

[3] See V. A. Hurowitz, The Mesopotamian God Image from Womb to Tomb, JAOS 123, 1, 2003

[4] Sefer Torah – scroll containing the hand-written Torah which is used ritually in the synagogue service

sacred world. As a result, ancient icons and certain relics are held sacred by Christians, as are the very stones of the Western Wall for Jews. The reality however is that for most true believers the icon, the holy scroll or the statue simply represents a conduit to the deity and a place of focus for their thoughts and for their worship.

Anyone who did misunderstand this distinction and worshipped the sacred object in and of itself, rather than as a symbol or a part of the sacred world, would certainly be an idolater. Indeed, a good working definition of idolatry is **'to mistake the symbol for the reference'**. Fundamentalists of all text based religions are particularly prone to this sort of idolatry. They often appear to take a completely literal approach to their sacred texts, while ignoring the symbolism they contain. Rabbi Jonathan Wittenberg, echoing traditional ideas expressed in the Talmud, eloquently described this danger:[5]

> *'One whose world is divided clearly into 'us' and 'them' by virtue of race or religion; one who worships absolutely texts and slogans; one who is incited to hate and who incites others; one who has lost the capacity for reverence; one who has lost the capacity for questioning, - such a person's conduct is idolatrous. The object of their worship may be their leader, their people, their religion, or even hate and violence itself. But it's godless; it's idolatry.*
>
> *One to whom life is precious beyond the boundaries of 'us' and 'them'; one who remembers reverence; one who feels the fear of doing wrong; one who strives to do good to others; one who understands, even in conflict, that the consequence of hate is more hate; one who seeks the presence of God, beyond the formulae of texts and the format of rituals; - such a person's conduct is truly pious. Such a person seeks and worships the God of all flesh.*
>
> *If only we all knew this and were faithful to it all the time.'*

To put this another way, a way that would have resonance for those familiar with the eastern religions' perspective on these matters, it is idolatry not only to worship a fixed image of God in metal or stone, but also to have belief in a rigid mental image of God and how He operates. To believe that one knows what God is, what God wants from human beings and exactly what rules God wants us to obey can, and indeed should, also be considered a form of idolatry. Certainly the

---

[5] *This text is taken from an e-mail to the community of the New North London Synagogue during the 2nd Israel-Lebanon war of 2006.*

monotheist's paternalistic and authoritarian image of God can appear idolatrous to those brought up with a different religious perspective. If one accepts this argument, then it follows that fundamentalists of all persuasions are, without exception, idolaters.

As soon as there is fundamental belief in a set of principles that are entirely right - and often set in stone for all time - then this belief can be used to justify, exonerate and motivate any act carried out in its service. Unspeakable acts are even more likely to occur if the believer holds his or her belief to be the sole truth for us all. Such a single vision held by those with power is what all of us must fear. This is what Isaiah Berlin called, with obvious allusion, a 'final solution' – regardless of whether it comes from religious or secular motives. Berlin wrote:[6]

> *One belief more than any other is responsible for the slaughter of individuals on the altar of great historical ideals, some religious, others secular, some political, others moral. This is the belief that somewhere in the past or future, in divine revelation or in the mind of an individual thinker, in the pronouncement of history or science, or in the simple heart of an uncorrupted good man there is a final solution.*

Secular man has had his share of these ideological certainties, these truths or final solutions that have punctuated history with tragedy. Sadly, the historical record also seldom lacks examples of barbarism being practiced in the name of religion. Nor is the situation any different today. Religions, with their seemingly clear answers about how to live, are regularly hijacked by those who use them to spread a spirit of holy intolerance, often with fatal results for those caught up in these delusions.

The combination of priests and rabbis, mullahs and popes with political and military power has seldom if ever been one that shows tolerance. The record of religion is stained with murder and oppression in the name of gods. The murderers considered themselves to be moral men – doing God's work – and were often rewarded by their co-religionists for their diligence. As Rabbi Wittenberg pointed out, such individuals in reality were idolaters and sadly there are still many such people affecting our world today from positions of power.

---

[6] *Paraphrased by Rabbi Jonathan Sacks, quoted in the Jewish Chronicle 14th September 2007*

Looking at this problem from a theological point of view, there are considered to be two alternative ways of describing god, known as apophatic and cataphatic. Apophatic theology describes what god is not; for example - god is unknowable or indescribable. By contrast, cataphatic theology describes what god is like - god the shepherd, the father or the king.

It is cataphatic theology, if its analogies are taken literally, that can lead to the idolatry described above. By its nature, cataphatic theology limits or restricts god. As a simple example, god the father would appear to lack a feminine side. By contrast, mystics of all religious backgrounds, but especially those from the East, tend to take an apophatic approach. They feel that the most dangerous graven images are fixed ideas of god, and they say that the supreme vision which they seek can only come when they have rid themselves of every idea of god whatsoever.

This leads to a paradoxical position where monotheists consider Hindus, for example, as idolaters as they have many 'graven images' of their many gods. From a Hindu perspective however the 'idols' are just some of the infinite number of masks that *Brahman* (God) can wear, for God is all of creation, including ourselves, simultaneously. They in turn consider the monotheistic concept of the Divine King in his heavenly court either as a simplistic childlike picture of God or as a concept that would tend to block off any direct experience of the divine. It is precisely such a transforming, direct experience that the devout of the orient seek in their spiritual quest. By contrast, strict monotheists aim to be good subjects of their Divine King and to obey his commandments ever more assiduously. In general though, they are not attempting to encounter God directly during this life.

The monotheist might further protest that, while a symbolic sculpture of one god might be acceptable, how can one believe in so many idols representing so many separate gods? Commonly for polytheists these gods symbolically represent different aspects of divinity or a deity with responsibility for certain aspects of the adherent's life. A Hindu worshipper may select which deity to worship according to their situation and needs of the moment without denying the divinity of the rest. Curiously, if we examine Judaism we find that a similar concept has also been cleverly incorporated.

In Judaism, we can represent different aspects of the divine by using many different names for our one and only deity. Whether we want to pray to the feminine aspect of God, to the comforting aspect, to the military leader, the father, the judge, the creator, the reviver of the dead, the granter of fertility, the inscrutable, the merciful or the redeemer, or indeed many other attributes, Judaism has a different name by which God can be addressed.[7] This is not polytheism; it is monotheism intelligently accommodating basic human needs. However, when recognised for what it is we obtain an insight into the polytheistic approach. Long before Judaism, a wise Hindu sacred text stated:

Truth[8] is one; wise men call it by many names.

In practice, if not in theology, one can see that in this regard the systems are not actually so far apart. As discussed in Chapter 1, it was recognised very early in the development of religion that the concept of a heavenly sky god who created the world single-handedly and dwelt far away in heaven was too remote to help ordinary people with their quotidian needs. Judaism (in a practical way) acknowledges this too by offering us more accessible links to the divine. We have such symbols as the Friday night candles, the *mezuzah* to kiss for luck and the *sefer Torah* scroll to venerate. In pagan (or natural) religions, divine attributes could be incorporated into a wide variety of objects, creatures or abstract ideas, which then became objects of worship (and hence were viewed as gods). For example, in the early days of the development of mathematics, individual numbers were treated as magical and as being imbued with particular powers. Such ideas were also absorbed into the monotheistic religions with the Jewish concept of *Gematria*[9] or the Islamic one of *Khisab al Jumal*. The Bible is full of numbers with symbolic and even mystical meanings.

Those who study religion sometimes consider the gods in terms of them being 'exchange objects'.[10] People pray or sacrifice to them in

---

[7] *More than 80 ways are used to refer to Judaism's one God. See the appendix p.221 for a list.*

[8] *The Sanskrit word translated here as truth can also mean 'god' or 'reality'. This quote 'Ekam sat vipraha bahudha vadanti' appears in the first mandala (book) of the Rig Veda (64.46).*

[9] *Gematria is a system to discover purported hidden meanings in texts based on the numerical value of words. In Hebrew, every letter also represents a number. Therefore, the numerical value of any word can be calculated. By making correspondences between words with related values, an infinite number of interpretations become possible.*

[10] *Such as Rodney Stark, professor of Comparative Religion at Washington University. See his book 'One True God'. Princeton U.P. 2001*

exchange for their protection or some other tangible benefit such as fertility. In early religious history there were many minor gods such as local rain gods that helped their village alone. Over time there has been an irresistible trend towards more powerful gods controlling, for example, the whole land rather than the village, and in charge of all the weather rather than just the rain. This trend reached its logical end-point with the development of monotheism. It can easily be understood that the more powerful the god, the easier it became to 'market' it to the population.

The urge that believers in the 'one true God' had to spread the word greatly increased the spread of monotheism. Unlike polytheists, they often deliberately set out to convert others by whatever combination of missionary activity or conquest suited their political circumstances. While Judaism today does not proselytise, it did so actively and effectively in the Greco-Roman world.[11]

The reality is that pure monotheism – where there is truly only one divine being without a supporting cast of minor supernatural creatures – is rare, as it is too intellectual and 'unnatural' for the large majority of people. One can see in all mythology and indeed in all effective fiction that each and every god or hero requires either to have a weakness or to have a reasonably powerful opponent. Without such an Achilles heel, heroes are not credible as they could simply solve whatever problem faced them without effort or challenge. Dull stories would result from such protagonists, and a perfect (and perhaps dull) world would result from such a perfect God. I hardly need to point out that we do not live in such a perfect world.

The core godless philosophy of Buddhism likewise seems to be too difficult for all but the ascetics and serious thinkers of the east. The practice of popular Buddhism is, in reality, replete with a pantheon of gods ironically including Buddha himself. Similarly, Judaism, Christianity and Islam dilute their strict monotheism with an assembly of minor supernatural creatures, such as cherubim and angels. As Christianity spread globally it even incorporated some pre-existing local

---

[11] *'Proselyte' derives from Greek for 'newcomer'. Voluntary proselytes were extremely numerous in the Greco-Roman world, which partly accounts for the large Jewish population in the Roman Empire. There were also the 'godfearers' who took on most Jewish attributes, but held back from certain obligations (e.g. circumcision.)*

gods and brought them 'into the church' as intercessors in the form of new Christian saints!

In Judaism, these divine beings with lesser powers are definitely subordinate to God. There is a heavenly court, with Satan (the adversary) and the angels. Such supernatural beings seem to address a human need for less remote deities, as well as helping to provide a possible explanation for the existence of evil.

An alternative, less remote way of approaching the Divine, which is used by followers of all three monotheistic religions, is the veneration of shrines. These are often the graves of sages or other revered individuals. Special powers are often ascribed to such places, for example the ability to grant fertility, and people sometimes make long pilgrimages to pray at these sites. While this behaviour is not generally part of the mainstream teaching of the religions, little is usually done to discourage it. Wise religious leaders understand the need for such outlets. In Judaism, especially among the ultra-orthodox, this type of practice is increasing.

Looked at objectively, this type of behaviour can be seen as a form of the ancient practice of ancestor worship incorporated into monotheism. For the supplicants, God is too remote so the spirits of their righteous ancestors are applied to in the hope that they will intercede on their behalf with the Deity.[12]

From ancestor worship, we move to another way of approaching the divine using a different intercessor, an idol. The very idea of idol worship is anathema when viewed through our culturally biased spectacles. However, we must stop a moment and think what this actually entails. In Judaism, we too have an object made by artisans which is imbued with sanctity and treated with the utmost respect. We adorn it with fine cloth and precious metals, even jewels, and bow down to it. Initiates know well that the Torah scroll itself is not being worshipped, that worshippers believe it to contain the words of God and therefore revere it as sacred. To an outside observer, however, this difference could be too subtle to be noticed. To give another example, Eastern Orthodox Christians pray gazing at an icon (a painting of Christ, the Virgin Mary or a Saint). They focus their religious emotion

---

[12]The kabbalistic book, the 'Zohar' says the dead sages can indeed intercede with God on behalf of supplicants.

on the intercessor portrayed on the icon and for them it becomes a window into the sacred world. Should the icon be considered as an idol? Surely not.

Observant Jews and Christians could be upset to have their sacred objects compared to idols, yet they seem unable to understand that such symbolism works in a similar way for the sacred objects of other religions. If we can accept the *sefer Torah* and the icon as symbols of and conduits to the divine, rather than as idols, then why not take a similar approach to a statue of Vishnu or Ganesh?

One thing, perhaps, all would agree to be a form of idol worship is excessive materialism, the worship of money. This can affect secular and religious, monotheist and polytheist alike, and is a sad feature of modern life. Amos Oz described it well:

> *When I look around me, I see so many people working harder than they should, in order to make more money than they need, which they use to buy things they don't want, in order to impress people they don't care about.*

Polytheists usually have a shrine with a representation of their favourite god in their home. In the Hebrew Bible similar household gods are referred to as the *teraphim*. Again, Judaism did not eliminate these ideas. It transformed them. Hence we have the *mezuzah* which, interestingly, since mediæval times has also contained, in addition to the sacred text, a lucky or magic charm.[13] This has given rise to the superstitious, popular custom of kissing the *mezuzah* for luck upon entering and leaving a house. A continuing theme in religious history is how little is original and how much is syncretism; the development of one religious practice on the back of another. As the dominant religion of a place changes with time, it is usual for the existing holy places to remain unchanged, being adapted to the new practice. Even the dates of old festivals are often retained with new rituals being introduced.

A more fundamental difference between belief systems is that for a monotheist God is transcendent, which means that He is remote, above and outside of this world. However God is not held to be immanent; in other words, although God may be everywhere; God is not present in everything. By contrast, for a polytheist God is both

---

[13] *see 'Superstition' - Chapter 12 p. 202 - for details*

immanent, and so present in all of creation (both animate and inanimate); and also transcendent. This leads to huge differences of philosophy. It becomes perfectly logical for a believer in an immanent god to say that the spirit of the divine is present in an idol, for god is in everything, including both idols and more importantly human beings.

Interestingly, in Jewish tradition at an earlier stage of our development, we also had a man-made object in which the spirit of the divine dwelt, and was stored and transported. This was the Ark of the Covenant which anthropologists would now classify as a *fetish object*. It was so important that it is represented symbolically in every synagogue as the ark for storing the Torah scrolls. Later, the claim that God had 'taken up residence' in the temple strengthened the argument for those wanting to centre the religion on Jerusalem. This 'residence' ended with the Babylonian conquest and in Ezekiel's vision of the chariot[14] one can interpret the bizarre symbolism as a vision of God departing his temple prior to its destruction.

When religions are compared, it is often found that there are more similarities than differences once the superficial layers and details are stripped back. This is not really surprising given that religions sprang up apparently spontaneously in all parts of the world. The explanation can only be that religion answered a psychological need of human beings. It would appear that religion developed in response to humanity's fears and insecurities and also in response to the quest for spirituality. That is, religion helped both the need to be in touch with the numinous and in alleviating the burden of human being's knowledge of their transience and inevitable death.

Religion also provided a mechanism for giving 'answers' to the metaphysical questions that some members of the human race were troubled with. Most of humanity seems unable to accept the apparently random nature of many events. Our brains seem to be wired to want to believe that all events are ordered and have a purpose and that all of life is being controlled from somewhere.

The psychologist, Carl Jung, developed a theory of the 'collective unconscious'. The theory claims that everyone, from whatever background, has a genetic predisposition to symbolize human

---

[14] *Ezekiel 1*

situations in certain ways. Jung called these symbols 'archetypes' and believed that such archetypes can be found in all the religions and mythologies of the world.

Jung's front door in Kusnacht, Switzerland

For Jung, gods are the personification of these symbols. It is interesting to note that Jung personally showed how important he felt their influence on the psyche was, as he had the following words carved over his front door and subsequently inscribed on his grave.[15]

Vocatus atque non vocatus deus aderit.
(Called or not called, the god will be present.)

In his book on the psychology of religious belief,[16] M.D. Faber produced a persuasive thesis as to how belief is perpetuated. He says that as they grow, infants go from full dependence on their caregiver, through a transitional stage of semi-dependence, to ultimate full independence. In the beginning, during the full dependence stage the infant's psyche becomes completely attuned to having all its needs met by a human caregiver (usually the mother) – and this mechanism is strongly imprinted.

It is during the transitional stage that the psyche is open to the religious idea of supernatural parental ministration and protection. At this stage, the psyche easily accepts the idea of a God who will love and protect the child throughout its life; of a divine parent who will always be there when the child can no longer call on its natural ones.

The mechanism to accept these ideas is (Faber argues) deeply imprinted during the transitional stage of development. This is a period when children make use of transitional objects – both physical (such as a blanket they won't be parted from) and psychic (such as belief in fairies, Santa Claus, angels and God). With increasing maturity, children gradually set most of these transitional objects and concepts aside – primarily as a result of parental or peer pressure. They discover or are

---

[15] *Jung explained this quotation of a response from the Delphic oracle as meaning; yes, the god will be on the spot, but in what form and to what purpose?*
[16] *M.D. Faber. 'The Psychological Roots of Religious Belief'. Prometheus Books 2004*

told that fairies and Santa Claus don't really exist. In relation to God, they are often either left to decide for themselves or more commonly, have belief reinforced by the behaviour of parents and society. The social pressure exerted by respected adults and by the leaders of a society is an incredibly strong influence in obtaining the conformity of the great majority of young people.

The earliest religious motivation, though, was surely fear. Danger was ever-present and a solitary person had little control. As the poet, A. E. Housman wrote:[17]

> *'I, a stranger and afraid*
> *In a world I never made.'*

The concept of having a higher power on one's side and so improving one's chances in all aspects of life, from trivial things like winning a game to serious matters of actual survival, was and remains an incredibly attractive one for many people. For these people it is well worth performing the ritual procedures, sacrifices or affordable donations that society's holy men demand in order to propitiate the god(s) of one's local culture. The strength of mind to give up such a transitional object (as God) and face the lottery of life alone was not, and still is not, possessed by many.

Let us now examine several human issues and compare how monotheists and polytheists respond to them:
  o   the place of the individual in society
  o   the separate but related issues of evil, suffering and divine justice
  o   the question of tolerance for outsiders or people with other beliefs
As you read the following sections, consider which belief system you feel offers the better responses for each issue.

• **The individual**
The difference in the role of the individual within the different religious traditions can be more easily understood in relation to the concept of time. In most polytheistic religions and in Buddhist philosophy too, time can be considered as being circular, events recurring just like the

---

[17] from *Last Poems 1922* – untitled - (first line – 'The laws of God, the laws of man')

seasons. In a similar way, lifetimes recur as souls are reincarnated and so one individual life is of little consequence. Maintaining the traditional nature of society is all important, and so non-conformity or individuality is discouraged. History too will repeat itself, and therefore a single person cannot change events significantly.

By contrast, for the monotheist for whom the deity has already acted in historical time, it is clear that time is linear, and change and progress are indeed possible. Talented individuals seem more likely to fulfil their potential within this framework, as the history of the West bears out, although the fundamentalist religious have often done their best to delay and deny progress. However, issues such as global warming show that by no means all of the changes have turned out to be true progress.

- **Evil**

Why does God allow it? If God is all powerful and just, then why do righteous people sometimes suffer and wicked ones prosper? The monotheistic religions have continuously struggled with this problem and have failed to find a convincing response. For dualists the answer is straightforward. The lesser God is responsible for all the evil in the world. The higher God is not (yet) powerful enough to stop evil. Polytheists can successfully use a version of this explanation too, with deities of varying morality each one lacking full omnipotence.[18]

- **Suffering**

For the polytheist the general rule is to accept suffering as a given. Only the gods could alter things and one must appease the gods to avoid making things worse or suffering oneself. Believers in monotheism, despite having no theological explanation of innocent suffering, are able to act both individually and collectively in historical time to make changes. As an example, public health has generally been given a higher priority in monotheistic societies.

Within different religious systems there are differences in the degree to which adherents will act to reduce suffering. Taoism, for example, is an extremely conservative belief system which, as mentioned earlier, was criticised that, 'they would not move themselves to pluck out a single

---

[18] *See Chapter 8 for a fuller exploration of this important issue.*

hair, even if by doing so they could save the world'. In psychological terms this acceptance of suffering as an unalterable situation may be a practical help for many individuals in coping with their difficult day to day experiences.

•   **Divine Justice**

Blinkered to what seems strong evidence to the contrary, monotheistic religions believe in a provident God that distributes reward and punishment fairly and justly to each individual. Apparent injustices are sometimes 'explained' away using the concept that God will make up for these wrongs in the world to come. A paradoxical manifestation of this belief in a provident God is often heard after a major accident or natural disaster. A survivor typically says words to the effect: 'God was looking out for me and saved my life'. They seldom consider that this type of statement is offensive to those killed or injured. Does the person making this claim really believe he was so much more worthy of divine intervention than the victims? Had God been minded to intervene at all, then why not prevent the entire incident in the first place?

Polytheists generally believe in rebirth of the soul and that suffering in this life is a result of misdeeds in a past one. The gods do not concern themselves with individual cases. In many ways, both systems use similar techniques to sidestep apparent divine injustice. One blames the past, the other looks to the future, with perfect justice arriving either in the world to come or when the Messiah arrives; but both tacitly agree that there is no justice in the world we live in. Both also demand obedience to their own code of behaviour in this life by offering the rewards of heaven for the monotheist and a better future incarnation (or ultimately release from reincarnation) for the polytheist. 'Jam tomorrow' is a common theme. There appears to be nothing of merit in either such attempt to rationalise and excuse human suffering, especially as both systems conclude that ultimately individuals get their just reward. I beg to differ.

•   **Tolerance**

For a polytheist it is very easy to incorporate another people's god or belief system into one's world view, or to recognise a foreign god as the overseas version of a god known locally by another name. This more tolerant attitude can only help reduce one of the main causes of strife between neighbours. A serious problem in believing in one God, who is a universal transcendent God, is that of exclusivity. One implicitly excludes as equal members of the human race those who do not share this belief. They are considered to be at best unenlightened and at worst subhuman. This even applies to other monotheists who apparently believe in the identical God, but with a different label. History is littered with the evil that such intolerance has led to. It is interesting and extremely sad to observe how differences of opinion, sometimes over seemingly minor details, within the same religion can so easily lead to charges of heresy and to the intense intolerance of heretics by their co-religionists.

It is clear that the polytheist is more tolerant of the monotheist than the other way round. As Schopenhauer wrote succinctly:

> *Indeed, intolerance is essential only to monotheism; an only God is by nature a jealous God who will not allow another to live. On the other hand, polytheistic gods are naturally tolerant: they live and let live.*

For similar reasons, it is primarily the monotheistic religions that engage in missionary activities. Polytheists are comfortable with their deities and happy for their neighbour either to share them or worship alternatives. Conversion is not an issue. They can always add a new god to their belief structure, as we would add a new dish to our diet while still continuing to enjoy all our old favourites. Monotheists by contrast, believing they worship the one true God, feel an urge to share this 'Truth' with others. This caused trouble in the polytheistic world. When the missionaries effectively claimed all other gods to be false they came into inevitable conflict with polytheistic societies. One result was the persecution of Jews and Christians in the Roman world. Initially the Romans actually saw monotheists as being atheists, for they denied the divinity of all the 'existing' Roman gods, and for them atheism was a crime. Nevertheless, in time the missionaries were effective. They were 'selling' a very desirable product. A God who was much more powerful than the local gods and one that promised to give his new followers real benefits in exchange for their allegiance. This was a God who, by contrast to the Roman gods, related to individual human beings.

This discussion demonstrates that neither belief system has all the answers, while each responds better to at least some of the questions. There doesn't appear to be a single compelling argument that demonstrates the superiority of monotheism although it is clearly more attractive to many people with its claims of a powerful God that takes a personal interest in and gives divine rewards to those following the rules. Perhaps this has been the reason for its success.

It also doesn't really seem to matter much whether we divide the multiple aspects of the divine into different gods or whether we give many different names to the same one God. Each named aspect of God answers a different human need. Of course, this discussion could be extended to debate whether god(s) are nothing more than a human invention to help deal with the species' own psychological needs.

It is interesting to see how these ideas have been incorporated into the main world religions of today. For simplicity, these can be divided into eastern and western religious traditions. The former covers the main religions of India, China and Japan while the latter includes the three major monotheistic faiths. The words *theism* and *monism* are helpful in this discussion. The essential difference between these terms is that:

- o theism posits that a transcendent God or gods exist *separately* from the universe
- o monism considers that all is one 'substance'. There is no fundamental separation between the physical universe and the immanent god(s).

• Mutual attitudes of (western) theistic and (eastern) monistic religions

How these very different philosophies of religion treat votaries of the other is very illuminating. Theists have always looked harshly on manifestations of monism. They interpret such monistic ideas as the individual claiming to be (a part of) God as blasphemy, or when they see the immanent God worshipped through such symbols as the sun, the moon or a sculpture as idolatry.

For such 'crimes' adherents of monism have been persecuted throughout western religious history. Those whose monistic ideas were expressed within their own religious traditions have been particularly persecuted as heretics; e.g. Meister Eckhart in Christianity, Spinoza in Judaism[19] and the Sufis (in general) in Islam.[20]

The eastern (monistic) religions by contrast are much more relaxed in their attitudes to theism. In general they do not condemn it but look on it as a 'lower' form of the truth. It is considered to be a stage the seeker after truth may pass through on his quest. Indeed they, rather patronisingly, consider that theistic systems are suitable for ensuring morality among the masses, while the higher monistic religions can achieve personal liberation for the more enlightened.

There is room here for no more than an overview of this fascinating subject. To read more about the similarities and differences between east and west a good starting point would be Joseph Campbell's fascinating and very readable four volume work, 'The Masks of God.'

The table points out and summarises (with inevitable generalisations) of the main contrasts between these religious traditions.[21]

Western religion – Theism	Eastern religion – Monism
One God, who is transcendent (i.e. above and outside the world)	The Absolute Reality (equivalent to, but different from the western idea of God) is both transcendent and immanent. (The divine is not just everywhere but in everything)
Male God created the world. This world is outside of him	Female goddess created the world. This world is part of her body
An individual's return to God requires divine revelation and instruction	Return to and experience of the Absolute Reality requires no revelation, but to re-cognise (alter one's perception)
God often has anthropomorphic characteristics. Can even be considered to have a 'personality'	The Absolute Reality (God) is a process, a truth or a state of being. There is no concept of such a God with personal characteristics (though lesser gods may have them)

---

[19] *Spinoza is usually considered a pantheist; that is as having a monist belief that God and nature (or God and the universe) are effectively one and the same.*

[20] *al-Hallaj d. 922CE was an early martyr.*

[21] *There is some crossover between east and west. Esoteric forms of western religion such as Kabbalah and Sufism incorporate many eastern concepts.*

Western religion – Theism	Eastern religion – Monism
World origin: First chaos then order	World origin: *either* a steady state with no beginning (cf. Aristotle's ideas) *or* a continuing cycle of chaos > order > chaos etc.
Mankind is separated from God by a historical event (and so must return via history). (thus time is linear - historical)	We are separated from God by a psychological event. Thus individuals must return by a psychological or inward event. No outside revelation is required. (thus time is circular - cyclical)
The universe is the work of a Creator God.	The universe has always existed.
God relates to man in a monarchical sense.	The immanent god is man in a mask.
Dogma and ritual are divinely revealed.	Dogma and ritual are of lesser importance.
The path to salvation depends on obeying holy law and doing good works, or of simple faith in God.	The path to salvation is by acquiring knowledge or wisdom; i.e. the ability to see things as they really are.
The purpose of salvation is to reach heaven or paradise or to escape hell.	The purpose of salvation is to emerge from the suffering of the world and to achieve *nirvana, moksha,* blissfulness.
The most important ritual elements revolve around worship (prayer) and sacraments.	The most important ritual elements revolve around meditation and achievement of altered states of consciousness.
Evil and suffering are due to sins against the laws of God	Evil and suffering are due to ignorance and self delusion
Individuals receive distributive justice – as they sow, so shall they reap.	Individual's fate in this life is determined at birth, and is dependent on their previous incarnation
An individual's contact with God is through worship. Prayer mainly consists of doxology[22] and entreaty.	Contact with the divine is achieved by meditation and knowledge.
Religion – *re-ligio* (Latin) to link back or bind *The link is God to man.*	Yoga - *yuj* (Sanskrit) to link, join or unite *The link is self to itself.*

[22] *Doxology – prayer praising God, flattering and complimenting Him*

Relativism

Between theism and monism is a further position – relativism. This holds that God or the ultimate reality is unknowable – beyond human ability to comprehend. Knowledge is always attained from a particular perspective, and is therefore relative (to that viewpoint). No statements of absolute truth can be made concerning the nature of God. The syncretic Baha'i religion is relativistic and incorporates both monism and theism. In its ritual, it uses both prayer and meditation and it describes time as moving in a spiral.

Chinese and Japanese religious practice is also syncretistic and relativistic. Commonly, people in these countries 'mix and match' their religious practice. A Chinese family for example may use Confucian practice to celebrate a birth and have a Christian marriage and Buddhist rituals on death.

The individual and society within western and eastern cultural traditions

These religious differences inevitably strongly influence both the general culture and the approach to life of individuals and entire societies in both the East and the West. In the East, until the increasing western influence of recent times, there had been little change over the centuries. In the West, by contrast, the influence of the monotheisms was dominant until the Enlightenment. Then there was a significant change and subsequently enlightenment values were widely embraced.

In the table that follows, it would have been possible to include a third (minority) column for those areas where pre-enlightenment monotheism still dominates. Such areas would include conservative Islamic states and the areas where ultra-Orthodox Jews maintain their separate way of life. As these societies are small in comparison with east and west, this group has been omitted but bear in mind that the western column would have been very different in pre-enlightenment times. Remember too, that these are generalisations and so not necessarily applicable to individual practice.

	Modern Western Tradition	**Eastern Tradition**
The Individual	Each of us is unique, and if we are to give any gift to the world, it must be from our own experience and the fulfilment of our own potential.	The individual is formed as if 'in a mould'. He/she has exact duties and must not try to break out from performing them.
Religion or Spirituality	The duty of a religious person is to love God and obey his commandments as laid down in the sacred texts of the person's religion.	The aim of a spiritual person is to achieve the traditional wisdom of his religion, to gain direct experience of the divine and to be released from the endless cycle of reincarnation.
The Teacher	A good western teacher guides students to develop an individual picture of themselves so that they can develop their potential in their own unique way. The traditional corpus of knowledge is taught as a possible point of departure.	Spiritually, a guru can guide one down the traditional and established path - a path which he is further along, and the student's aim is to follow in his guru's footsteps. Original thought is not encouraged, nor is the forging of a new or individual path. There are a few gurus, however, who do teach that they have no answers to give and that each individual has to 'work it out' for themselves.
The Arts	Similarly, in the arts one learns techniques from a master, but then develops ones own style and ideas. In the west the duty of art is to progress.	In the arts, one learns from the master in order to continue in the established tradition, by producing similar work.

7

The Chosen People - a Galactic Perspective

—————————

There is no nation, it seems, which has not been promised the whole Earth.
Elias Canetti

T he concept of chosenness is not unusual, especially among local
religions (which Judaism itself once was). It appears to be a
basic human habit to consider oneself and one's group as
special and it seems reasonable, even logical, to consider that the group
who worship a particular god are of special concern to, or have in some
way been chosen by that god. The paradoxical nature of this circular
logic seems clear only to those looking from the outside. Voltaire put it
succinctly:

> *God created man in his image and man promptly returned the compliment.*

Local religions have certain typical features. They usually have a sacred
place or places where the god appeared or some other important event
took place and which is kept as a place of worship or pilgrimage.
Commonly there is also a blessed or Holy Land, which is invariably
that of the religion's original adherents, and whose inhabitants are
specially treated by their god. As Robert Ingersoll pointed out in 1872
when surveying the religions of early civilisations:[1]

—————————

[1] *Robert G. Ingersoll. The Gods. 1872*

'Each nation has created a god, and the god has always resembled his creators. He hated and loved what they hated and loved and he was invariably found on the side of those in power. Each god was intensely patriotic and detested all nations but his own.'

When a local religion transformed their local god into the Universal One, who then became the sole God for all humankind, it had a logical problem to overcome. How could it communicate this new information to the rest of humanity? God never seemed interested in helping his followers with such communication and, in general, the world's other people seemed disinterested, as they were quite satisfied with the deities they already had.

Only two methods were available to spread the word. The religion could either proselytise by sending missionaries, ideally to make high profile conversions, as Christianity did so successfully in the Roman Empire, or convert people by the sword. The latter method was particularly effective in the ancient world as success in conquest was 'known' to be linked to the protection of a powerful god. Combine this with the knowledge that most people, faced with a choice of convert or die, will take the first option; one can then understand how religion began its relationship with war and violence. Both methods have been used by those with firm belief that their God was the only true God. The method selected seemed to depend primarily on their political and military strength at the time. As discussed elsewhere, while all religions were spread by their adherents only believers in monotheism actively proselytised, gaining converts both voluntarily and by force.

Judaism practiced forced conversion during Hasmonean times (see Chapter 3) and proselytised actively in Roman times. Once Christianity became the imperial religion, this activity ceased and for political reasons Judaism stopped actively seeking converts.

Christianity also had active missionaries in the Roman Empire. In the early 4th century, it achieved the masterstroke of converting first Emperor Constantine's mother, Helena, and then the Emperor himself. Following this, they had wealth and military strength on their side and this imperial power was not withheld in converting pagans within the Empire. Christian missionary activity was no longer required, and ceased until the 17th century with the advent of the colonial era.

From its beginning, **Islam** obtained followers by a combination of conversion and conquest, with the religion spreading incredibly rapidly after the death of Mohammed in 632 CE. The catalyst for this success was undoubtedly the military campaigns of conquest mounted by the Umayyad dynasty.

A truly universal God, who wished to reveal important information to humanity, should have been able to foresee the drawbacks of doing this by revelation only to one small people, with all the mistrust that such an act would inevitably cause among its neighbours. One would imagine that had He so wished, God could have found a way of revealing such important information to all humanity. Did God not care about the majority who never got a chance to hear 'the truth'? What of those people who lived before His revelation? Did they have no moral guidance?

If the monotheist's universal God 'chose' the people who believe in him to be his 'light unto the nations' then there is an even greater recipe for trouble. Even a Deity unable to foresee the future, but who simply possessed knowledge of human psychology should have predicted that the other nations would not consider themselves to be in darkness and accordingly would not welcome this 'light'.

We must therefore find it logically improbable that a truly universal and transcendent God would choose one race above the rest. Would a parent of a large family be wise to choose one child above its other siblings? Even more improbable is for such a *universal* deity to order the slaughter of one people by another.[2] As Freud rightly commented:

'*Along with the belief in a single God religious intolerance was inevitably born.*'

The tenet of Judaism that all gods but ours are false gods and that worshipping other gods is not only misguided but evil, can only lead to intolerance. Jews holding this orthodox view can be considered no different to any other believer in a single, exclusive religion, for each such religion claims the justification of 'truth'.

Those who believe themselves to be in possession of such an exclusive truth are able to use the 'logic' of monotheistic belief and say that they

---

[2] *e.g. Ai - Joshua 8:18-29*

must obey the revealed will of this all powerful God. Any who do so rigidly and unquestioningly fall squarely within my definition of fundamentalist. Such behaviour could result in them being able to carry out even unspeakable acts with a clear moral conscience. Steven Weinberg put it as follows:[3]

> 'With or without religion, you would have good people doing good things and evil people doing evil things. But for good people to do evil things, that takes religion.'

In this statement, the word religion should be extended to include ideology. It can apply to any of Isaiah Berlin's 'final solutions' or certainties that were discussed in the previous chapter.

One may also question what constitutes a good person. Howard Bloom[4] discussed the heiress Bertha Krupp[5] who, during the second World War regularly visited Krupp workers who were ill and gave generously to those who were in need. She considered herself warm, compassionate and giving. However, although fully aware of them, she had no conscience or concerns about the slave labour camps run by her son, in which people (Slavs and Jews) were kept in inhuman conditions and worked to death. Such people were referred to by Bertha (and other Germans at the time) as *stücke* (livestock).

The indictment of religion is that, like all ideologies that claim to know the truth, it sometimes exploits a weakness in human beings. It seems that even good people are capable of unspeakable acts if manipulated correctly, and religion is one of the various ways this manipulation can occur.[6] As Alexander Solzhenitsyn wrote movingly:

> If only there were evil people somewhere insidiously committing evil deeds, and it was necessary only to separate them from the rest of us and destroy them. But the line dividing good and evil cuts through the heart of every human being, and who is willing to destroy a piece of his own heart?

---

[3] *Stephen Weinberg – Nobel Laureate (Physics – USA) quoted in the New York Times 20th April 1999*
[4] *In 'The Lucifer Principle Atlantic Monthly Press 1999'*
[5] *Bertha Krupp was heiress to the Krupp dynasty, Germany's largest industrial empire (coal, steel and armaments) of the 19th and 20th centuries. She is remembered by the name Big Bertha, which was given to the long range German artillery pieces during the Second World War.*
[6] *Also see the classic experimental work of psychologist Professor Stanley Milgram. He 'persuaded' ordinary people to inflict pain on others. Consider too the Stanford prison experiment - see bibliography-Philip Zimbardo*

Double standards of morality have been a constant of human and religious history, particularly in time of war. They are to be found in the *Tanach* where, for example, God's chosen people are told to kill all the conquered men after the successful siege of a city.[7] It mattered not that this behaviour was incompatible with the commandment 'Thou shall not kill'. The anthropologist Margaret Mead commented that every human group, in effect, makes the rule not to not kill members of their own group, but everyone outside is fair game.

Double standards like this, easily lead to racism and the orthodox in particular are at risk. One Jewish group has indeed incorporated what appears to be racist theology into their belief system. According to a central text of the Lubavitch, *'Tanya'*, there is an actual difference between the soul of a Jew and that of a gentile, such that a gentile is incapable of truly doing good deeds. Any good they apparently do is purely for self glorification.[8] This is a dangerous and indeed racist idea and is contrary to normative Jewish belief. It is mentioned here as we must be ever vigilant to the danger of such ideas infecting the religion.

The paradigm of a chosen people treating the resultant non-chosen group as inferior and so to some degree sub-human, has led to callous behaviour throughout history. The example from *'Tanya'* shows the insidious way such ideas can infiltrate the mainstream. In most wars, each antagonist has claimed to have God on its side despite the paradoxical nature of such claims. A.C. Grayling summed up the religious approach to war as:[9]

> *Faith is what I die for, dogma is what I kill for.*

As discussed in Chapter 3, prior to the prophets' introduction of exclusivity to Yahweh, it was acceptable in Israelite practice for other nations to have their own god (monolatry). Then the prophets of the Yahweh-alone movement began to preach that other people's gods are idols or devils. The *Tanach* includes the statement:[10]

אין אלוהים בכל הארץ כי אם בישראל....

> '.... *there is no God in the whole world except in Israel.*'

---

[7] *Deuteronomy 20:10-15*

[8] *See appendix p.242 for more details concerning these ideas*

[9] *A.C. Grayling. Against All Gods. Oberon Masters. 2007*

[10] *2 Kings 5:15*

By promoting such ideas, Judaism effectively claimed that the rest of humankind is godless and second class. Is this a reasonable belief for a theist? It certainly seems a step down the road to intolerance.

With the centring of the early sacrificial Israelite religion on Jerusalem, a paradoxical situation developed. Judaism had a universal God whom it was only possible to worship (i.e. sacrifice to) in Jerusalem. This centralisation of the religion also led to conflict with the Samaritans, a northern Israelite group who followed the Torah but wished to continue to sacrifice at their traditional holy places on Mount Gerizim (Nablus). Jews and Samaritans split over this issue and went their separate ways. Later, when the Jews were politically and militarily stronger, they attempted to wipe them out - a single tragic example of religious intolerance for a competing 'truth'.

The Jewish concept of *covenant* takes the idea of chosenness even further. While chosenness is a concept that excludes the principles of plurality, covenant is actually a political alliance with God.

A tribal deity generally reflects the moral values and cultural attitudes of a specific people at a particular historic time, in this case that of Iron Age Hebrews. It is certainly true though, that during the events of the *Tanach* God is transformed from tribal to universal, and that the moral consciousness of his people also evolved as God was challenged by the passion and the suffering of the individual.

Sadly, the interest that God took in his chosen people seems to have been short term. God appears to stop taking an active part in history even before the end of events related in the *Tanach*. The covenant with the Jews seems to be discarded, and He withdrew from this brief foray into human affairs. This apparent abandonment of his chosen people is another theological problem. It appears to this student of Jewish history that the Jewish people have been un-chosen.

The abandonment and breaching of the covenant by God occurs in parallel to God's character transforming from tribal to universal during the course of the *Tanach*. This appears to show that, in practical terms, the biblical authors understood the incompatibility of the ideas of universality and chosenness. The later, more ethical, universal God that emerged is the one taken up as Judaism developed after the Exile.

However, belief in the chosen people and in the covenant with God remained too central to the religion to be discarded, as perhaps these elitist ideas should have been.

Looking at the concept of a chosen people from a wider perspective further brings home how parochial it is and makes it even more difficult to accept. When considering the Jewish people in relation to 'God's universe' it is impossible for us to conceive how totally insignificant they are, both in terms of size and of the period of time for which they were chosen. To approach this, let us begin by restricting ourselves to the small planet Earth and considering the animal world and the place of our human species within it. We, being human centred, naturally tend to consider *Homo sapiens* as the summit and focus of God's attention. It seems completely natural that our sacred text records our species as being made in the image of God. However, we need to bear in mind that we are just one of well over a million animal species.

When the famous geneticist, J.B.S. Haldane was asked by a theologian what conclusions he could draw about the Creator from studies of the animal kingdom, he replied, 'an inordinate fondness for beetles'. Haldane was referring to what seems to be a disproportionately high number of species belonging to the order *Coleoptera* (beetles). At more than 300,000 they account for something like one in four of all known animal species in the world. Other species have a claim for special treatment too. Douglas Adams wrote:

> *Man [has] always assumed that he was more intelligent than dolphins because he had achieved so much, - the wheel, New York, wars and so on - while all the dolphins had ever done was muck about in the water having a good time. But conversely, the dolphins had always believed that they were far more intelligent than man - for precisely the same reason.*

As well as the attention the Creator paid to beetles and dolphins, should we ignore the effort expended on the great variety of parasites, bacteria and viruses? These were presumably deliberately created to bring disease to the other species. Our arrogance in believing that we humans were created in God's image had already been questioned by the Greeks. The philosopher, Xenophanes (c. 570-480 BCE) wrote:

The Ethiopians say that their gods are flat-nosed and black, while the Thracians say theirs have blue eyes and blond hair. Yet if oxen or horses or lions had hands and could draw and sculpt like men, then the horses would draw their gods like horses, and oxen like oxen; and they would each shape the bodies of gods in the image of themselves.

Bearing this in mind and trying to ignore the distracting possibility that beetles, not humans, were created in the image of God, let us now look at the physical universe we all inhabit. Remember that when the Jewish theology of the chosen people developed, the cosmology current at that time was used as a background in writing the *Tanach*. This told of a three tiered flat Earth, which was the centre of everything. The world we inhabit was the middle layer, with *sheol* or some form of underworld below. Above us were the heavens, where God lived along with the heavenly bodies, the sun, moon and all the stars.

Now contrast this with our current knowledge of the size and structure of the universe. Israel covers a tiny portion of our planet. This planet, Earth, is just one of several satellites orbiting around our local star, that seat of many ancient divinities, which we call the sun. We also know that our local Galaxy,[11] the Milky Way, contains somewhere between 200 and 400 *billion* such stars – an incomprehensibly large number. Our entire solar system is but a minute speck within this Galaxy. Consider further; for the Milky Way, with all its stars and solar systems is just one part of a cluster made up of 50 galaxies. This in turn makes up only one of 100 such clusters comprising the Virgo supercluster.

If we are now feeling rather modest about our planet's importance to the universe it is perhaps because we have already far exceeded our human ability to comprehend such large numbers of stars, planets and the huge distances involved. Travelling at the speed of light it would take 200 million years to pass from our planet's position near one edge of the Virgo supercluster and reach the opposite side. But we are nowhere near finished. Clusters of galaxies are separated by immense voids in space, and this cluster is but one of thousands of clusters of galaxies in a universe whose limits are still unknown.

---

[11] *By convention, astronomers distinguish the Galaxy in which planet Earth resides from the others, by using a capital G. We can enjoy the coincidental use of a capital G for both our God and our Galaxy.*

In an attempt to try and get back to a human scale, this means that there are at least 10 huge galaxies in space for every single human being on planet Earth.[12] It is also unknown whether our universe is unique (as no one has ever seen the edge) or whether other universes may exist beyond, a concept known as the multiverse.

For the sole God of this universe to have selected a small portion of just one animal species on this tiny planet (lost in the vastness of space) for his particular attention may now seem unlikely, but let's stay with it. Keeping in mind that as a grain of sand is to the Earth, so the Earth is to the universe; we must start to consider the length of time God remained interested in his chosen people. This must be related to the time that has passed since first the universe and then much later the Earth came into existence. Once more, we have to deal with numbers that the human brain is not well designed to relate to. To help, let's borrow a concept that can put this into perspective.[13] Planet Earth has been around for about 4.5 billion years. Imagine this time as a story told evenly over the course of a 900 page book. This is a chunky tome, think of Moby Dick, Middlemarch or The Brothers Karamazov.

Each single page of this book represents the enormous period of 5 million years. Not until page 200 do Earth's first life forms (bacteria) appear. It then takes until page 810 for land plants and 830 for land animals to arrive. On page 887, a huge catastrophe[14] wipes out over half the species that had so far evolved. Dinosaurs are among those that disappear for ever. On the next page, India collides with Asia, and the Himalayas begin to be formed. Only on page 890, a mere 10 pages before the end, do mammals become dominant. The first hominids do not appear until page 899 – the next to last page. Our species, *Homo sapiens* finally arrives at the beginning of the last line at the very bottom of the last page! This complete line finishes the book with the words, THE END. Somewhere around the letter 'N' is the time assigned to Abraham, and Judaism dates only from the final 'D'. The subsequent full stop represents the most recent millennium.

---

[12] *Estimates are 100 billion galaxies and 6.5 billion humans, actually over 15 to 1.*

[13] *With gratitude to Professor David Park and his fascinating book 'The Grand Contraption' for this idea, which I have extended*

[14] *The Cretaceous-Tertiary extinction thought to have been caused by an asteroid striking the Earth*

Now consider again the Jewish people in relation to both the size and age of the universe. Did the universe's supreme power really choose to single out this tiny speck of humanity on its even tinier speck of the universe for his personal attention, and then discard them after the equivalent of less than one letter in a 900 page book? A relationship, which if compared to a long human lifespan of 100 years, would have lasted less than 8 minutes, the length of time we might spend drinking a cup of coffee.[15]

Bear in mind also that the book represented only the history of planet Earth. The best estimate for the age of the entire universe is 13.5 billion years. We therefore need two additional 900 page volumes to tell the full story since 'creation'. Now, looking forward it is estimated that in 1 billion years (200 pages) the Earth will become too hot for humans to survive.[16] Another 4.5 billion years forward (a further 900 page volume) and the sun will run out of hydrogen fuel at its core and be transformed into a red giant. Planet Earth may survive a further 2 billion years before spiralling to a vaporous death.

Our species, uniquely, have had an awareness of the spiritual (as evidenced by burial sites and painted figures) since the earliest times we have evidence of their existence. Divine revelation (in its Jewish version at least) seems to have been long delayed and was not to the entire species but only to a small people living in a tiny geographical area of one remote planet.

Is it really sensible to believe that a universal God intervened directly in the history of this small people for just a few hundred years, a divine split second? Even for those who believe in a universal God it must be hard to understand why He would behave thus. 'God's ways are mysterious, and we cannot understand or comprehend them' would probably be the believer's truly felt, but unhelpful explanation.

---

[15] *Calculation based on a universe aged 13.5 billion years and a generous 2000 year interest in the Jews*
[16] *This ignores global warming, the temperature increase being purely due to the increase in the sun's brightness.*

8

The insoluble problem of divine justice and evil

Go up to the ancient ruin heaps and walk around;
Look at the skulls of the lowly and the great.
Which belongs to one who did evil, and which to one who did good?
The Dialogue of Pessimism[1]

Within the western tradition two important assumptions are made by most religious people. First, that life in some way has a meaning or purpose and secondly, that God treats his devotees justly. In respect of justice, there has always been the need to explain why sometimes, even for the faithful, this fairness is not apparent and that human suffering is so widespread.

Theodicy (a term simply meaning an explanation of how a just God can coexist with evil) has challenged sages and philosophers down the centuries[2] but remains for the monotheistic religions the insoluble problem it has always been. For many Jews today, living in the shadow of the Holocaust, it is a major obstacle interfering with belief in the God of tradition.

The *Tanach* gives several different answers to the problem of suffering, not all of which are compatible with each other.[3] For the prophets the

---

[1] *The Dialogue of Pessimism was written in Mesopotamia during the 14th century BCE*
[2] *The term theodicy (unlike the problem) only dates from the Enlightenment, having been coined by Leibnitz.*
[3] *Apart from the prophets and Job discussed here, Kohelet (Ecclesiastes) clearly influenced by Hellenism shows a picture favoured also by Eastern religion, that suffering is simply the nature of reality, while Daniel gives the second century BCE apocalyptic Jewish view of cosmic evil forces loose in the world – essentially a dualist opinion.*

matter is simple. God is angry with his people who have sinned and He is the one meting out the justified punishment. This was used to account for the destruction of the first temple and the Exile. In later times, it became apparent that collective punishment where all the people suffered together was not justice and the question soon arose of why righteous individuals sometimes suffered while some of the wicked prospered.

The prime text used to debate this issue in Judaism is the Book of Job, perhaps the most challenging book of the *Tanach*. Let us begin our inquiry by looking at this ancient story of a perfectly good and pious man, with a seemingly perfect life, who lost everything - his possessions, his children and his health as a result of a bet made in heaven. The core of the book concerns Job's search for an explanation of his suffering, in particular from God. What follows is a great simplification but is a personal, overall understanding of the text in relation to this issue. We will then survey wider Jewish responses to evil and to the Shoah in particular and look briefly at religious responses in general. The reader is invited to decide if any of the responses can be accepted.

The Book of Job, when stripped of its wonderful poetry and examined from a theological point of view, sets out to reconcile the following three statements each of which it holds to be true:

> A. Job is a righteous man who suffers.
> B. There is one all powerful God capable of intervening in human affairs.
> C. God is just and dispenses reward and punishment fairly.

The reader understands that, by simple logic, all three statements cannot be true – so which one is false?

In the narrative, Job's friends put forward the mainstream religious arguments for suffering[4] and try to convince him that it is A - perhaps Job is really not so righteous. Maybe he has sinned in some way, possibly without even being aware of it, and so he deserves his terrible punishment. Had this been true, there would have been no dilemma.

---

[4] *The friends' main arguments are; 1. Job has sinned without intending to. 2. Job is suffering in order to receive a spiritual education (suffering as discipline). 3. Job was in some way guilty at birth.*

However, both God and the Satan confirm Job's righteousness at the opening of the story. Also, given the events of the book and the realities of our own life experience, we are aware that indeed righteous individuals sometimes suffer and evil ones may prosper. Accordingly, statement A must be accepted as true; the righteous do indeed sometimes suffer.

Some commentators feel that statement B (one powerful intervening God) is the false one. God wants to be just but has not (or no longer has) the power to intervene in human affairs.[5] With reference to the Book of Job, this is a weak argument. God's existence and power are not at issue here. As to God's existence, He is an active participant in the story and in any event, without God[6] there is no theodicy issue to address. As for power and intervention, God does indeed intervene. He appears from the whirlwind although not to respond to the serious indictment made against him, rather to show his power and arguably to bully Job into submission. Like a consummate politician, he ignores the question we all want answered. Following his own agenda, his response is to say: 'You cannot know my ways, nor understand my creation. An individual man is of little importance to my plan, how dare you complain at your treatment?' That Job recanted and dropped his charge against God's justice was perhaps due to his terror at the experience, or possibly a realisation of the futility of his quest. Therefore, within the book, proposition B must also be accepted as true.

Job himself justifiably challenges statement C (God is just). One could argue that God implicitly agreed with him for his response to Job is full of power, but has little to say about justice. In God's only reference to this issue, He, with some irony, reprimands Job, 'Would you impugn my justice?'[7] The reader, meanwhile, knows perfectly well that Job has a cast iron case to do precisely that. Near the end of the book, God specifically says that Job's friends, who we know were simply proposing the standard religious explanations of suffering, had not spoken

---

[5] *Such concepts as God's withdrawal from history, or God hiding His face are proposed. The existence of both an all powerful God and evil allows for the philosophical argument that a good man can be more moral than God. The argument goes: Evil and injustice are rampant in the world. A moral man would try and remove them, but cannot. An all powerful God can remove them, but does not (after Epicurus).*

[6] *Strictly an omnipotent, omniscient, just and active God*

[7] *Job 40:8 - the verse concludes 'Would you condemn me that you might be right?' The Book of Job is surprisingly full of irony.*

correctly.[8] One can only understand this as God implying that the traditional religious understanding of sin being punished and virtue rewarded (distributive justice) is mistaken. This would seem to substantiate God's knowledge of, and seeming complicity in, the unjust treatment of man. To the extent that this issue is resolved in the text, no evidence whatsoever has been brought for God's justice. Accordingly, statement C has not been validated and with respect to the Book of Job, distributive justice from God cannot be accepted as true.

By the end of the book, Job seems to accept that both God's ways and the reason for suffering on Earth are beyond human understanding and that righteous individuals do indeed sometimes suffer. It appears that he was reconciled to the reason for his suffering remaining mysterious primarily because he had experienced God personally and directly. Interestingly, this is the last time God speaks in the *Tanach*. He fades out of the narrative in subsequent books, perhaps implying that He had nothing further to say on this or any other subject.

A subsidiary issue underlying discussion of these matters has always been: 'What is the origin of evil? Does it derive from God or man?' In Judaism, the origin would seem to be from God who, after all, created the tree of knowledge of good and evil before He created Adam and Eve. Furthermore, in Isaiah, God says explicitly that he created evil:[9]

יוצר אור ובורא חשך עושה שלום ובורא רע אני יהוה עשה כל אלה.

> *I produce light, and create darkness; I make peace, and create evil;*
> *I am Yahweh that does all these things.*

This concept so troubled the rabbis that when this verse appears in the daily liturgy the word evil was changed. The blessing is now to God who:[10]

> *produces light and creates darkness, who makes peace and creates* **everything.**

The compilers of the liturgy appear to have thought it would be too troubling for the faithful to be reminded daily and in such a clearly stated manner, of monotheism's biggest theological problem. If there is

---

[8] *This rebuttal of the friends' arguments comes in the prose section at the end of the book, which like the prose at the beginning is thought to be a later addition. The main work is composed in the form of a poem.*

[9] *In Isaiah 45:7 - also in Job 40 God discusses His creation of Behemoth and Leviathan, saying in effect, 'These things of darkness, I acknowledge mine'.*

[10] יוצר אור ובורא חשך עושה שלום ובורא את הכל *From the morning service blessings before the Shema prayer.*

only one God, He and only He must be ultimately responsible for all
the evil in the world as well as all the good. If He alone created human
beings, the butterfly and the giant panda then He alone must also have
created the malaria parasite and the human immunodeficiency virus.[11]
As the psalmist wrote:[12]

מה רבו מעשיך, יהוה- כלם, בחכמה עשית, מלאה הארץ, קנינך.

*How manifest are your works, O Lord; in wisdom have you made them
all: the Earth is full of your creatures.*

The verse quoted from Isaiah is thought to have originally been
intended to oppose the dualist concept of Zoroastrianism which
strongly influenced the development of Judaism and was very powerful
during Isaiah's time. Zoroastrianism holds that a separate, though
lesser, deity is responsible for evil. There is a cosmic battle going on
between the two gods and man's role is to assist the ultimate triumph
of good over evil. This demonstrates that dualist religions do have a
credible theodicy, while monotheism still searches for one. It is
probable that the Book of Job was also influenced by Zoroastrianism,
for the story has two known Babylonian antecedents and the Satan (the
adversary) who appears at the beginning of the book in later times
becomes the devil, the negative counterpart of God, which is somewhat
awkwardly incorporated into monotheism.

For other prophets too, the concept of suffering being caused by God
(as collective punishment for sin) seemed to cause no difficulty. Amos
for example asks:[13]

אם תהיה רעה בעיר, ויהוה לא עשה?

Shall evil befall a city, and it not be caused by God?

It has been argued that among what Israel Knohl calls 'the Divine
Symphony' of the biblical sources, the Torah contains one dissenting
voice to this concept that evil ultimately originates from God.[14] The
priestly source, the composer of the first of Genesis' two creation

---

[11] *responsible for HIV/AIDS*
[12] *Psalm 104:24*
[13] *Amos 3:6. This passage is written in such a way that the question is clearly intended to be answered, 'No'.*
[14] *The Divine Symphony, Israel Knohl, JPS 2003. For more about the biblical sources see Chapter 11.*

stories, writes of pre-existing malign forces on Earth before the creation of life began on the newly formed planet:[15]

הארץ היתה תהו ובהו וחשך על פני תהום ורוח אלהים מרחפת על פני המים.

And the Earth was unformed and void, with darkness over the surface of the deep; and the spirit of God hovered upon the surface of the waters.

This verse allows for the interpretation that the 'unformed and void Earth, darkness and deep waters', represent the forces of chaos and evil that existed prior to the creation of life and that these forces continue to exist and are responsible for evil. However, the argument is weak, for in normative Judaism there is no continuing struggle between these opposing supernatural forces. Given also that in the previous sentence in Genesis the Earth had just been created by God, it would be reasonable to consider that these malign forces were created alongside it. If this is so, then the responsibility for evil must remain with God.

If asked to show a single occasion where the Torah shows evil and suffering being caused directly by God, one must consider the story of the Tower of Babel:[16]

הבה נרדה ונבלה שם שפתם אשר לא ישמעו איש שפת רעהו.

Come, let us go down, and there confound their language, so that they shall not understand one another's speech.

Such an event, had it really occurred, would have been a direct cause of an unimaginable amount of human suffering. Surely, no moral, just, good or benevolent universal God could do such a thing? Inability to comprehend the foreigner has led to the concept of the barbarian and to intolerance and violence throughout human history. The only motives God could have for such an act would be to delay human progress and hinder understanding and tolerance between ethnic groups.

If this story is correctly understood as *mythos*, it reads as a foundation legend purporting to explain the origin of all the world's different languages. It is interesting though, to speculate for a moment on a benevolent creator God that had taken the opportunity to give all of

---

[15] *Genesis 1:2*
[16] *Genesis 11:7*

mankind the same language. What a different world we would be living in today.

Another controversial example of God's justice is the first murder in the Bible. The prime cause of Cain's jealousy of his brother Abel was God's stated preference for Abel's animal sacrifice over Cain's 'fruit of the soil'.[17] A strange God that showed such favouritism in the full knowledge of the violence it would unleash. A good parent would never show such partiality between twins. Again, an interpretation of the story as *mythos*, such as that given in Chapter 2, makes more sense.

An interesting story concerning the lack of justice in this life appears in the Talmud. It tells how Rabbi Elisha ben Abuyah[18] once saw a child, on the instructions of his father, climb a tree and shoo away the mother bird so he could take her eggs. Honouring one's parents and sending away the mother bird are the only two *mitzvot*[19] for the observance of which the Torah promises the reward of long life.[20] When this child, who was simultaneously carrying out both these commandments, fell from the tree and was killed, ben Abuyah concluded, 'there is no justice and there is no judge.'

Arguments on theodicy became tragically relevant last century with the Shoah. It is still probably too soon, even over sixty years on, for the full effects of that atrocity to be comprehended. Nevertheless, there can be little doubt that God has a case to answer. Some theological explanation is required for the deaths of so many innocent children. What about the babies, why were they punished?

Many Jewish thinkers have struggled with this dilemma and a wide range of responses have been offered by them. Others have chosen not to address the issue, or at least not in public, and this too is understandable. For those interested, I have compiled a brief summary of their responses below.

Jewish responses to the Shoah

1.   Shoah as punishment for Jewish sin

---

[17] *Genesis 4:3-4*

[18] *Kiddushin 39b -ben Abuya later lost his faith and subsequently the Talmud refers to him as Acher (another).*

[19] *mitzvah pl. mitzvot – religious commandments under Jewish law.*

[20] *Honouring parents (10 commandments) - Deuteronomy 5:16; Mother bird mitzvah - Deuteronomy 22:6-7.*

This is the traditional Orthodox Jewish response to persecution or catastrophe. It is the prime response of the prophets and Job's comforters. It is also the tradition of the Talmud which, when discussing suffering, gives a key statement:[21]

If a man sees that painful sufferings visit him, let him examine his conduct.

This was the initial response in relation to the Shoah also. However, there has been no agreement as to the sin being punished. The wide range of sins suggested include Zionism, opposition to Zionism, not performing the *mitzvot*, assimilation, sins committed in a previous life and Reform Judaism. Rabbi Menachem Schneerson (Lubavitch) opposed all these views and stated that the view of the Holocaust as punishment for Jewish sin was unconscionable, and that the tragedy of the Shoah was unanswerable.

2. God is dead

This argument states: if there is a God of history, we must see the Shoah as punishment for sin. However, there is no sin that could warrant the death of a million children. Therefore, there cannot be a God who is active in history.

3. God hiding his face

Several thinkers discuss the concept of *hester panim* הסתר פנים[22] or of God hiding his face and withdrawing from history for a period of time. For all practical purposes, this is similar to the argument that God is dead, except that one can hope that his withdrawal is temporary and that He may at some future time choose to re-engage with human affairs.

4. Divine revelation

Another proposition[23] considers the Shoah as tantamount to a divine revelation, like that at Sinai, but opposite in nature. That is, a revelation of the possibility of God's absence from the world.

5. Human wickedness

This approach argues that there is no religious significance whatsoever. The Shoah should be seen as a supreme example of human wickedness

---

[21] *Talmud. Berakhot 5a. If the examination reveals no sin, then the cause is given as lack of Torah study.*
[22] *This is taken from Job 13:24*
[23] *See 'Breaking the Tablets' by David Weiss Halivni. Rowman Littlefield 2007*

and the proper Jewish response should be to carry on in the traditional manner.

6. Emil Fackenheim's 614th commandment

Fackenheim 'commands':

Do not grant Hitler a posthumous victory. Do not forget, and do not assimilate.

This may be valid as a coping mechanism, but does not address the main question. It also addresses the victims rather than the perpetrators and deliberately puts unwarranted guilt on any member of the victim group who freely chooses to assimilate. It also wrongly assumes that Hitler was primarily trying to eliminate Judaism, the religion, rather than Jews, the people. Hitler's genocide was racial, not religious. Assimilated Jews, the ultra-religious and anyone with one quarter Jewish 'blood' were equally targeted. Conversion to Christianity would not save a Jew, unlike during persecutions of the past that were religious.

7. Never again

Meir Kahane argued that the Jew must defend himself and be strong. This is another coping strategy, but one that does not address the issue under discussion. It is also a response that can lead to violence and fundamentalism.[24]

8. Restorative fire

This suffering is part of God's plan and has a purpose.

'*The fire that destroys our bodies is the fire that will restore the Jewish people*'.[25]

This type of response suggests that the Shoah was necessary to allow for the foundation of the State of Israel or as an essential part of some other divine plan. Before this idea can be accepted one must consider the opinion of Dostoevsky's Ivan Karamazov that even if it could be shown that the torture of one innocent baby would in some way lead to the saving of countless other lives, he would still refuse to allow that baby to be tortured.[26]

9. The covenant renewed

Rabbi Irving Greenberg asked and answered:

---

[24] *Baruch Goldstein followed Meir Kahane's ideas. In 1999 he murdered 29 Moslems who were at prayer.*
[25] *This is widely attributed as having been the last words of Rabbi Elchanan Wasserman before he was murdered in the Shoah. The attribution is disputed however.*
[26] *The Brothers Karamazov - Book V Chapter 5*

'Why were the Nazis so frightened of the Jews?'
'Because the Jewish religion is superior'!

Judaism must redraft the covenant making the Jewish people the senior and God the junior partner. Rabbi Greenberg also said that it is obscene to speak of God in the presence of burning children.

10. The work of Satan

This is a logical but essentially dualist answer. As discussed elsewhere, Judaism is not pure monotheism, i.e. there is not one single supernatural being alone, but one very powerful and also several less powerful supernatural entities (angels, archangels, the Satan etc.). Nevertheless, if we believe that the evil entity had enough power to cause the Shoah, we have moved to a dualist belief system.

11. Silence

Faced with suffering on this scale and the pitiful inadequacy of other theological responses, this response states that it may be more respectful to the victims and perhaps less blasphemous, to respond in the way of Aaron on hearing of the death of his sons, killed by God:[27]

'and Aaron was silent – וידם אהרן'

12. Failure to engage

Among Jewish leaders in the aftermath of the Shoah, a surprisingly common 'response' has been a failure to engage with the issue. Many leading rabbis and Jewish thinkers have had little original to say, and appear to avoid this issue, at least in public.

13. Unconditional faith

Viktor Frankl's notion of faith is black and white. He wrote, 'I personally think that either belief in God is unconditional or is not belief at all. If it is unconditional, it will stand and face the fact that six million died in the Nazi Holocaust.' This statement suggests that belief can never coexist with doubt, and that most people's faith can be strong enough to deal with the shattering reality of the mechanistic mass murder of the Shoah.

---

[27] *Leviticus 10:3 Nadab and Abihu were killed by God for making unauthorised fire.*

This brief summary shows how thinkers within a specific religion responded to a specific devastating evil. However, the continuous presence of evil (albeit at a lower level) has always presented a major theological problem for all religions that believe in the existence of an active, just deity. The problem was well stated by the thirteenth century Catholic theologian Thomas Aquinas to demonstrate a possible error in his 'proofs' for the existence of God:[28]

> *It seems that God does not exist because: if either one of two opposites has*
> *infinite power, then it would completely destroy the opposing one.*
> *But the name God means that He is infinite goodness.*
> *Accordingly, if God exists, evil would have been completely destroyed.*
> *But evil is still present in the world.*
> *Therefore God does not exist.*

In many ways Aquinas was restating a much earlier argument made by the Greek philosopher Epicurus[29] who put it as follows:

> *Does God want to prevent evil, but is not able?   Then He is not omnipotent.*
> *Is God able to prevent evil, but not willing?   Then He is malevolent.*
> *Is God both able and willing?   Then where does evil come from?*
> *Is He neither able nor willing?   Then why call him God?*

Many explanations of the presence of evil have been proposed. This

fact alone should tell us that none of them are fully satisfactory. None have yet properly answered Epicurus' 2300 year old questions. The main explanations or theodicies that religious thinkers of the world have come up with are summarised below. These ideas may be held singly or in combination. Some explanations only

> *Ruins of Carmo Convent. This convent was*
> *destroyed, alongside most of Lisbon's*
> *churches, in the 1755 earthquake. About*
> *80,000 people were killed.*

---

[28] *Thomas Aquinas. c. 1225-1274. Summa Theologiae Ia, 2, 3 obj.*
[29] *Epicurus - 341-270 BCE*

purport to explain moral evil, others also include natural evil. Moral evil is evil directly attributable to man's deeds, while natural evil relates to suffering caused by 'acts of nature' such as earthquake, tsunami etc.

Natural evil presents its own problems, as was exemplified by the Lisbon earthquake of 1755. This major tragedy occurred on the morning of All Saints' Day when most of the Catholic faithful were in church. Many of the churches collapsed and thousands were killed where they prayed. This led to something of a crisis of confidence among the faithful who asked such questions as: 'Why were the churches destroyed yet the brothels spared?'

Again, I am including a brief summary of theological answers, this time from worldwide sources. Many books are available which discuss the merits and problems of these responses in more detail. The theodicies can be divided into three groups, attributing responsibility for evil to:

- the attributes of man
- the design of the world
- supernatural being/s.

Explanations that hold man responsible

The monotheistic religions tend to favour theodicies that fit into this group. Man, not God, is to blame for evil. This group of explanations makes no attempt to explain natural evil.

1. Free will
If humans cannot sometimes choose to do evil, they do not have true free will.

This is the traditional Judeo-Christian view, and that of some Moslems (the Mu'tazila). It leads to the question of why God created man, knowing how much suffering this would lead to. This is usually answered that in the long run the good will outweigh the bad.

2. Ignorance
Suffering is a result of human failure to see things as they really are.

This concept (*avidya*) is taught by the Advaita school of Hinduism. The physical world possesses an illusion of reality (*maya*). Under this illusion we seek the material things of this world and are led into greed and passion, for reality is concealed. Suffering inevitably results from such behaviour. This concept was developed by the Buddha as the four noble truths[30] (*ariya-satya*). The ultimate cause of suffering then is ignorance of reality. The wheel of life (which is a circular chain of events) says ignorance leads to sensation which leads to craving and hence to suffering. The cure is wisdom and following the Eightfold Path. In Gnostic religion too, the evil of the material (dark) world can be countered by the acquisition of knowledge or wisdom (gnosis).

3. Distributive Justice
Evil and suffering are the result of reward and punishment for human actions.

In Judaism, the existence of distributive justice, normally during the individual's time on Earth is the fundamental position, both within the Bible and the liturgy. For example Psalm 145:20 states:

שומר יהוה את-כל אהביו, ואת כל-הרשעים ישמיד

Yahweh looks after those who love him, but He destroys the wicked.

The law of *karma* in Hinduism and Buddhism says that every event that occurs is caused by previous events. If suffering occurs it is as a result of evil deeds done by that person in the past. This includes past lives from which the person has been reincarnated.

In the Bible[31] and the Koran this idea is also present, with vertical distribution of justice, so that as well as being punished for one's own sins one can be punished as a descendent of a wrongdoer 'unto the third or fourth generation'. In Judaism, Christianity and Islam 'guilt' follows the bloodline, whereas in eastern religions it, arguably more fairly, follows the individual via her or his reincarnations. The Talmudic rabbis were generally complete believers in distributive justice, on many occasions fitting punishment to crime by stating which sin 'caused' which illness or problem, a tradition that continues with the *rebbes* of certain ultra-orthodox communities until today.

4. Original sin
Christian doctrine that evil is inherent in human beings.

---

[30] *1. All aspects of our worldly life lead to suffering (*duhka*), birth, sickness, decay, death. This even includes pleasurable experiences as they are ephemeral and ultimately unsatisfying. 2. The root cause of this suffering is craving for sensory pleasure, and attachment to things of the world. 3. The way to cease suffering is to stop craving, and so achieve Nirvana. 4. The path to achieve the cessation of suffering is the Noble Eightfold Path.*
[31] *Exodus 20:5; 34:7.9 et. al.*

In the Garden of Eden humans had the possibility of not sinning and thus of not suffering. By their free-will, Adam and Eve did sin and were consequently exiled from Eden and sent into this world. This is the Christian concept of 'The fall of man'. Now, outside Eden, there is no longer the possibility of avoiding sin. As Adam and Eve's children, our nature is inherently flawed and thus tends towards evil.[32] Although this idea is not accepted by normative Judaism, for some kabbalists (influenced by Christianity) Eve's first sin is considered to have caused a disruption in the upper worlds and this is the source of evil.

In Baha'i scripture, human nature is seen as having two aspects, animal and spiritual. The animal side will lead to evil if not balanced by the spiritual.

5. Spiritual growth or salvation
Suffering is part of spiritual education.

In Job, Eliphaz and Elihu[33] offer the theodicy of suffering as discipline, as a means towards repentance. This idea, together with that of suffering as education from God is also found in the New Testament and the Koran.[34] This is sometimes called 'the instrumental theory of suffering', the theory that suffering is an instrument of God's purpose for humankind. Suffering can be seen as a test of faith, an obstacle to be overcome, an opportunity for sacrifice, detachment and spiritual growth. In Judaism, the Talmudic argument of 'afflictions of love'[35] makes suffering represent chosenness and so paradoxically demonstrates God's love. This idea was later extended into the concept of martyrdom or *kiddush ha'shem* - קידוש השם.[36]

This can also be taken further where suffering becomes a mechanism for salvation, so that even if the suffering is not survived it gives the subject extra credit in the world to come. Pope John Paul II claimed, 'All human suffering, all pain, all infirmity contains a promise of salvation, a promise of joy.'

---

[32] *The first record we have of this idea is in the writings of ben Sira c.200 BCE. It was introduced to Christianity by St. Augustine (354-430 CE), being accepted by Western Christianity but to some extent resisted by Eastern Orthodox Christians.*
[33] *Job 5:17; 33:14-33: 36:2-21*
[34] *New Testament 1 Peter 1:6-7; Koran 2:156; 29:2*
[35] *Baba Metseva 85b*
[36] *Kiddush ha'shem (Sanctification of God's name - becoming a martyr rather than compromising one's beliefs This concept came into use during the anti-Semitic outrages of the Crusades, leading to many incidents of suicide.*

6. Curse by fellow man

In primal religion and among the superstitious everywhere, it is believed that certain individuals have the power to cast curses that will bring bad luck, illness or even death to their intended victim.

Even today, many people still believe in the concept of the 'evil eye'. This is a superstition that certain individuals are able to cause bad luck (or worse) on others by 'casting an evil eye' on them. This belief has a long pedigree dating back at least to biblical times.

Explanations involving the design of the world

1. Denial of genuine evil

There are only varying degrees of good, and what appears to be evil is only so relative to the higher degrees of good that exist.

This view was originated by the philosopher Plotinus. He made two assertions:

- The universe as a whole is perfect and good.
- The perfection of being requires that every level of existence must come into being (principle of plenitude).

As there are different levels of being, there must be different levels of goodness. Since these lower levels of goodness necessarily exist as part of the perfect whole, they are part of the greater good. There is, therefore, no genuine evil in the world, if by evil we mean that without which the world would be better.

St Augustine and St Thomas Aquinas took up this view into Christian thought, arguing that nothing is created evil by nature; humanity's moral evil is only evil by will. Furthermore, evil is only allowed to exist in the universe so that there may be a greater good. If God had not permitted this amount of evil, then a very much greater amount of good would also be absent.

2. Best of all possible worlds

This world contains the greatest amount of good and the smallest amount of evil that it was possible for God to have created.

Following on from the arguments of Augustine and Aquinas above, Leibnitz (1646-1716) asserted that there were many universes that God could have created, but since God is good he created (necessarily) the best of all possible worlds. This was also proposed by Plato in the Timæus. In early Islam (Mu'tazili position) a moral obligation was placed on God to create the best possible world.

In one kabbalistic explanation of evil, it is characterised as a natural waste product from an organic process, like the dregs left when making a good wine. Creation was as perfect as it could have been but, as in other processes, some inevitable waste by-product is formed, in this case evil. In another kabbalistic idea, evil is an entity which is not in its right place. Every act of God, when it is in the place allotted to it in creation, is good. If dislocated, it can become evil.

3. Necessity of evil
If evil ceased to exist then so must good. One cannot exist without the other.

The Kogi Indians of Colombia have this belief, and Taoist philosophy also stresses the need for a balance between such opposites as good and evil, darkness and light.

Explanations attributing responsibility to supernatural being(s)

1. Evil being(s)
Evil and suffering are the result of the actions of supernatural being(s) (e.g. Satan), or an inherent tendency in creation to oppose God.

This concept may well have originated with the dualistic religion of Zoroastrianism in which we see the struggle of the evil deity, Angra Mainyu or Ahriman, against the good God, Ahura Mazda.

In primal religions and many eastern religions evil spirits play a prominent role. These can become angry and need propitiating to stop them causing suffering. A common belief is that after death souls become malevolent beings and roam the Earth trying to harm humans. Most religions have a ritual for use in warding off or exorcising such spirits.

As discussed earlier, the Jewish priestly source of the first creation story implies that evil forces pre-existed on Earth before humans were created, allowing the proposition that these forces continue and are responsible for evil. However, in contrast to Zoroastrianism and Eastern religion there is no struggle in early Judaism between such opposing supernatural forces. Later, in the 2nd century BCE, almost certainly in reaction to Greek persecution of observant Jews, a new explanation for evil was required. The traditional prophetic view of suffering as punishment for sin no longer rang true as those 'sinners' who adopted Greek ideas were seen to be prospering while observant Jews suffered.

This led to the apocalyptic literature, of which Daniel was an early example. This genre claimed that cosmic forces of evil were loose in the world and came close to a dualist view of a battle between good and evil. The Devil (Satan, Iblis[37]) developed directly from these ideas. God has temporarily, or voluntarily, suspended his omnipotence and allowed cosmic evil forces or the Devil to cause suffering and evil in the world. Usually, this will continue until some eschatological[38] event such as the coming of the messiah. Later, in esoteric kabbalistic Judaism the essentially dualist concept of the *sitra achra* (the other side) develops. Apocalyptic ideas also became very powerful in Christian thought.

2. God is dead
Withdrawal of supernatural involvement in human affairs.

This concept proposes that a deity who was once active in human affairs has either 'died' or chosen to withdraw (temporarily or permanently) from direct involvement in human affairs, leaving man's evil instincts unchecked. The Jewish concept of *hester panim* (God hiding his face) discussed earlier is an example.

The idea that God created the world but then left it to run according to the impersonal laws of nature was first stated by the 9th century Islamic philosopher Mu'annar.[39] Spinoza, in the 17th century, believed this too, famously stating that God is identical with nature (pantheism). For Spinoza, religion was superstition perpetuated by fear.

3. Action of God or Gods
Good and evil both originate from God(s)

Hindu deities have both positive and negative sides. Natural evil originates from the negative side. Shiva is both a loving god, full of

---

[37] *Iblis and Shaytan are the names of the Devil in the Koran.*
[38] *Eschatology – dealing with the end of days; how the world will end*
[39] *Mu'ammar b. Abbad al-Salami*

grace and also the destroyer. The dance of Shiva simultaneously creates and destroys the world. (The illustration shows Shiva Nataraja, Lord of

the Dance[40]). In Orthodox Islam and traditional Christianity, the belief is that all events are predetermined by God. In this view God is fully responsible for every event, good or evil, that occurs. Every event is to be accepted as the will of God, without question. In the Jewish *Tanach* most sources imply that the origin of evil is from God[41] although, as already discussed, the P (priestly) source has an implicit idea of pre-existing evil forces.[42]

4. Justice in the afterlife
Or 'jam tomorrow'.

Justice is, for whatever reason, limited in this life, but all will be made right after our death by a just deity who will judge us posthumously and in one way or another reward or punish us in some form of afterlife or reincarnation. In Judaism, this appears in Talmudic writings, probably influenced in part by Christianity.[43]

Postscript: Kant once wrote that that traditional theodicy is a case where the defence is worse than the charge.[44] It is worth considering all of the above 'explanations' with that in mind. Perhaps it is time to face the unpalatable fact that many believers know in their hearts – that much of suffering is entirely random. The individual was not selected to suffer, was not picked out to be punished, but was simply in the wrong place at the wrong time. This is so whether their suffering was caused by catching an infectious disease, a transport accident, a natural disaster or a terrorist attack. After surveying the weakness of the theological

---

[40] *Shiva Nataraja's dance is the tandava, which simultaneously creates, maintains, and destroy the universe.*

[41] *Isaiah 45:7; Job 40:15 et seq.; Lamentations 3:38; Job 2:10; Ecclesiastes 7:14 The serpent in Genesis 2 (J creation story) is a symbol of evil, and was created by God.*

[42] *Exodus 1:2 as quoted above, and the idea is also present in the P text (Lev. 16:5-10) concerning the scapegoat for Azazel.*

[43] *These writings appear around 325-400 CE in Ta'anit, Baba Metseva, Kiddushin & Pirkei Avot.*

[44] *Immanuel Kant 'On the failure of all attempted philosophical theodicies'.*

responses and observing the life stories of those we know well, is it really tenable to hold a belief that our ultimate fate in this life is a reward or punishment for our actions?

So does religion have nothing useful to contribute to this issue which is central to the lives of so many? Possibly not in terms of explaining unknown causes. These will continue to be seen as random by the sceptic and unknowable by the believer. However, as an aid in coping with suffering, religion can be very helpful for some. Not the religion of those orthodox rabbis who would blame a faulty *mezuzah* for the suffering of a child, or who come up with other such obscenities, but the more practical support of community and the spiritual insights of sensitive religious leaders.

Having started this search for an answer to the problem of evil by looking at the Book of Job and then searching, with no real success, for answers both within Jewish tradition and then around the world, perhaps we should return to the range of responses found in the Hebrew Bible.

Kohelet or Ecclesiastes is a late book and certainly one that contains Greek and pagan influences.[45] It was brave of the rabbis to include such an arguably nihilistic work in the canon. We should be grateful to them for doing so, as it can be considered the most profound book of the *Tanach*. It is also the most honest. For *Kohelet*, as for followers of the eastern religions and philosophies, suffering is an integral and unalterable part of the world we inhabit. He makes no attempt to explain or justify it, the implication being that it can neither be explained nor justified.

Kohelet simply accepts the random nature of suffering that can affect any of us, righteous or wicked, at any time and that ultimately we all will suffer and die. *Kohelet* neither offers us the avoidance of sin as a means of preventing suffering nor the consolation of life after death as compensation for it. His philosophy is *carpe diem*.[46] Even though pleasure, like everything else, is ephemeral, *Kohelet* teaches that we should still enjoy the good things of life while we can.

---

[45] *Specifically in the way the author considers fate and fortune to influence the date of a man's death.*

[46] *carpe diem – (Latin) Seize the day. Live and enjoy life in the here and now. In the words of Robert Herrick's poem, 'Gather ye rosebuds while ye may.'*

While not providing an explanation for suffering, *Kohelet* shows us that friendship can be a great help to us in coping when we suffer. This same coping mechanism was well described by the psychiatrist Victor Frankl, in his enlightening book *Man's Search for Meaning*, in which he discusses his Holocaust experiences in relation to his work on the human psyche. Both *Kohelet* and Frankl find that 'two are better than one'. A person does much better in a pair than as a solitary being and this is true even in the worst of circumstances. Let us conclude this survey of explanations for evil with the pathos of *Kohelet* reflecting on suffering and on how much worse it is for those who suffer alone.[47]

But I returned and considered all the oppressions that go on under the sun; and to see the tears of the oppressed, who had no comforter; and on the side of their oppressors they had power, but they had no comforter. And so I praised the dead that are already dead more than the living that are yet alive; but better than them both is he that has not yet been born, who has not seen the evil work that is done under the sun. Again, I considered all labour and all excelling at work, that it just a man's rivalry with his neighbour. This also is futility and striving after wind.

The fool folds his hands together, and eats his own flesh. Better is a handful of quietness, than both hands full of labour and the striving after wind. Then I returned and saw futility under the sun. There is one that is alone, without a companion; he has neither son nor brother; yet is there no end to his labour, nor is his eye satisfied with riches: 'for whom then do I labour, and deny my soul of pleasure?' This also is futility, yes, it is a grievous business.

Two are better than one; because they have a good reward for their labour. For if they fall, the one will lift up his fellow; but woe to him that is alone when he falls, and has not another to lift him up. Again, if two lie together, then they have warmth; but how can one be warm alone? And if a man fights against him that is alone, two shall withstand him; for a triple cord is not easily broken.

---

[47] *Kohelet 4:1-12*

Part three

Problems with
Jewish practice

9

We expect ethics, tolerance and compassion, but may find only pietism and the use of guilt.

Religion is a moral code to live by, rather than a purpose in its own right that gives believers the right to deny rationality and humanity.
Will Hutton

It would seem both logical and natural to expect higher levels of ethical behaviour, tolerance and compassion from individuals claiming to be religious than from those in the population at large. In the real world, sadly, it is disappointing to find this not to be the case. On an individual level, one finds the full spectrum of human behaviour among those in the faith community in the same way as one does in the general population, but there is no unequivocal evidence that their distribution is significantly different among either group.

In this chapter, we will not be considering individual examples of behaviour, as both wonderful and diabolical activity can be found in both groups, and such anecdotal evidence concerning individuals will take us no further. What is more instructive is to look at the ethos that informs the behaviour of the orthodox community. That is to say, we must consider the values transmitted by the educational system and demonstrated in the public behaviour and attitudes of the leaders who are the role models of the community.

The community being looked at here is only that of the orthodox and the *haredim* or ultra-orthodox Jews. The reasons for this were given in the introduction and I would stress that many of the problems to be discussed have already been addressed by other branches of Judaism.

Currently in Israel, there is a particular problem because the *haredim* control the decision making process relating to marriage, divorce and conversion among the Jewish population. This applies to the entire spectrum of Jews as there is no alternative civil option, even for the secular on whom they impose their sometimes uncompassionate decisions. Such decisions cause considerable resentment to build up.

Looking for examples of ethical behaviour, tolerance and compassion among the leaders of the *haredi* community can often be a disappointing and disheartening experience. Their attitude to their fellow man outside of their own group (even including other orthodox with different affiliations) is often in the range of antagonistic to openly racist. Tolerance seems to be in very short supply when dealing with issues concerning any alternative life style to their own. Compassion, or even an attitude of live and let live is rarely found, nor is the use of violence always condemned. If the reader considers these claims to be too strong it is necessary only to read public statements by leaders of these communities on almost any controversial topic (such as women's rights, homosexuality or secular education) for this to be confirmed.[1]

These attitudes within the leadership lead to orthodox youngsters sometimes venting their intolerance in a violent way, as has been seen on many occasions in Israel since the founding of the state. Examples include throwing stones at cars being driven on the Sabbath, violence against women attempting to sit at the front of segregated buses,[2] aggressive and intimidating behaviour to stop archæologists carrying out work at certain sites and violent opposition to a gay pride festival in Jerusalem. The perpetrators were often students from certain *yeshivot* (seminaries) whose actions could have been curtailed by those in authority over them. If they were not encouraging this behaviour, then they usually looked the other way and certainly hardly ever spoke out in public against such violence.

---

[1] *Examples of this type of behaviour are often reported in the Israeli press. Many are listed online at www.failed-messiah.com*

[2] *Buses where women are forced to sit at the back, reminiscent of the racially segregated buses of half a century ago in the USA, now operate in haredi areas of Israel.*

In Jerusalem today, there is even a 'modesty guard' that operates in Taliban style by intimidating those who live in orthodox areas and do not conform to orthodox norms of dress and behaviour.[3] As such areas now take in former secular areas this includes long standing residents, who the orthodox aim to force out.

Even more serious were the pronouncements of certain religious leaders among the settlers, which were tantamount to incitement to murder, in the period before the assassination of Yitzhak Rabin (1996). This created the climate in which a religious Jew, Yigal Amir, could carry out this awful crime for which he has shown no remorse. He still believes he was acting in the name of God and in the interests of the Jewish people. The assassination was celebrated as a victory by these extreme groups. The background of this period within the religious world is well described in the chilling book 'Murder in the Name of God'.[4]

The moral problem of which this violence is an extreme example is recognised by some in the orthodox community. Rabbi Shlomo Riskin addressed it in the language of the orthodox by suggesting that the messiah will not come until:[5]

> *'the image of the religious Jew is of one who personifies ethical probity and moral righteousness, rather than one who punctiliously observes the Sabbath and puts on phylacteries each day.'*

Jewish Religious Courts *(Batei Din)* often demonstrate this image problem by failing to show compassion for an individual's personal situation, or not trying hard enough to find a humane way around laws which sometimes lead to oppression and suffering. Despite Hillel's wonderful expression of the Golden Rule being the whole Torah,[6] subsequent rabbis have generally failed to follow his approach. They enforce often archaic laws without reference to the individual human

---

[3] *Such excesses are regularly reported by Haaretz newspaper, among others. For a 2008 report see: http://www.haaretz.com/hasen/spages/1013163.html*
[4] *The authors, Michael Karpin & Ira Friedman, describe the use by extremists of the pulsa da-nura curse, and the proposal to use the archaic din rodef and din moser (duty to kill a Jew who imperils other Jews or turns them in to authority) to place a death sentence on the Prime Minister. See bibliography for book details.*
[5] *Rabbi Shlomo Riskin, Chief Rabbi of Efrat writing in the Jerusalem Post 7th March 2008*
[6] *Hillel was reportedly asked to summarise the Torah while standing on one leg. He responded, 'What is hateful to you do not do to your fellowman. That is the entire Torah, all the rest is commentary. Go study.' (Talmud Shabbat 31a).*

distress and suffering their actions may cause. Examples where individuals' personal lives can be seriously affected by a religious court include:

- treatment of *agunot* [7]
- not allowing a divorcée and a Cohen to marry
- the general discriminatory treatment of people who through no fault of their own are branded as *mamzerim*
- refusal to accept converts to Judaism who have been converted by almost any other community, and even reversing conversions carried out long ago by a fully orthodox rabbi
- treatment of women in general (see Chapter 11)

Decisions of the *Batei Din* on these matters, whatever their seeming validity to the *dayanim* (judges), commonly fail to show evidence of human compassion or individual justice. Even aspiring to tolerance is too much for some. When the Orthodox Chief Rabbi of Britain, Jonathan Sacks, wrote that we should be tolerant of other religions and implied that we may have things to learn from them he was forced by his *dayanim* to withdraw his remarks and change a book already published.[8] The *dayanim* correctly pointed out that Judaism is not tolerant of idol worshippers (such as Hindus from the orthodox perspective) and claimed Judaism has nothing to learn from other faiths.

Part of the concern of these religious leaders is that tolerance may lead to Jews being exposed to, and possibly attracted by, ideas not sanctioned by orthodoxy. They fear such exposure may diminish their faith. This fear may indeed be well founded. It is arguable that if the ultra-orthodox were allowed a wide general education many of them would leave the fold, but the narrow upbringing they receive makes an exit strategy into the 'outside world' very difficult and effectively traps any dissenters.

A similar fear was demonstrated by the behaviour of Rabbi Shneur Zalman (the founder of Lubavitch)[9] at the beginning of the 19th century

---

[7] *agunot – so called chained women, whose husbands either refuse to grant them a divorce, or have disappeared*

[8] *J. Sacks, 'The Dignity of Difference' 1st edition. Sacks amended these remarks in subsequent editions.*

[9] *Lubavitch (also known as Chabad are one of the several ultra-Orthodox Hassidic movements, where the followers venerate their leader (rebbe) in a way alien to normative Judaism. Recently this became so extreme that many followers of the last Rebbe, Menachem Schneerson, consider him to be the messiah. When he died in 1994 they did not appoint a successor, and he is still 'consulted' posthumously. The followers of Rabbi Nachman of Bratslav are another prominent example of this. (See the discussion on shrines and ancestor worship p.109)*

when Napoleon was fighting Tsar Alexander 1 for control of the Pale of Settlement. This was an area where large numbers of poverty-stricken Jews lived under a harsh anti-Semitic regime. Victory for Napoleon offered the prospect of freedom and prosperity. Victory for the Tsar would keep Jews impoverished and endangered. Surprisingly, Rabbi Shneur Zalman prayed for the Tsar to defeat Napoleon. When asked why, he explained that he considered Napoleon's enlightenment values and the emancipation of the Jews to be a greater danger to the Jewish future than the Tsar's anti-Semitism and pogroms.

The religious commentator Karen Armstrong feels that while religions are generally compassionate, the human beings who make up their adherents are not. There is seldom any compassion at all found among people debating religious dogma. Often in disputes between different religious groups, the more closely connected they are, the worse the behaviour. One sees this in Britain in the behaviour of successive Orthodox Chief Rabbis.[10] They have no difficulty sharing a platform with Bishops or Imams, but refuse to do so with Reform Rabbis. The comedian Emo Philips captured this attitude among the religious:

Once I saw this guy on a bridge about to jump.
I said, 'Don't do it!'
He said, 'Nobody loves me.'
I said, 'God loves you. Do you believe in God?'
He said, 'Yes.'
I said, 'Are you a Christian or a Jew?'
He said, 'A Christian.'
I said, 'Me, too! Protestant or Catholic?'
He said, 'Protestant.'
I said, 'Me, too! What franchise?'
He said, 'Baptist.'
I said, 'Me, too! Northern Baptist or Southern Baptist?'
He said, 'Northern Baptist.'
I said, 'Me, too! Northern Conservative Baptist or Northern Liberal Baptist?'
He said, 'Northern Conservative Baptist.'

---

[10] *Rabbi Jonathan Sacks refused to attend the funeral of Rabbi Hugo Gryn, an extremely respected and prominent member of the Jewish community fearing it would show recognition of a Reform Rabbi. Sacks demonstrates exactly the dichotomy being discussed, reputedly being tolerant and compassionate in his personal life, but often unable (because of the orthodox interpretation of halachah) to practice this in his public actions.*

*I said, 'Me, too! Northern Conservative Baptist Great Lakes Region, or
Northern Conservative Baptist Eastern Region?'*
He said, 'Northern Conservative Baptist Great Lakes Region.'
*I said, 'Me, too!' Northern Conservative Baptist Great Lakes Region
Council of 1879, or Northern Conservative Baptist Great Lakes Region
Council of 1912?'*
*He said, 'Northern Conservative Baptist Great Lakes Region Council of
1912.'*
I said, 'Die, heretic!' And I pushed him off.

Anthropologists who look at close-knit groups which have a high
degree of internal trust have found that this is invariably accompanied
by a degree of xenophobia. In a close-knit community where children
can trust those people of the same 'sort' as their parents, they also need
to be taught not to trust outsiders. In a more integrated society this is
less of a problem.

Xenophobic attitudes are, in any case, familiar from the *Tanach*. Other
nations and their practices are routinely described in intolerant
language. Even in the later books, when the prophets preach a more
ethical form of religion and of a truly monotheistic universal God, this
attitude to neighbouring nations does not soften. The prophets
continue to refer to them in pejorative terms, in many cases effectively
cursing them. Such attitudes colour the Talmud too.

Returning now to consider the ethos of Orthodox Judaism. If one
looks at the emotion favoured by a culture to encourage individuals to
conform to its norms, one finds that societies divide into shame
cultures and guilt cultures. The ancient classical world was a shame
culture. With shame one loses face, and if caught breaking the rules
must hide one's face. If the shame is too bad then exile (or even
suicide) may be an appropriate sanction. Eastern cultures are also
generally shame cultures.

The use of guilt was primarily a development within the Judeo-
Christian world. As an example of this, the guilt associated with
sexuality and the prurience concerning the human body came into
Judaism from Christianity. For an individual, the emotion of guilt can
move ethics forward and improve behaviour as it is self policing. (One
feels guilt immediately on doing something one considers wrong, but

shame only on being discovered by others.) It also strengthens the concepts of atonement and of making reparations to the victim.

These advantages unfortunately have a price. Guilt is an emotion that can be easily manipulated by those in a position of power such as teachers or religious leaders. These individuals (especially those from the more conservative pole of the monotheistic religions) routinely peddle a doctrine that anyone straying from the behaviour sanctioned by them is guilty of sin, and will be punished during this life by suffering, disease, infertility or family tragedy, or failing that will be eternally punished in the world to come. They reinforce this doctrine after a tragic event by their dreadful habit of explaining it as God's punishment for one sin or another.

The whole concept of heaven or the world to come depends on the emotion of guilt to maintain its powerful hold on susceptible minds. It can be used as a form of blackmail which is particularly objectionable when used to modify the behaviour of the young.

As for the more Christian concept of hell and eternal punishment[11] (and bearing in mind the concept of predetermination) John Stuart Mill wrote correctly:[12]

> *There is something truly disgusting and wicked in thought that God purposefully creates beings to fill hell who cannot in any way be held responsible for their actions when God himself chooses to lead them astray.'*

The concepts of divine judgement and the world to come, along with that of guilt, have been used and abused by teachers from church, mosque and synagogue alike. Many young minds have been traumatised by such teachings over many centuries. One example in Judaism is the natural and harmless activity of masturbation which is taught to be a serious offence. Incidentally, this law is only aimed at boys, the rabbis apparently never considered such an activity possible for girls. Any boys and young men in the orthodox world who succumb to this temptation, are left feeling guilty of a major sin. For their part, girls and young women, who are forbidden any form of contact with the opposite sex,

---

[11] *The ideas of heaven, hell and the devil came into Judaism and Christianity from Zoroastrianism. Christianity (especially Catholicism) developed these ideas much more fully than Judaism.*
[12] *John Stuart Mill (1806-1873) 'The Utility of Religion'. Predetermination is the concept that a person's behaviour is known or 'predetermined' by God from the time of their birth.*

both physical and social, may find their natural development repressed or may suffer severe guilt if they break this rigid code even in some minor way.

By contrast, many teachers who propagate these feelings of guilt among their students appear to display smugness, self satisfaction, and sanctimoniousness as they observe religious commandments to the letter. They manifest these attitudes of religious elitism in the way they judge and categorise both students and outsiders according to their level of observance and also by their lack of respect for those Jews who interpret their shared religion differently. Even other rabbis are judged on the strictness of their interpretations rather than their wisdom, tolerance or humanity. As Rabbi Riskin implied, it is a serious criticism of the practice of many Orthodox Jews that the detailed observance of these many religious laws, which govern all aspects of their behaviour, can take priority over ethics in their lives.

There are ethical laws that if obeyed should modify such behaviour; Leviticus 19:11 clearly says:

ולא-תכחשו ולא-תשקרו, איש בעמיתו

You shall not deal deceitfully nor lie to one another

The ethos of the *haredi* community when carrying out business matters does not seem to prioritise such principles. It is apparent that matters such as how long to wait between consuming meat and milk are given a much higher priority in their lives.

Most religious laws are capable of a spectrum of interpretation ranging from relaxed to very strict. Extra merit seems to attach, in orthodox circles, to the person making the strictest interpretation, with individuals sometimes going to what seem to be ludicrous extremes. Such a level of observance has the effect of rendering a person unable (and usually with no desire) to function outside the parochial Jewish world. It may be argued that this is one of the intentions of these restrictive laws, to maintain the Jewish people by keeping them separate and so free from the temptation to go a step further and intermarry. Some consider that the kashrut laws, by effectively banning the eating of meals in non Jewish homes, have been the most important single factor in the Jews' survival as a distinct group.

Depending on one's point of view, obeying Kashrut laws may be considered to be a laudable aim. However, the level to which some take this observance results in behaviour that appears obsessive. Such behaviour is also divisive as, for example, rival authorities regulate kashrut for their own community, and sometimes do not accept the validity of other authorities. A spat between the Manchester and London authorities some years ago resulted in a compromise that each was to have authority only in its own area. Manchester certificated food was not deemed kosher if sold elsewhere. In an ironic letter to the Jewish Chronicle, a reader asked, if he bought a salt beef sandwich in Manchester to eat on his drive to London, at which service area must he stop to eat it before it ceased to be kosher?

To an outsider this is simply amusing but these matters are taken seriously by adherents. A significant number of men in the *haredi* community spend much of their lives studying the minutiae of the interpretation of such rules. They actually consider this the most important and valuable way they could spend their time. They don't appear to question whether they can believe in a God who micromanages every aspect of their behaviour and yet allows torture and genocide to remain unpunished in his world, along with so much preventable human suffering. To the outsider they appear to live narrow lives, not participating in much of the modern world or being aware of the wonder of ideas that originate outside their strongly defended intellectual boundaries. Perhaps they should consider what Saint Augustine wrote in the 4th century:

> *The world is a book, and those who do not travel read only a page.*

Pietism can also lead to intolerance, since individuals are judged and valued within the group primarily on their level of religious knowledge and observance of these arcane laws, rather than by their ethics or behaviour towards the less observant. In less orthodox and secular communities, by contrast, other people's religious observance is generally considered as a personal choice, without such judgments being made. Worse still is the orthodox conservatism toward new secular ideas. The orthodox are not tolerant or open minded to ideas or scholarship that might call established teachings into question.

Even more than that, some extreme groups even consider what they call 'secular thinking' to be a sin. They claim that everything is within the Torah (which for them includes the Talmud and even the statements of their own style of rabbis up to today). As an example, they are so conservative that in 2004 they banned books by an impeccably orthodox rabbi with an interest in zoology who had written about the animals of the *Tanach*. Although reasons for the ban were not given explicitly, it appears to have been simply the author's scientific method of thinking which offended them rather than any specific content of his books.[13] This type of religious approach was once summed up by a philosophy professor as, 'I *don't* think, therefore I am".

Religious history is littered with examples of such closed-minded attitudes. A library of an orthodox institution, even today, contains only approved books. Censorship and suppression of alternative opinion continues, and for this reason the internet is perceived by some as a threat. This censorship works in another way too, for most believers also censor themselves. They would no more pick up and read a book that questioned their beliefs than read pornography.

It appears to many outsiders, that a religious lifestyle in which every aspect of one's personal behaviour is so circumscribed and which simultaneously maintains a blinkered approach to secular knowledge, has gone down a blind alley. Those who follow this way of life may find themselves obsessed with the letter rather than the spirit of the law.

Modernity is utilised selectively, technicalities being used to avoid being bound by some religious laws.[14] For example, on Shabbat the observant will not use a lift, but a Shabbat lift (which runs continuously and wastefully on a pre-programmed cycle) is acceptable. The orthodox will not generally carry objects outside the house on Shabbat lest they contravene some rather complex laws. If, however, an *eruv*[15] (an artificial boundary) has been constructed, then they are confident that such carrying is allowed within its limits. They will not write on Shabbat, but a Shabbat pen (which has ink that fades after about 72

---

[13] *For more details on this controversy and an insight into the world of the ultra-Orthodox Jew see* http://www.zootorah.com/controversy/default.html

[14] *This concept of using technicalities to legally 'break laws' goes back to Talmudic times. Hillel devised a contract to circumvent the law abolishing debts during the Sabbatical year (every seventh year). This meant people would not stop lending money because they were worried the borrower could legally default in the Sabbatical year.*

[15] *An eruv completely encircles an area and clarifies its status, so ensuring that carrying within it is always in accordance with* halachah *(Jewish Law). A wire strung on poles is commonly used. Typically, there are different interpretations of what constitutes a legitimate eruv, such that some orthodox groups do not recognise an eruv constructed by others.*

hours) is now available to overcome this prohibition (although it is not in widespread use). These are by no means the most peculiar of the convoluted, man made rules and loopholes that some allow to order their lives.

Whilst the choice of the orthodox to behave in ways outsiders might find strange is to be defended, provided no one else is harmed or seriously inconvenienced, it would seem reasonable to expect the orthodox to allow the non-orthodox the same freedom of behaviour.

Sadly this does not seem to come naturally. When the orthodox have political power, their instinct is to curtail activities that may be based on personal or ethical choice but are in conflict with their interpretation of *halachah* (Jewish law). One can regularly see this demonstrated in the policies of the religious political parties in Israel.

Taking a wider view, we should also consider the concept of heresy in religious history. In many ways heresy may be considered as a thought-crime. The whole concept is a restriction of personal freedom and invariably the stronger group show no compassion whatsoever towards those they declare heretics, whether groups or individuals.

Heresy can simply be the result of thinking a different way about dogma. Such alternative thinking is not encouraged by the educational system and the general way of bringing up children among the orthodox. This is often kept deliberately narrow – even basic and non-controversial subjects such as mathematics are hardly taught in ultra-religious schools, partly for fear that they may encourage 'secular thinking'.

The main focus in the orthodox world is on observance, ethics are secondary. One does not question the *halachah*, one observes it in the manner laid down by the rabbi of the community. Indeed the traditional meaning of life is given to Jews at the end of the most philosophical work in the Jewish canon, Ecclesiastes: [16]

---

[16] *Ecclesiastes 12:12-14; which follows the precedent of Deuteronomy 10:12-13. This is not, however, the opinion of the author of Ecclesiastes (Kohelet) himself, but that of an editor who added the last six verses (including the above) to bring what otherwise could be considered a nihilistic philosophy back into the mainstream. The book would possibly otherwise not have made it into the canon.*

Of making many books there is no end; and much study wearies the flesh.
The end of the matter, all having been heard:
Fear God, and keep his commandments; *for this applies to all*
men. For God will judge every act, every secret deed, whether good or evil.

In monotheistic religion, to break God's commandments is to commit
sin but a sin is not necessarily the same thing as immoral behaviour. In
this regard, Bertrand Russell wrote that he found the whole concept of
sin puzzling. He could understand sin when it caused unnecessary
suffering but not that in some circumstances it is actually a sin to
prevent suffering (euthanasia). In Judaism, it can be a sin simply to eat
the wrong food, or to carry out a trivial action on the Sabbath. In other
words, sin is simply transgressing a religious rule; it commonly has
nothing to do with morality. This seems an odd emphasis for a religion
that considers itself ethical.

Anyone who observes the lack of justice and the degree of suffering in
the world would surely empathise with an old Jewish saying, 'If God
lived on Earth, man would throw stones at him'. With this in mind, is it
at all possible to contemplate a God who would concern himself (or
want his people to concern themselves) with such minutiae as the
provenance of salt, or even water[17] consumed at Passover, while
apparently indifferent to the suffering of starving children.

That morality is often not the chief concern of religious practice was
once again cleverly satirised by Emo Philips:

> *When I was young I used to pray to God every night for a new bicycle.*
> *Then I realised that wasn't how God works.*
> *So I went out and stole one, and prayed for forgiveness.*

Prayer is indeed central for Judaism. An early rabbinic saying has it that
prayer is greater than good deeds. So what does this prayer consist of?
In general it is either petition or praise. On examination, these two
concepts seem a little odd. For a petition to be answered, one requires a
God who is active in human affairs, indeed one that micromanages
them. The evidence of history reveals no such God; nor does evidence
show that an individual who prays is no more likely to win a race or
avoid a plane crash. As for doxologies, or prayers lauding God for his

---

[17] *The entire water supply to Jerusalem is changed at Passover to well water, as the normal supply (which of*
course is cleaned and treated) comes from the Sea of Galilee, where fishermen sometimes use bread to attract fish!

perfection, firstly they appear sycophantic. Secondly, if such a perfect God existed would He really want the human beings he created spending their time praising him, when there was so much work needed to improve his world? One might imagine that God has higher priorities than listening to all this praise.

There is no doubt that prayer can help individuals psychologically, in the way that practices such as meditation do. Whether there are any greater psychological benefits from chanting the Jewish liturgy, that of another religion or simply a mantra, seems unlikely. It would appear to be the case that each individual just needs to find a method that resonates within their own psyche.

Prayer, when carried out in public, also strengthens bonds with the community which in turn strengthens belief in its efficacy and that of the ritual which surrounds it. When one sees respected elders, alongside ones friends and family all engaged in prayer, and have been exposed to this from an early age it is natural to consider that it must be valid and effective.

Another aspect of tolerance is free speech and debate. It is always difficult to have a dialogue with very observant Jews on matters such as those discussed in this book. Jonathan Miller,[18] who experienced this too, put it very well. He said that in debate with an Orthodox Jew he used the arguments of the university while his opponent used those of the *yeshiva*.[19] This meant that true debate seldom occurred. Rational evidence based argument (which the ultra-orthodox sometimes dismiss as secular thinking), like that set out in Chapter 5 for the multi-authorship of the Torah, is often met by the orthodox with such comments as, 'Oh, no one really accepts that nowadays'. This, of course, is true in the very restricted milieu in which such people move, and they may well have been told it by their *rebbe*. But have the observant ever examined the widespread evidence to the contrary, given that this information is carefully excluded from the libraries of their *yeshivot*? If presented with such evidence they tend to treat it like *trefe* (non-kosher) meat and refuse to engage with it.

---

[18] *The theatre and opera director, and Jewish born atheist*
[19] *yeshiva, plural yeshivot – a Jewish seminary*

In debate, the orthodox sometimes appear to patronise their opponent by making statements like – 'This is too subtle for someone who hasn't *really* studied the Talmud to understand.' They can seldom be pinned down by logic – their arguments seem to disappear in a pious fog. As Steven Weinberg said:

'All logical argument can be defeated by the simple refusal to think logically.'

An example is an argument frequently rehearsed by the orthodox when 'dealing' with the mythic content of the Torah. They ask, 'did Jews lay down their lives just for folktales and myth?' A moment's consideration shows this question to be without relevance. Looking widely, it is certain that some of the people who have died for their faith in a religion or ideology have been misguided, but that is not the point. It does not matter whether they were Jew or Moslem, Albigensian or antinomian, or holder of any other belief, the fact that they died bravely does not validate (or invalidate) their theology or ideology. In most cases, their death is simply a sign of the intolerance of those who killed them. Of course, this does not apply to those extremists who follow the tradition that began with the Jewish zealot and has now been refined by the suicide bomber. For such individuals, it is a sign of their rigidity of mind and of their misunderstanding of myth which leads them to wrongly believe that they die as martyrs doing God's work.

Anthropologists find one of the features of religion in general is that dogma is complex and often deliberately expressed in ways that make it difficult to comprehend. It sounds as if it makes sense, but on closer examination becomes more obscure rather than clearer. The pious fog of obfuscation closes in. Tertullian must have already been aware of this in the late second century CE when he wrote:[20]

The son of God died. This is to be believed because it makes no sense. And he was buried, and he rose again. This fact is certain, because it is impossible.

A more recent Christian example comes from Pope John-Paul II who 'explained' to the faithful:

Jesus is the incarnate word, a single and indivisible person.

Try to clarify that sentence if you can, or join the many that are lost in the fog. The fact is, the faithful who hear it proclaimed by the Pope will

---

[20] *Tertullian. De carne Christi (On the flesh of Christ) 5*

believe it without ever understanding it. Mainstream Judaism is fortunately much freer of dogma and so less prone to this syndrome, but any who start to travel the byways of mysticism or Kabbalah will soon find the visibility reducing. Even within the mainstream, attempting to pin down the exact role within Judaism of angels and other heavenly creatures can be difficult.

Many Orthodox Jews are quite happy to accept the laws and traditions without questioning them. They are understandably comfortable in the waters in which they swim and don't want to come on to dry land to discuss these matters with the rest of us. Either they may have some deep seated insecurity that if they lose the argument they may never get back into the water again or more likely they are so secure in their beliefs that they don't want to expend effort in discussing them with an *apikoros* - who is a lost soul anyway.

It should of course be remembered that pietism leading to intolerance is by no means a uniquely Jewish characteristic. Many anti-Semites were extremely pious Christians. An example was France's King Louis IX who in 1242 banned and burned the Talmud, calling it a vicious attack on the person of Jesus. He once claimed that the only way to debate with a Jew was to kill him with 'a good thrust in the belly as far as the sword will go'.[21] He also started the first inquisition and led two crusades against Islam. With such a track record of 'pious behaviour' it can be little surprise that he was canonised after his death as a saint of the Roman Catholic Church.

So far we have discussed primarily the intolerance of religious leaders towards individuals, rather than that of a religion against its perceived enemies. When considering organised religions, the excesses of some – such as their culpability for the Crusades, the Inquisition, or the behaviour of the Taliban, has led some Jewish apologists to argue that Judaism as a whole has been innocent of such behaviour.[22] They conveniently forget that this type of intolerance can only produce such widespread terror when the religion has political and military power to support it. In Judaism's history this has only happened twice, in Hasmonean and in modern times.

---

[21] 'The Life of St. Louis' by John of Joinville.
[22] For example, David Hazony's essay claiming this in the Jewish Chronicle of 11 January 2008. This was refuted by the author in a letter published the following week.

The Hasmonean state resulted from the first ever war of religion, and their military record demonstrated exactly the holy intolerance we are discussing. Defeated people were offered the choice of conversion to Judaism or death. In what (using today's values) can only be considered as an attempted genocide, John Hyrcanus tried to wipe out the Samaritans, attacked their unprotected cities and destroyed their holy places. This is not behaviour the Jewish people can be proud of. During this period, Judaism also introduced to the world the new concepts of terrorists prepared to use violence against civilians to stir up holy war (the Sicarii) and religious martyrs who were prepared to die, rather than compromise their beliefs.

We may consider by way of mitigation, that ordinarily it is unfair to judge behaviour of a bygone age by today's standards, as the accepted norms of morality were different then. (Whether such mitigation can be used logically by those who believe morality is unchanging is another matter.) However, one must factor in the mores of the time, especially the contemporary approach to war.

In the lead up to the disastrous Bar Kochba revolt against Rome, which ended Jewish political power for almost two millennia and led to huge Jewish loss of life, no less a figure than Rabbi Akiva was the key supporter of Simon bar Kochba, believing him to be the Messiah sent by God. Rabbi Akiva persuaded the *Sanhedrin* to support him and this brought about, arguably, the blackest chapter in Jewish history prior to the Shoah.

It is too early for history to judge the modern state of Israel in this regard, but we must be ever vigilant lest those with fundamentalist views are given more power.

On the world stage Judaism may not have been responsible for many of the outrages perpetrated in the name of religion, but possibly this is not because our theology is better, but more likely because for long periods Jews have been politically and militarily weak. Military power in the hands of priests, rabbis, popes and mullahs or indeed anyone else, whether religious or secular, who believes themselves to be in possession of 'the truth', has never been a happy combination.

10

Is Judaism really Torah True, or do Jews practice moral relativism?

> *Truth in religion is simply the opinion that has survived.*
> Oscar Wilde

Religious Jews quite commonly refer to the unchanging practice of 'Torah true Judaism'. If asked to clarify what this means, they explain that there is an absolute moral position on certain issues which coincides with that described or legislated about in the Torah. They may go on to say that they are 'following the Divine law that has lasted over 3000 years and shown its superiority to the current fashion for moral relativism'.

If this position is examined and deconstructed, no single part of it withstands scrutiny. The phrase 'Torah true Judaism' would seem to imply adherence to the laws given by God to Moses which were recorded in the Torah and then subsequently fixed for all time.[1] The Jewish reality, however, is nothing like that. As we have seen, theological ideas have changed radically over time as the people have been faced with new historical realities. Arguably, it has been the ability to innovate theologically that has maintained the religion while most of the contemporary religions and cultures have disappeared. Let us

---

[1] *In orthodox tradition, the Mishnah was also given with the Torah, but putting aside the historical issues, logically it would seem strange, even schizophrenic, for God to both give and overrule a law at the same time.*

remind ourselves of these major theological changes that were discussed in Chapter 3:

- the slow evolution from monolatry to monotheism
- the Deuteronomic theodicy of a God who rewards and punishes individual justly
- the centralisation of religious practice on Jerusalem
- the theodicy produced in response to exile. Powerful nations can be used by God as a means to punish his people (collectively) for their faithlessness.
- the development of the synagogue during the Exile to allow ritual practices to take place anywhere
- the compilation of the Torah from its constituent texts (and its successful promulgation as civil law in Yehud)
- the apocalyptic literature with its eschatological ideas (which later contributed to the disasters of the Jewish revolts against Rome). This new theology was developed when it was found that the previous theodicy was not working when under the Greeks, the faithful were suffering and those rejecting the religion prospering.
- the reinvention of Judaism after being crushed by Rome. The breakthrough idea was the Oral Law, which included belief in *Torah min hashamayim*.[2]

Divine revelation *(Torah min hashamayim)* and the writing and dating of the Torah were discussed in Chapter 5, but even leaving the findings of modern scholarship aside - the laws in the Torah are not primarily the laws which observant Jews consider themselves bound by today, or indeed those they have obeyed since Talmudic times. There are two indisputable reasons for this. Firstly, there are a small number of laws that contradict each other, yet both appear in the Torah.[3] Someone has to adjudicate which of these should be obeyed and which ignored. Secondly, and much more importantly, despite religious diatribes against it, moral relativism is a historical fact of life. Morality really has evolved or, at the very least, changed over time and such changes

---

[2] *Torah min hashamayim – Torah from heaven. The Jewish concept that the Torah was dictated by God to Moses at Sinai, and has remained unchanged ever since.*

[3] *Examples: i. concerning the cooking of the Passover sacrifice, Deuteronomy 16:7 vs. Exodus 12:9*

ii. concerning the treatment of slaves, Exodus 21:1-11 vs. Leviticus 25:39-41

iii. concerning divination, Leviticus 19:26 vs. Exodus 28:30 These and other examples are caused by the heterogeneous nature of the work (multi-authorship). The Temple scroll of the Essenes is a version of the Torah with these contradictions resolved which overcomes these problems with the text.

rendered some Torah laws inappropriate and in need of reform even quite early on in Jewish history.

For an example, let us look at the Torah's law on the procedure to deal with a woman suspected by her husband of adultery, which involves the use of trial by ordeal. This bizarre procedure is described in great detail at Numbers 5:11-31.[4] In brief, it instructs the suspicious husband to take his wife to the priest, who after burning a barley-flour sacrifice to God, makes the woman drink a noxious potion in order to induce a spell. This magic spell causes the woman's body to 'prove' her guilt or innocence by the way it reacts to what she drank.

By Torah standards, twenty one verses of instruction on one topic suggest it merits serious attention and should not be easily dismissed. Nevertheless, this arcane practice was repealed early on by the rabbis, partly because the open invocation of magic was no longer morally acceptable in Talmudic times. Moral relativism was already active in the Jewish world. The rabbis of old had realised that parts of the Torah had become outdated and they were confident enough to give themselves the power to sideline these Torah laws and replace them with new laws of their own.[5] Interestingly, in this instance it is also true that one of the reasons given by the Talmud for suspending this law was the uncontrollable number of cases of adultery that were occurring.[6]

Another example of a Torah instruction 'overruled' by the rabbis is that of the rebellious son. The Torah states:[7]

> *If a man has a stubborn and rebellious son, who will not listen to the voice of his father, or the voice of his mother, even though they discipline him, he will not listen to them; then his father and his mother shall lay hold of him, and bring him out to the elders of his city, and to the gate of his place; and they shall say to the elders of his city: 'This our son is stubborn and rebellious, he does not listen to our voice; he is a glutton, and a drunkard.' And all the men of his city shall stone him until he dies; so shall you put away the evil from your midst; and all Israel shall hear, and be afraid.*

---

[4] *This part of the Torah derives from the Priestly (P) source. (See Chapter 5 for explanation of sources).*
[5] *As discussed in the Talmudic tractates of Gittin (36a-b) and Yevamot (89b-90b)*
[6] *Mishnah Sotah 9.9. Rabbi Yohanan ben Zakai said that women could be expected to undergo trial by ordeal only if the men were pure, and this was no longer the case.*
[7] *Deuteronomy 21:18-21*

This punishment is not only seen as excessive by us today, but was clearly already deemed excessive in Talmudic times. Rebellious youth is an age-old problem. There is no evidence of stoning ever being carried out for this crime as the Talmudic rabbis used a technique known as *midrash metsamtsem* - מדרש מצמצם in order to effectively annul the law.[8] This technique works by adding one onerous condition after another, each and every one of which has to be fulfilled for a death sentence to be passed. For all practical purposes the law was annulled.

These examples make clear that in practice the Talmud, not the Torah, has become Judaism's rule book, and that it is the rabbis, not the Torah, that have the last word. Any idea that God had revealed laws in the Torah that were fixed and unchangeable for all time was overturned long ago. Arguments sometimes made by the orthodox that we cannot pick and choose which laws to obey, can be clearly seen as hypocrisy as the Talmudic rabbis themselves did exactly that. They were fully aware that in some cases they had 'overruled God' and even wryly allude to it in a story concerning a dispute between the rabbis of the *Sanhedrin*[9] about the ritual purity of a reconstructed oven. This is a précis of the story:[10]

> *In the debate, Rabbi Eliezer[11] made his case using all his skill in argument, but despite this all the other rabbis disagreed with him. After he saw that he was not able to persuade his colleagues, he appealed directly for God's help and then said, 'If the law is as I say this carob tree will prove it'. A miracle took place and the carob tree moved several hundred cubits, but the other rabbis said, 'One does not use a carob tree as proof.'*

> *Rabbi Eliezer then appealed again to God for further signs, and He made water in a pipe flow backwards and the walls of the study house lean inwards, but the rabbis once again refused to accept the validity of these clear divine interventions.*

> *Finally Rabbi Eliezer said, 'If the law is as I say it should be, let heaven prove it'. God's voice came down from heaven saying, 'What are you next to Rabbi Eliezer, for the law always agrees with what he says?' Defiantly, the rabbis still refused to accept this, Rabbi Jeremiah arguing that since the*

---

[8] *m. Sanhedrin 8*
[9] *Sanhedrin – religious high court*
[10] *Talmud Baba Metzia 59a-b*
[11] *Rabbi Eliezer was from the School of Shammai, the others in this story from that of Hillel. This story is set a few years before the bar Kochba revolt (132-134 CE).*

Torah has already been given we do not pay attention to heavenly voices for God has already written, 'Incline to the majority'.

The Gemarra (commentary) relates that many years later Rabbi Natan met the Prophet Elijah and asked him, 'What was God doing when the rabbis refused to accept his heavenly voice?' Elijah replied, 'God laughed and said: 'My children have defeated Me, My children have defeated Me!''

Another traditional story tells of God allowing Moses to return to Earth and eavesdrop on a Talmudic discussion led by Rabbi Akiva. Moses listened to it and grew increasingly perplexed as he didn't recognise anything he had heard as having come from the Torah. Finally, to his consternation, he heard Rabbi Akiva remark that he was saying nothing new, only speaking in the tradition received directly from Moses at Sinai.

There is an interesting parallel here with Dostoevsky's great Parable of

The Catholic Inquisition - interrogation in progress

the Grand Inquisitor. This is a brilliant satire of Christianity and especially of the Catholic Church. In the story:

Christ returns to Earth, to 16th century Spain the day after a grand auto de fé,[12] where almost 100 heretics had been burned with great ceremony for the greater glory of God. Jesus draws a crowd, performs miracles, and even raises a young girl from the dead.

The Grand Inquisitor realises who he is, understands that Christ has returned and immediately acts to arrest him and then sentences him to death. Late at night before he is to be executed at dawn, the Inquisitor visits Christ's prison cell to talk to him.

He criticises Jesus for the 'mistakes' that he had made when last on Earth; for having resisted worldly wealth and earthly power, and for not using magic

---

[12] *auto de fé (Mediæval Spanish — act of faith) - strictly this refers to the public procession and ceremony of sentencing the 'guilty' as determined (often by torture) by the Inquisition. The 'guilty' were handed over to the secular authorities to be 'relaxed' (a euphemism for burned). The phrase auto de fé commonly (as here) but technically wrongly, is used to refer to the actual burning at the stake of these heretics.*

powers to avoid danger. The Inquisitor says that this meant that he had left a legacy for his church and for his followers of poverty, powerlessness and free moral choice. The Catholic Church had been doing its best for centuries to overcome this difficult burden that it had been left with, and Jesus could not (by his return) be allowed to undo all these centuries of hard work.[13]

Just as the Catholic Church, both in Dostoevsky's story and in the underlying reality, have changed and overruled Jesus' original teaching, so too the rabbis in Talmudic times clearly believed that they could overrule the Torah and outvote God!

The stories of Rabbi Eliezer and Rabbi Akiva confirm that adherence to long accepted Jewish practice can more correctly be dubbed 'Talmud true Judaism'. Any claim of 3000, or even 2000 years of unchanging practice is also disingenuous; the Babylonian Talmud was not completed until after 500 CE. The only peoples who have a claim to be 'Torah true' are the Samaritans, the Sadducees and the Karaites. The Samaritans, who were discussed earlier, split from Judaism in 424 BCE and follow only their Torah and the book of Joshua, without other books or interpretations. The Sadducees also rejected the Oral Law, but as their way of life was rigidly linked to temple practice, they failed to survive as a group for long after its destruction. Karaism is a more recent 'heresy'[14] which also holds only the *Tanach* to be sacred, not the Talmud.

Looking at the question of legislating on moral issues more philosophically, a thinking person today has to decide how to respond to a straightforward question:

Should morality be based on ethics or on religious commandments?

---

[13] *Paraphrased from 'The Brothers Karamazov', although this story seems in many ways like a free standing novella, independent of the rest of the book.*

[14] *Origins of Karaism are unclear. Karaites claim descent from the Sadducees, but the more accepted opinion is that the sect was started by Anan ben David in the eighth century CE. Maimonides wrote that the Karaites are to be considered among the heretics and it is a great mitzvah to kill a heretic (Hilchos Mamrim 3:2). However, at the same time Maimonides held (ibid 3:3) that most Karaites and others who deny the Oral Torah are misled by their parents (tinok she'nishba - captive baby). Maimonides said one raised by sinners cannot be held accountable for their own sins because they were never shown the truth. The effective death penalty outlined above would then no longer apply. Ultra-Orthodox groups today who offer 'conversions' to ordinary Jews forgive their earlier sins using this same reasoning. They weren't real sins as their parents had left them ignorant of 'the truth'!*

Ethics are always a work in progress, as society develops and comes up with new answers and also has to deal with new questions. Jewish religious commandments *(mitzvot)* have now effectively become a closed book as today's orthodox rabbis no longer have the confidence to update laws. Accordingly, Jewish law has become fossilised, almost impervious to new ideas and remains firmly fixed in the past.

If one accepts as true (and as an ideal way to live) a 'morality package' based on ancient sources *(mitzvot)*, a major problem may arise. In the course of daily life, circumstances might occur where the package is in conflict with the morality one 'believes in' based on reason and conscience (ethics). Mark Twain illustrates such a conflict when Huckleberry Finn decides to help Jim, the runaway slave, even though he'd been taught during his whole upbringing that doing such a thing would inevitably lead to him being consigned to hell. 'Well, I guess I'll go to hell then', he says – and follows his conscience.

In a Jewish context, examples where following the rabbinic law conflicts with many people's moral conscience are not hard to find. Is the current treatment of *agunot* morally defensible? Should not the whole concept of a *mamzer* be consigned to the past? What of the position of homosexuals in Judaism? Morality does change with time. One could venture to say that most of us feel this is usually for the better, though one must never be complacent that such progress will not be reversed. Slavery is not acceptable to any of us but the Torah was written in a time when it was common practice and so it had to address the issue. Indeed, its stance could be considered enlightened if judged by the standards of the time of its composition, but the majority of humanity has caught up and has now left those once relatively enlightened laws far behind.

Another example of a moral position that started as absolute and became relative is usury. The Torah unambiguously says that lending money at interest is forbidden.[15] The Talmud extends and clarifies the prohibition; usury was still prohibited. In late mediæval times, probably for economic reasons, there was pressure to change this law and the practice was no longer considered morally wrong (an opinion now shared by most Christians but not by Moslems). A legal way was

---

[15] *Exodus 22:24, Leviticus 25:35-37, Deuteronomy 23:20-21. Deuteronomy allows for usury when lending to foreigners.*

needed to enable interest to be charged and in due course the rabbis helpfully came up with a solution to circumvent this now inconvenient law, the legal fiction of *hetter iskah*.[16] This has become so routinely accepted that today interest bearing transactions are freely carried out in accordance with Jewish law by simply adding the words *al-pi hetter iskah*[17] to the contract. Indeed, many Jews are no longer aware that, in principle, usury is forbidden to them. A changed view of morality from that of both Torah and Talmud was clearly demonstrated by the rabbis.

Accordingly, both absolute morality and Torah true Judaism are revealed as fictions. There have never been any such things. Some laws need to change with time. Orthodox Judaism used to update its laws to reflect this but generally no longer allows itself to do so.[18] The claims that one cannot change divine law and that morality is absolute rather than relative, simply do not match the facts. Nevertheless, such claims seem to remain fundamental to the position of the religious community.

The orthodox also sometimes use an argument found in Dostoevsky's Brothers Karamazov, that if God does not exist, everything is permitted.[19] Within Judaism, such a proposition could only be valid if God's laws for humankind, as stated in his revelation, the Torah, were clear and immutable. But, as has been demonstrated, this is not the case. Some 'immoralities' and inconsistencies were 'corrected' by the Talmudic rabbis. The Talmud in its turn is now over-ripe for updating. Anyone disputing that statement should consider examples such as the Talmud's ideas on the origins of disease or the causes of infertility, to say nothing of its misogynist attitudes.

The proposition that morality is based on following God's commandments also leaves open the question as to whether there were any moral men before the time of the (traditional) revelation at Sinai. Were the Children of Israel in Egypt without a moral compass or any

---

[16] *Hetter iskah, meaning the permission to form a partnership was a legal fiction formulated by a synod of rabbis and leaders in Poland and Lithuania headed by Joshua ben Alexander ha-Kohen Falk in 1607.*

[17] *al-pi hetter iskah – in accordance with hetter iskah*

[18] *Rabbi Louis Jacobs book,' A Tree of Life, Littman Library 1984, offers an excellent discussion of how Judaism used to revise laws to adapt to new situations.*

[19] *This is often mistakenly given as if it were a direct quote; as if it were Dostoevsky's opinion put into the mouth of one of his characters. In fact these words do not appear in this or in similar form anywhere in the book, but they are a fair summary of the views given to Ivan Karamazov by the author.*

ethics because the Torah had not yet been revealed? What of the large portion of humanity with no revealed religious law book or those with sacred texts that reveal rules that conflict with Judaism? Did God play tricks by revealing false texts to them or are their texts of human origin and only ours came from God?

Our law code was, according to tradition, issued in two forms, the written and the oral. Traditionalists believe that God issued both the written instruction and the oral amendments simultaneously: a rather strange form of revelation. One would have expected a perfect God to have got the drafting right first time, especially if morality is absolute. It is interesting to note that in contract law, if the parties claim that both written and oral agreements exist, precedence is given to that in writing. In Judaism it is the reverse, the Oral Law being the basis of *halachah* and the arbiter of (absolute) morality.

If it is true that there is one absolute morality which God wanted to reveal to his chosen, why did He keep this secret from the majority of the world's population? Revealing it to such a small people, the Hebrews, has resulted in only a tiny percentage of people living according to this 'absolute morality code'.

It is also quite patronising for religious people to imply that atheists and agnostics cannot be moral – and have no source of morality. For the religious it is generally taken as a given that the source of morality and ethics is God (or the gods). This proposition was already effectively disputed by Plato.[20] Stated briefly he argued:

> *If good behaviour is that which God approves, does He approve of it because it is good, or is it good because He approves of it?*
>
> *If the former, then goodness exists independently of God.*
> *If the latter, then the choice is arbitrary and not meritorious in its own right.*
>
> *In such a case, to call God good is not very helpful, as all it means is, 'God is what God approves of'.*

If God cannot be the source of ethics and morality, then what is? This is a question that western ethical theory sets out to answer. As is to be expected, there is no agreement among philosophers but three main

---

[20] *In 'The Euthyphro' c. 400 BCE*

concepts have emerged over many centuries of thought. Simplified, these are:

- Virtue theory (after Aristotle). This promotes the cultivation of *the virtues* (valued character traits) in order to achieve human flourishing.
- Deontological approach (after Kant). This says that we should concentrate on carrying out our duty or what is right in itself, regardless of the immediate consequences of such actions.
- Utilitarianism (after Bentham). This states that we should arrange things in such a way as to result in the maximum possible amount of happiness and the minimum amount of unhappiness among all those affected by a particular action.

The best answer may involve taking something from each concept. However, we must all decide individually on that or whether we actually prefer to accept a ready made theological package. The latter is attractive to many people, perhaps because it seems to offer certainty. However, Bertrand Russell pointed out that a theological package induces a dogmatic belief that we have knowledge, when in fact we have ignorance. He felt uncertainty to be painful but something that must be endured if we wish to live without comforting fairy tales. In a recent book, Sam Harris was even more forthright:[21]

It is time we realized that to presume knowledge where one only has pious hope is a species of evil.

To accept the argument that morality is relative and can be seen to vary with place and time, is a long way from accepting that relative morality means that 'anything goes'. Rather, it means that in a sensible society the moral code which is observed and taught to children should be based on ethics, with the precise details of the code the subject of ongoing democratic debate.

What would seem a reasonable basis for morality is that people should be free to behave as they wish in their personal lives provided that by doing so, they do not interfere with other people's rights to do the same. Only where there is conflict between competing rights, need society step in and determine a law. As for laws claiming supernatural

---

[21] *Sam Harris 'The End of Faith'. Norton 2004*

or Divine origin, it must always be a voluntary individual choice whether to bind oneself to them. It is totally immoral to force others to obey such laws in the way religions with political power have done (and are still doing) down the ages. Outrages such as persecution of heretics, the burning of so called witches and the Inquisition have no ethical basis, and are clear evidence of the selective approach to morality by all religions.

In general, the morality of a society seems more related to the degree of freedom enjoyed by its people, combined with effective protection for its minorities, than whether it is religious or not. The greatest moral dangers are in societies run by leaders who 'know the truth' for their people. Their ideology may be religious or secular – but they feel themselves free to carry out immoral acts in its name. In such a repressive atmosphere it is much harder for ordinary people to act morally. In pluralistic societies minority views are more likely to be taken into account and tolerance is more commonly demonstrated.

Ethically based relative morality[22] does not mean that anything is permitted as the absolutists allege. It simply means that laws can adapt to changing circumstances, always keeping such ethical considerations as the Golden Rule in mind. Certainly there are some absolutes in morality, which would be recognised by religious and atheist thinkers alike. There are many more situations where accepted morality has changed significantly with time, and may reasonably be expected to change again in the future.

What can be concluded from a consideration of these issues is that there is no absolute position moral for all time. While we might arrogantly think that a twenty first century moral standpoint is the definitive one, history teaches us that, given time, views on morality will inevitably change and change again.

Those who uphold the concept of absolute morality ignore both the evidence of history and the reality of changes to Jewish law and practice. Such changes have occurred in response to some (although

---

[22] *As the term is used here, a few 'extreme relativists' certainly exist. They argue that if a society practices, say, slavery or child sacrifice, such behaviour is acceptable for that society. This shows the complexity of this subject, but reinforces the need for an ethical approach rather than the extremes of a rigid law code or 'anything goes'.*

critics would say too few) of the changes in normative moral practice since biblical times.

To conclude this discussion, here is a copy of a satirical email sent in the form of an open letter to Laura Schlessinger, a radio and TV personality in the U.S.A., by one of her listeners. Dr. Schlessinger dispenses advice to callers into her radio show. On air in 2001, she said that as an observant Orthodox Jew and in accordance with Leviticus, she viewed homosexuality as an abomination that cannot be condoned in any circumstance. A listener, James Gibson responded:

Dear Dr. Laura,

Thank you for doing so much to educate people regarding God's Law. I have learned a great deal from your show, and I try to share that knowledge with as many people as I can. When someone tries to defend the homosexual lifestyle, for example, I simply remind them that Leviticus 18:22 clearly states it to be an abomination. End of debate. I do need some advice from you, however, regarding some of the specific laws and how to follow them.

a) When I burn a bull on the altar as a sacrifice, I know it creates a pleasing odour for the Lord (Leviticus 1:9). The problem is my neighbours. They claim the odour is not pleasing to them. Should I smite them?

b) I would like to sell my daughter into slavery, as sanctioned in Exodus 21:7. In this day and age, what do you think would be a fair price for her?

c) I know that I am allowed no contact with a woman while she is in her period of menstrual uncleanliness (Leviticus 15:19-24). The problem is, how do I tell? I have tried asking, but most women take offence.

d) Leviticus 25:44 states that I may indeed possess slaves, both male and female, provided they are purchased from neighbouring nations. A friend of mine claims that this applies to Mexicans, but not Canadians. Can you clarify? Why can't I own Canadians?

e) I have a neighbour who insists on working on the Sabbath. Exodus 35:2 clearly states he should be put to death. Am I morally obligated to kill him myself?

f) A friend of mine feels that even though eating shellfish is an abomination (Leviticus 11:10), it is a lesser abomination than homosexuality. I don't agree. Can you settle this?

g) Leviticus 21:20 states that I may not approach the altar of God if I have a defect in my sight. I have to admit that I wear reading glasses. Does my vision have to be 20/20, or is there some wiggle room here?

h) Most of my male friends get their hair trimmed, including the hair around their temples, even though this is expressly forbidden by Leviticus 19:27. How should they die?

i) I know from Leviticus 11:6-8 that touching the skin of a dead pig makes me unclean, but may I still play football if I wear gloves?

j) My uncle has a farm. He violates Leviticus 19:19 by planting two different crops in the same field, as does his wife by wearing garments made of two different kinds of thread, (cotton /polyester blend). He also tends to curse and blaspheme a lot. Is it really necessary that we go to all the trouble to burn them to death at a private family affair like we do with people who sleep with their in-laws? (Leviticus 20:14)

I know you have studied these things extensively, so I am confident you can help. Thank you again for reminding us that God's word is eternal and unchanging.

Your devoted disciple and adoring fan,

James Gibson.

11

Are women second class in Orthodox Judaism?

History, real solemn history, I cannot be interested in.... I read it a little as a duty; but it tells me nothing that does not either vex or weary me. The quarrels of popes and kings, with wars and pestilences in every page; the men all so good for nothing, and hardly any women at all - it is very tiresome.

Jane Austen (Northanger Abbey)

To outsiders, especially the secular and the liberal, it is quite apparent that women are treated as inferior to men by Orthodox Judaism. These outside appearances notwithstanding, Orthodox Jews of both sexes sometimes claim this is not so. They contend that the roles and responsibilities of men and women are simply different, a difference made inevitable by biology. They sometimes add that a woman's natural role is primarily that of homemaker and child-rearer.

Without even addressing the outdated and patronising nature of this last statement, any argument on the lines of 'equal but different' is completely untenable as will become clear if one considers the following evidence of the long standing misogynist tradition and practice within Orthodox Judaism.

Most of these issues have been addressed by the non-orthodox communities which are much more enlightened on this issue. However, nominally orthodox but often less observant women, belonging to institutions such as Britain's United Synagogue, still find themselves bound by many of these attitudes and rules in matters of family law, as do all Jews who live in Israel, whether religious or secular. All the same, I reiterate that most of what follows applies primarily to the ultra-religious.

Attitudes of inferior treatment of women were first recorded in the Bible whose stories, as exemplified below, reflect the mores of the time in which they were written.

- When Adam and Eve were expelled from the Garden of Eden (as a result of the first woman's sin) God said to his secondary human creation, Eve:[1] 'Your urge shall be for your husband, he shall rule over you.' Womankind is put in her place from the start.

- When God asked Abraham to sacrifice his son, Isaac he reprieved him at the eleventh hour.[2] By contrast, when Jephthah was required to sacrifice his only child (a daughter who isn't dignified with a name) she was not reprieved, despite spending two months under sentence of death.[3]

- When the Torah was revealed to the Children of Israel at Sinai it was apparently only to the men. Before the revelation, Moses instructed the 'people' not to go near a woman.[4] Accordingly, the Hebrew word used for *people* (עם) both in this sentence and in the rest of this chapter can logically only refer to men. The presence of women would have apparently rendered the men unclean in the sight of God!

- A common punishment for women in the *Tanach* was to be made infertile. This never happened to a man. Even today infertility (in women) is considered as a divine punishment among many orthodox believers – a cruel concept which adds greatly to the suffering of these women.

- When a census of Israel is taken God instructs Moses only to record the names of the men.[5]

---

[1] *Genesis 3:16*
[2] *Genesis 22*
[3] *Judges 11:39 - some consider this story as a transposition of the Greek myth of Agamemnon sacrificing his daughter Iphigenia.*
[4] *Exodus 19:15*
[5] *Numbers 1:2*

The books of the *Tanach* have overwhelmingly male actors, both human and divine; females are either written out, anonymous or disposable.[6] Women within the text have no property rights, can be given as chattels in marriage, and even can have vows between them and God revoked by their husbands or fathers.[7] With this imbalance at the centre of the religion (even though such bias is to be expected of writing of that period) it has been very difficult for women to achieve even a modicum of equality within the confines of the orthodox world.

Consider the ceremony of *brit milah* (circumcision) which, somewhat uncomfortably to a modern sensibility, is intended to symbolise the covenant between God and the Children of Israel. Women simply could not be more excluded. Would a God who values both genders equally, choose a symbol for his relationship with his special people that excludes half of them?

There is neither a celebratory ritual to mark a girl's birth, nor (in the more orthodox communities) is there one to mark her coming of age – while her brother celebrates his bar mitzvah. Even when her parents die a daughter cannot say the mourner's prayer (*kaddish*) in public.

If the *Tanach*'s primary view of women is as chattels and can, at best, be called paternalistic, the Talmud – which in some cases reinterprets and neutralises bad laws of the Torah[8] – also shows little enlightenment in its treatment of women. There is no doubt that misogynist attitudes were widespread among the traditional and respected Jewish (male) religious figures who composed it. Rabbi Eliezer said that teaching a woman Torah was tantamount to teaching her lechery.[9] Another Talmudic rabbi stated even more outrageously:[10]

אשה חמת מלא צואה ופיה מלא דם

A woman is a sack full of excrement and her opening is full of blood.

---

6 *Examples: Adam & Eve have two sons. Cain (having murdered Abel) is exiled to Nod, where he (miraculously) finds a nameless woman to continue the human line. All the genealogies of the Torah list only men. Aaron is called the firstborn, despite Miriam being older. Miriam's poem is called a song of Moses, etc.*
7 *Numbers 30:3-15 contrasts the discriminatory treatment of men and women who make vows to God.*
8 *See Chapter 10 for more details and examples.*
9 *Sotah 3:4*
10 *Shabbat 152a.* חמת *is literally a water-skin, a leather bag for carrying fluid;* צואה *is faeces.* ופיה *literally means 'and her mouth' (a euphemism as the reference is clearly to menstrual blood). The sentence finishes, 'yet all run after her -* והכל רצין אהריה*'.*

Elsewhere in the Talmud various rabbis describe women as lazy, jealous, vain and gluttonous, prone to gossip and particularly prone to the occult and witchcraft. The tractate of *Mishnah, Nashim* (women) essentially deals with men's rights over them. The Talmud spells out a wife's duties towards her husband:[11]

ואלו מלאכות שהאשה עושה לבעלה טוחנת ואופה ומכבסת מבשלת ומניקה
את בנה מצעת לו המטה ועושה בצמר.

The following are the kinds of work a woman performs for her husband: grinding corn, baking bread, washing clothes, cooking, suckling her child, making ready his bed and working in wool.

A woman's subservient position is confirmed when the Talmud says that even if a married woman wants to visit her parent's house her husband's permission is required.[12] Maimonides said that a woman who refused to wash her husband's feet should be chastised with a rod![13] Fortunately, the texts do contain some balancing statements. A man must provide his wife (at the very least) with food, clothing and conjugal rights.[14] Sexual relations (*onah*) are a woman's right in marriage not a man's so not everything is negative. The Talmud also advises that a man should consult with his wife on all matters[15] and provides for punishment for men committing the grave crime of wife beating.[16]

In Jewish marriage and divorce law, the man has the prerogative. For example, a man is obligated to see his prospective wife before their marriage, there is no such requirement for a woman. As for divorce, without her husband's cooperation a woman simply cannot obtain one; while the Talmudic law for a man states:[17]

הזורק גט לאשתו והיא בתוך ביתה או בתוך חצרה הרי זו מגורשת

If a man throws a get (a bill of divorce) to his wife while she is in her house or in her courtyard, she is thereby divorced.

---

[11] *Ketubot 59b Mishnah. In return the Talmud says a man must provide his wife (at minimum) with food, clothing and sex. Sex (onah) is a woman's right in marriage not a man's so not everything is negative.*
[12] *Kiddushin 30b*
[13] *Mishneh torah hilchot Ishut 21:7-10*
[14] *This appears in Exodus 21:20 and is confirmed by the Talmud.*
[15] *Baba metzia 59a*
[16] *Mishneh torah Hilchot hovel umazik 4:16-18*
[17] *Gittin 8:1 Mishnah*

This blatant inequality in divorce law has led to the inexcusable treatment of *agunot* ('chained' women) who can be left in a permanent state of limbo, not being allowed to get on with their lives or remarry if their husbands cannot or will not give them a *get*. This can affect women whose husbands are missing, whether lost in battle, at sea or otherwise; or whose husbands are mentally or physically incapable of giving a valid *get*. Then, of course, there are those men who refuse to grant a divorce out of spite, or to extort something from the women. Altogether, a significant number of women are affected by this failure of *halachah*.

If they had the will, the all male rabbinate could resolve this injustice by using the type of creative thinking they employed to change the law on usury (described in the last chapter). It is a scandal that they have so far chosen not to do so. It is not surprising though, for the rabbinical courts have a well earned reputation for favouring the man in all manner of divorce cases. Other outdated and demeaning traditions such as levirate marriage[18] and the *halitzah*[19] ceremony also still remain within the orthodox tradition.

In the *Shulchan Aruch*[20] there is a prohibition against a man passing between two pigs, two dogs and two women. A particularly cruel *Mishnah* states that the punishment for failing to correctly observe the three women's *mitzvot* (religious duties)[21] is death in childbirth. This made such an impression on some women that they took steps to have inscribed on their tombstones how meticulously they had carried them out. Would a God who values all humanity really carry out such an awful punishment on women for such petty offences? Imagine how cruel it would be for a woman to die in childbirth still believing this to be her punishment from God and convinced that she will carry this moral stain with her into the next world. Given the number of childbirths orthodox women typically undergo and the high mortality rates of former times, many traumatised women must have gone to

---

[18] *Levirate marriage (yibum), if a man dies childless, his brother must marry the widow and a child he then fathers will be considered to be the child of his late brother.*

[19] *Halitzah (Hebrew: 'drawing off') a demeaning ritual to free a widow from the biblical obligation of levirate marriage. If the brother can't be found or is under age, the woman must wait until he is found or of age. This can place a woman in a situation similar to that of an agunah.*

[20] *Kitzur Shulchan Aruch 3:8. The Shulchan Aruch is a medieval compendium of Talmudic rules of everyday behaviour.*

[21] *Shabbat 31b For more details and photos of the women's tombstones see*
http://www.utoronto.ca/wjudaism/journal/vol3n2/Rosenwiller.pdf

their deaths 'knowing' this was God's will. One can understand the power of such moral blackmail to keep women subservient and dutifully observing the women's *mitzvot* for fear of such a fate.

The three women's *mitzvot* that are traditionally considered to be sufficient to fulfil women as far as religious observance is concerned are: lighting the Shabbat candles, separating the Hallah dough, and *niddah* – ritual purity. Readers may decide for themselves whether this distribution of *mitzvot* is discriminatory or 'equal but different'.

Other examples of Jewish practice where women are viewed differently than men (or discriminated against, depending on your view):

- During the morning prayers, men give thanks for not having been made a woman, while women thank God for being made 'according to your will'.
- After giving birth to a male baby a woman is ritually unclean for one week, after a female birth for two weeks.[22] This is only one example of the laws of *niddah* (impurity) which are still strictly observed by women in ultra-orthodox households. In such households a menstruating woman will not even touch an item that is to be handled by a man for fear of making him unclean. This can extend as far as a doorknob!
- In orthodox practice, a woman is not permitted to say the *Kaddish* prayer at a funeral, at the *shivah* (the week of mourning) or in the synagogue, regardless of whether she is the closest or the only near relative of the deceased. This applies after the death of a parent, a sibling or even a child.
- A married orthodox man can visit a non-Jewish prostitute without being considered to commit adultery. Can this be equated with the level of modesty both of appearance and behaviour required of a Jewish woman within this culture?
- Polygamy was legal until the 11th century CE in Ashkenazi tradition and it is still accepted in Sephardic Judaism where not prohibited by the law of the land.
- Women are among those disqualified from testifying as witnesses.[23] According to natural justice, a woman's evidence is of

---

22 *Leviticus 12:1-5*
23 *Yad, Edut 9:1. Jerusalem Talmud Sanhedrin 3:9*

equal value to a man's, yet in an orthodox religious court she is simply not listened to. So much for equality or justice. It is of course also true that a man's evidence is valued differently according to his status. The evidence of a Jew who, for example, does not observe the Sabbath is also ignored in some Jewish courts.

- Given that they are not even trusted to be witnesses, it almost goes without saying that a woman cannot be a judge in a religious court.

- According to Talmudic law, a wife cannot inherit property from her husband, nor if there are sons can a daughter inherit from her father.[24]

A rabbinic prayer from the Talmudic period which confirms the inferior position of women is still to be found in many Orthodox Jewish prayer books:

> *'Praised be God that he has not created me a gentile! Praised be God that he has not created me a woman! Praised be God that he has not created me an ignoramus! Praised that he has not created me a gentile: 'For all gentiles are as nothing before him'.[25] Praised that he has not created me a woman because the woman is not obliged to fulfil the commandments. Praised that he has not created me an ignoramus for the ignorant man does not avoid sin.'*

As this litany of unfairness, injustice, discrimination and cruelty attests, the reality is that women are still very much second class within the orthodox Jewish community. This is true not only in their role in the home and their daily lives, but in their spiritual lives too. While Rabbi Eliezer's attitude to teaching women Torah persists among the *haredim*, the synagogue is primarily a male preserve among all orthodox communities; women have no obligation to attend. The ritual there involves only men; there is no speaking part at all for women.

A woman may not become a rabbi or a *chazan* (cantor), carry out any of the duties of a Cohen or a Levi, be called up to read from the Torah, open the Ark or even be counted for a *minyan* (a quorum necessary to say certain prayers). It cannot even be said that her status is better in ritual matters in the home, where it is sometimes argued she is treated

---

[24] *Baba Batra 109b; 111b; Bava Kama 42b; Ketubot 83b.*
[25] *Isaiah 40:17*

equally. In the dining room, a quorum of three is required to say the full form of grace – but once again the orthodox tradition is only to count the men – the women remain unseen and uncounted.

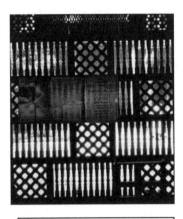

A woman's view of one Orthodox Synagogue through the *mechitza*

The only concession in the synagogue is that women may observe proceedings from a segregated area behind a *mechitza* – a screen or barrier. This allows them to see (sometimes with difficulty) but not to be seen by the men. Women are admitted to the main synagogue only on their wedding day (and that of their children) – and even then they have no speaking part. A woman's consent to marriage is given by silently accepting the ring from the groom.

A strong argument has been made that part of the imbalance in Judaism is due to the suppression of the goddess, or the female aspect of God within Jewish tradition. In the ancient world it was an almost universal situation for every god to have a consort. The consort had definite functions and, in many cultures, the female was the dominant one of the pair. While there are still some traces of the goddess in the *Tanach*, the degree to which this became anathema for at least some of the biblical writers is shown by the use of the term *abomination* - שפץ for the pagan goddess.[26] In nature religions, as in many religions of the East, the typical creation story is that of a goddess creating or giving birth to the Earth – which remains a part of her. This symbolism suggests that the Earth and all it contains (including mankind) are a part of the divine, and it follows that the gods are both immanent (present in all nature) and also transcendent (above and outside of the natural world).

In Judaism and the other monotheistic religions the creation story has a remote male God creating the Earth. The Earth is separated from God, making God purely transcendent. It is argued that the absence of a goddess in heaven is mimicked by the subjugation of women on Earth. Even those who do not accept this argument must admit the heavenly

---

[26] *The term abomination is used in 1 Kings 11:5 to refer to the pagan Ammonite goddess Milcom.*
ואחרי מלכם שפץ עמנים.

paradigm to be male dominated and this example has been continuously followed until today.

The orthodox community sometimes produce the stories of a few exceptional women who achieved much renown in the man's world of study and prayer. That a very few did achieve such feats was mainly in vain, as it did little to create a precedent and nothing to create a path for those who came after. These few brave women had to fight incredible prejudice and their (small) success is admirable, but the overwhelming majority of orthodox women are still strictly confined within a defined narrow role. They are kept too busy at home looking after the daily needs of their husband, their children and finally themselves. That a husband can take this for granted and, as is quite common among the orthodox today, even expect his wife also to work to earn an income so that he can spend his days in holy study is such a cruel distortion of values, that it can best be simply expressed as the exploitation of women.

On public transport in orthodox areas of Israel, segregated buses now operate on which women are relegated to the back seats. Women are also hidden from public view. In the strictly orthodox press and on orthodox web-sites, pictures of men do appear, but never women, however modestly dressed. As an example, in 2007 when the commission of enquiry into the Second Lebanon War was published, pictures of all the members of the commission were printed by an orthodox newspaper, except for the one female member – a distinguished law professor of mature years. It may also be that, apart from the alleged modesty issue, the orthodox men responsible for this discriminatory behaviour do not want to publicise as role models such independent women with successful careers.

The educational system in religious schools sets out to perpetuate these differences between the genders. One need only compare the syllabus for boys with that for girls to see this clearly.

The tradition of arranged marriages, which perpetuates the biblical Iron Age morality of treating women as chattels, is still alive and well in Orthodox Jewish circles. A woman who wants to achieve a good match within this system (and this is the most important goal set for her by her parents and peer group) has no choice but to conform to traditional values. She will be judged and graded by her conformity to the accepted norms of behaviour. She is, in any case, usually married off while still too young to have had any serious opportunity to consider, or even be aware in any meaningful sense, of alternative lifestyles or value systems.

Sadly, by the time most women of an independent nature realise that this is not the lifestyle they wish to follow they are usually trapped. They often have the responsibility of children and have had almost no secular education or experience in how to function in the world outside the *haredi* community. If they were to leave the security of this community, they would be likely to be cut off by their family as well as experiencing a good deal of guilt at rejecting their upbringing. This means that very few are strong enough to take such a step.

While there is no doubt that there are many women who are happy to live in this world, as there are people who are happy to conform to almost any social system, there is a great price to be paid by those women who think for themselves, ask questions or wish to express their individuality.

12

Superstition, Magic

and the Kabbalah

The general root of superstition is that man observes when things hit, and not when they miss; and commits to memory the one and passes over the other. Francis Bacon

S uperstition seems to answer a primal need for humanity by purporting to help avoid, or reduce, some of the ever-present risks of life and by seeming to give the individual a degree of control over future events. There is nothing more attractive to human beings than the idea that they can personally receive 'special treatment' from the supernatural realm in return for the performance of certain rites. Humankind finds it very difficult to accept the possibility that many events that affect their lives are entirely random.

It is surprisingly difficult to define the difference between superstition and religious faith. On analysis they have many characteristics in common – and may perhaps best be seen as different places along the same continuum. Both involve belief or reliance on propositions that must be accepted without evidence and thus a voluntary suspension of the individual's critical faculties. Perhaps a key difference is that superstition is belief in ideas that can be demonstrated experimentally to be false, while religious faith is belief in ideas that cannot be tested experimentally and so can neither be proved nor disproved. However, there is clearly a considerable degree of overlap and many religious beliefs that deal with events of this life do, on more detailed examination, fall into the category of superstition.

To demonstrate how difficult this issue is, consider the following. In a classic experiment an experimental psychologist[1] was able to induce superstitious behaviour in pigeons. He fed hungry birds by mechanically presenting them with food according to a predetermined schedule without any reference to the birds' behaviour. He observed that most birds developed rituals or dance routines which could only be intended to produce more food. Observation showed that whatever action the pigeon was carrying out immediately prior to the arrival of food, tended to be repeated and, as the experiment progressed, different birds were seen performing many strange and different routines.

Even more than pigeons, human beings seem conditioned to look for patterns and this occurs even when dealing with random events or those that are not susceptible to human influence. For example, the shaman's rain dance may well have developed in the same way as the pigeon's food dance. The shaman may have initially tried to find some pattern linking actions taken on those occasions it rained and comparing them to those when it didn't.

As religions developed further, sacrifices were offered to achieve the same purpose and later still, this evolved to include the use of prayer. In Judaism, the current ritual is to add petitions for rain to the central *amidah* prayer during the winter months. Readers may consider for themselves at which point along this continuum, *pigeon's dance – shaman's rain dance – sacrifice – prayer,* superstition ends and religion begins. If we were to perform a controlled experiment, would we expect any of them to actually influence the course of future events? Or could all of them be superstition?

The Enlightenment philosopher, David Hume[2] wrote how the practice of all religions seemed to consist of superstitious practices. He claimed this to be the main occupation of religions, rather than what he had expected – the promotion of morality, virtue and honesty. He wrote:

---

[1] *B F Skinner in 1947. Journal of experimental psychology 38:168-172, which is available online at* http://psychclassics.yorku.ca/Skinner/Pigeon/
[2] *David Hume 1711-1776 - in 'The Natural History of Religion'.*

It is certain, that, in every religion, however sublime the verbal definition which it gives of its divinity, many of the votaries, perhaps the greatest number, will still seek the divine favour, not by virtue and good morals, which alone are acceptable to a perfect being, but either by frivolous observances, by intemperate zeal, by rapturous ecstasies, or by the belief of mysterious and absurd opinions.

However, this chapter will not be primarily concerned with what some may consider as the superstition involved in mainstream Jewish belief, prayer and ritual, but with some of the more peripheral practices such as Kabbalah. Like a high percentage of people everywhere, both religious and secular, many Jews believe in and regularly carry out superstitious customs.

Orthodox Judaism adopts a somewhat hypocritical approach to traditional superstitions. While the *halachic* ban on magic and divination is clear,[3] superstitious practices carried out among the orthodox are almost never denounced. Indeed, practices such as the use of amulets and the attribution of magical powers to *mezuzot* are carried out by some of the community's most prominent rabbis. There is more than a suspicion of the mediæval in the *haredi* world.

Other superstitious ideas now to be considered have been popular over long periods among Jews. These are astrology and the zodiac, the evil eye concept and the Hamsa. As for the 'prohibited' practices of divination and soothsaying both these activities, along with other superstitious practices, occur without censure within the text of the *Tanach*[4] before subsequently becoming endemic among the traditions and behaviour of the Jews.

Astrology is significantly older than Judaism and is an interesting example of how a patently false belief system can persist for millennia. Even today, astrology has huge numbers of followers throughout the world despite the fact that long before it was discredited scientifically, Pythagoras had already made the rational observation that identical twins do not have the same life experiences, a comment repeated by Saint Augustine to equally little effect. It was also pointed out as far back as the Greek era, that two babies born at the same time and place,

---

[3] *Leviticus 19:26*

[4] *Soothsaying by the prophets is routine, see a list of other superstitious practices in the Tanach, appendix p.242*

one to a rich man and the other to a peasant or slave, tend not to have similar life experiences.

Astrology originated from observation of the night sky and mankind's attempts to make sense of it. It was soon realised that all but five of the observable heavenly bodies had regular predictable movements in the sky. The five exceptions moved seemingly as they wished, even sometimes changing direction. As a result of their seemingly random celestial journeys, they were called *planetes* (wanderers) and named for gods associated with having such apparently supernatural powers.[5] The search was then on for those who could give an explanation as to how the movements of these gods in the heavens would influence events on Earth. As always, there were some individuals who were able to convince others that they possessed such knowledge.

Other events that needed interpretation were unusual occurrences, such as eclipses, comets and even thunder and lightning, which were universally believed to be ordered by the gods. While, in those times, everyone considered such events as omens, 'wise' men were needed to explain exactly what they meant. As a result, astrology and the zodiac developed and became a very complex and sophisticated system of 'prediction'.

Zodiac on mosaic floor of Beit Alfa Synagogue
517 CE

Initially it was considered that it was only possible to 'read' the information concerning events related to kings and states but as the practitioners became more experienced and confident, they claimed to be able to advise ordinary individuals too.

---

[5] *Weekdays in many European languages were named after the Sun, Moon and the gods of these five wandering planets. In English some take their Norse form. French gives the Roman form better. They are Tiu or Mars – Tuesday/mardi, Woden or Mercury – Wednesday/mercredi, Thor or Jupiter – Thursday/jeudi, Frig or Venus – Friday/vendredi, and Saturn – Saturday/samedi.*

The zodiac has been integral to Jewish tradition and practice for 2000 years but the earliest examples of astrological signs we have come from Babylon and date from around 1500 BCE. These are carved into *kudurri* (property boundary markers) and cylinder seals. The entire zodiac is first found in the Hellenistic period, for example at the Temple of Hathor at Dendera, Egypt, built around 30 BCE. This is also the time of the earliest Jewish references to the zodiac found so far.[6] Astrology became so influential in Jewish culture that it was often used as the main design motif of mosaic floors in early synagogues (*see illustration*).

This tradition was still current when the seminal work of esoteric Judaism, the *Sefer Yezirah*, appeared sometime between the 8th and 10th century. This book is best known for containing the first version of the kabbalistic *sephirot*, but also deals with astrology. It associates the 12 signs of the zodiac with 12 of the Hebrew letters, with the 12 months of the Hebrew calendar and with 12 parts of the body (thus 'explaining' how the stars influence health).[7] These correspondences, along with some others of Jewish tradition are detailed in the table below.

Astrological sign	Hebrew name	Part of body	Hebrew month	Letter	Tribe of Israel & cardinal point	
Aries	תלה – lamb	head	Nisan	ה	Judah	E
Taurus	שור – bull	neck	Iyar	ו	Issachar	E
Gemini	תאומים - twins	shoulders	Sivan	ז	Zebulun	E
Cancer	סרטן – cancer	chest	Tammuz	ח	Reuven	S
Leo	אריה – lion	heart	Av	ט	Shimeon	S
Virgo	בתולה – virgin	stomach	Elul	י	Gad	S
Libra	מאזניים - scales	kidneys	Tishri	ל	Ephraim	W
Scorpio	עקרב -scorpion	genitals	Heshvan	נ	Menasseh	W
Sagittarius	קשת – bow	thighs	Kislev	ס	Benjamin	W
Capricorn	גדי – kid	knees	Tevet	ע	Dan	N
Aquarius	דלי – pail	calves	Shevat	צ	Asher	N
Pisces	דגים – fish	feet	Adar	ק	Naphtali	N

Zodiac references are incorporated into *piyutim* (Jewish liturgical poems) and also used as illustrations in Ashkenazi *machzorim* (festival prayer books) of the middle-ages. In the mid 11th century, a text dealing with Jewish astrology - *Baraita de Mazzalot*[8] appeared. In medieval times there was one Jewish school of thought that believed astrological influences

---

[6] *In the Qumran literature; 4Q138 (Brontologion); 4Q186 (Horoscope)*
[7] *Sefer yezirah 5:2 - there is also a correspondence with the 12 permutations of the letters in the tetragrammaton.*
[8] *Baraita of the Zodiac, a Baraita being a tradition of Jewish Oral Law that is not a part of the Mishnah.*

only affected gentiles. God gave special protection to the Jews, provided that they observed the commandments! Others were of the opinion, however, that Jews like all nations and religions were governed by the zodiac. They held Judaism to be governed by Aquarius, Christianity by Virgo and Islam by Cancer.

From the early 17th century, painted wooden ceilings in synagogues became popular in Poland. Astrological signs were commonly used to represent the heavens above the worshippers. These differed from the Byzantine mosaic floors as there was now no representation of the human body. Such ceilings were still being made in the early 20th century but sadly, all of these synagogues were destroyed in the Shoah. A few photographs and sketches are all that remain.

In the 18th century, the founder of *Hasidism*,[9] the Baal Shem Tov incorporated astrology and the zodiac into his magical practices. At the same time the zodiac was used as a motif for some Torah decorations, especially the crowns. Within sacred text itself, it was used to decorate the scrolls of Esther.

Other more personal Jewish examples of using the zodiac for good luck include:
- *wimpel* (swaddling belt): worn by the baby for his *brit* especially in Germany from the 16th century. These usually had the baby's name and his astrological symbol on them. They were donated to the synagogue on the baby's first visit and used to bind the *sefer Torah* on his bar mitzvah as well as on the Shabbat before his wedding.
- wedding cup decorations
- decoration on silver salvers for *pidyon ha'ben* (redemption of the first born)
- the expression *mazal tov* – or good sign which started at weddings (mazal means sign of the zodiac and from this has come to mean luck generally)
- *ketubot* (marriage contracts): zodiac decorations were common on these documents in 18th century Italy especially in Venice.

---

[9] *Hasidism - a Jewish mystical movement which was against Talmudic learning as a lifestyle and promoted the serving of God by word and deed.*

- amulets (*kameot*): these are lucky charms, commonly decorated with astrological and kabbalistic symbols to bring luck to the bearer. This tradition continues until today. Amulets blessed by a holy man or a revered *rebbe* are still widely accepted as being effective among the orthodox.

The **hamsa** is an old and still popular symbol for magical protection against the envious or evil eye, particularly among the Sephardi community. The word hamsa means 'five' in Arabic and refers to the digits of the hand. An alternative Islamic name for this charm is the Hand of Fatima, a reference to the daughter of Mohammed, while Jews sometimes call it the Hand of Miriam, after the sister of Moses and Aaron.

The *hamsa* appears both in a two-thumbed, bilaterally symmetrical form (as shown) and in a more natural form in which there is only one thumb. There is good archæological evidence to suggest that the downward-pointing protective *hamsa* predates both Judaism and Islam in the region and that it was associated with Tanit (the chief Goddess of Carthage) whose hand (or vulva in other images) wards off the evil eye. Its path into Jewish culture can be traced through Islam. Some variations on the *hamsa* feature the Shema prayer or doves or dove-shaped hands. There is also a Buddhist *hamsa* (known as *Abhaya* or the *Abhaya Mudra*) which has essentially the same connotations. This similarity has even led to speculation about an ancient Judeo-Buddhist community but the widespread nature of this symbol is more likely to be another example of syncretism.

The **evil eye** concept dates back at least as far as biblical Israel and was also widespread in ancient near eastern culture. Symbols to protect against the evil eye have been found on the prows of first millennium BCE ships and can still be found today on the tails of Turkish aircraft! It was, and is, believed that a person looking at another with envy (a particular example being a childless woman looking at a baby) can bring that person bad luck. There are many instances in both the *Tanach* and Talmud[10] of people casting the evil eye (עין הרע - *ayin hara*). Ashkenazi Jews use the Yiddish expression, *'keyn ayin hara'* (no evil eye) to ward off

---

[10] *An example: Rabbi Yohanan (in Bava Batra 75a, Sanhedrin 100a) was displeased by a certain student. He cast his eyes on him an he was turned to a pile of bones.*

bad luck after hearing praise or good news. Another talisman worn to fend off the evil eye is the kabbalistic red string.[11] This seems to have ancient roots and recently briefly became a fashion item.

The **Magen David** or Shield of David is perhaps the best known  Jewish symbol despite its recent adoption. The six pointed star is a protective device which seems to have become a Jewish symbol as late as the seventeenth century. It was in use as an esoteric symbol in places such as Tibet and Egypt much earlier. It was also used in magical circles to represent a blending of energy. The upward pointing triangle represents the physical realm (fire) while the downward one represents the spiritual realm (water). Given this background, it is not surprising to find that it was first popularised by the kabbalists.

A popular folk etymology has it that the Star of David was literally modelled after the Shield of David. In order to save metal, the shield was not made of metal but of leather spanned across the simplest metal frame that would hold the round shield: two interlocking triangles. There is absolutely no historical evidence for this. Jewish lore also links the symbol to the Seal of Solomon, the magical signet ring supposedly used by King Solomon to control demons and spirits.

The earliest Jewish literary source to mention the Shield of David is the *Eshkol Ha-Kofer* by Judah Hadassi (a Karaite) from the middle of the 12th century CE, where seven shields are used in an amulet for a *mezuzah*. It appears to have been in use as part of amulets before it was in use in formal Jewish contexts.

There are superstitious practices surrounding the **mezuzah** whose contents include an archaic lucky charm along with the Torah passages.[12] There is a popular custom of kissing the *mezuzah* for luck on leaving a house. Moreover, bad luck, accidents or illness are, as

---

[11] *There is in fact nothing in the Kabbalah concerning this. There is a Talmudic mention of the practice (Tosefta Shabbat Ch. 7-8), but this condemns it as a worthless, superstitious practice, close to idol-worship.*

[12] *Mezuzot also contain a lucky charm - kozo bemuksaz kozo -* כוזו במוכסז כוזו *which when decoded according to the Caesar or avgad -*אב'ג'ד *cipher (shift each letter 1 alphabetic position) reads* יהוה אלהינו יהוה, *the names of God from the opening of the Shema prayer. This practice dates from around the 14th century.*

discussed elsewhere, sometimes attributed by Orthodox Jews to the use of defective or incorrectly written *mezuzot*, which do not have the 'power' to protect.

Tefillin (phylacteries) probably derive from amulets. Indeed, *kameot* (amulets) and *tefillin* are discussed together in several places in the Talmud.[13] They were originally considered to have a protective function and one also occasionally hears of defective *tefillin* being blamed for personal tragedies. The Japanese religion, Shinto has something similar, *omamori*, cloth amulets containing inscriptions to 'protect' the wearer in various circumstances.

Following a personal tragedy, some rabbis' insensitive approach is to look at whether the victim had failed to perform some ritual properly, and to suggest the tragedy is a divine punishment. As with the 'comforters' view of Job, their first assumption is that the victim must have sinned. This cruel attitude creates guilt among believers when they 'sin' by breaking petty laws but presumably is intended to do just that.

Those with this mind-set treat good luck entirely differently. For example, such individuals who miss a plane which subsequently crashes killing all on board, will claim a miracle. God was their protector and caused them to be delayed in order to save their lives. There is a strange silence as to how the plane load of victims was selected for death by this same God who has been clearly shown to concern himself with the fate of individuals. Primo Levi wrote movingly of such a situation in his Auschwitz memoir.[14] A selection had just taken place in the hut to decide who was to live (for the time being) and who to die:

> *Now everyone is busy scraping the bottom of his bowl with his spoon so as not to waste the last drops of the soup; a confused metallic clatter, signifying the end of the day. Silence slowly prevails and then from my bunk on the top row, I see and hear old Kuhn praying aloud, with his beret on his head, swaying backwards and forwards violently. Kuhn is thanking God because he has not been chosen.*

> *Kuhn is out of his senses. Does he not see Beppo the Greek in the bunk next to him, Beppo who is twenty years old and is going to the gas chamber the day after tomorrow and knows it and lies there looking fixedly at the light without saying anything and without even thinking any more? Can Kuhn fail to recognize that*

---

[13] e.g. *Shabbat 60a, Kelim xxiii 9*

[14] Primo Levi. *Se questo è un uomo.1958 (If This Is A Man. 1960. Chapter: October 1944)*

next time it will be his turn? Does Kuhn not understand that what has happened today is an abomination, which no propitiatory prayer, no pardon, no expiation by the guilty, which nothing at all in the power of man can ever clean again?

If I was God, I would spit at Kuhn's prayer.

Another superstitious traditional Jewish practice is to change the Hebrew name of a person who is gravely ill so that the Angel of Death will be confused and unable to find his target. Those who do this perhaps remember the 'miracle' of an occasional individual who recovered and overlook the many that did not, giving excuses like the action had been left too late.

Among the Hassidic community superstition and belief in magic is endemic. The following is just one example. It is believed that the *rebbe*[15] contains *nitzotzot* – ניצוצות (holy sparks from God). At the Shabbat afternoon meal a large plate of food is placed before the *rebbe* who takes a morsel. He then pushes the plate away for the rest of the Hassidim (men only of course) to pounce on the *shayarim* – שיירים (leftovers) which they believe contain these holy sparks. In truth, the treatment of *rebbes* by their communities sometimes seems close to worship, and hence idolatry. The *rebbe's* photograph is often displayed prominently in the homes of his followers and is considered to bring luck and protection.

The tradition of revering sages goes back at least as far as the days of the Talmudic rabbis, many of whom had the reputation that they could heal the sick, cast the evil eye and perform many forms of magic. These abilities are recorded in the Talmud where they are fully accepted at face value, even claims as extreme as the ability to create life![16]

The *lulav* and *etrog*[17] originated as fertility symbols, while the *mezuzah* became a substitute for the household gods. These relics of minor 'idols' were transformed and incorporated into Judaism as they fulfil a human need for tangible symbols which a remote purely transcendent

---

[15] *A Hassidic rebbe is the leader of the community.*

[16] *Talmud Sanhedrin 67b, in a discussion on magic tells us, 'Rabbi Hanina and Rabbi Oshaya spent every Sabbath eve studying the laws of creation, by means of which they created a third-grown calf and ate it.'*

[17] *Lulav and etrog. Two of four species (ארבעת המינים) used ritually at Sukkot. These are: lulav (לולב) – a palm frond; hadass (הדס) –myrtle leaves; aravah (ערבה) –willow leaves; etrog (אתרוג) – citron fruit.*

deity cannot satisfy. Many kabbalistic ideas have also passed into both folk belief and informal Jewish practice as superstitions. As will be seen, Kabbalah itself is a wonderful mix of superstition, magick[18] and esoteric thought.

These examples of superstition, which are clearly influenced by their Jewish context, provide a fascinating insight into the history and very human experience of those who practice them. All respectable theologians discourage superstition while often, in practice, turning a blind eye to it. Given the essentially superstitious nature of many religious practices, this seems to be the mainstream Jewish approach too and it colours the stories of the *Tanach*.

The Kabbalah

The Kabbalah is a development of esoteric (mystical) Judaism. As with most religions, there has probably always been an esoteric side to Judaism. The prophetic tradition is essentially mystical, prophets being shaman like figures who had visions and felt themselves to be receiving direct instruction from God. There is a long history of such figures in the ancient world; soothsayers, diviners, oracles, ecstatics, seers, shamans and prophets. This tradition of receiving God's instruction firsthand continues into early Judaism, where the high priest used the *urim* and *thummin* [19]- האורים והתמים as a tool for this purpose when an important issue needed a decision.

Later, there is evidence of esotericism in both the circles of the Pharisees and the Essenes as can be seen in the Book of Enoch. By the first century CE the Merkavah mystics were in existence. Their ideas centred on the throne chariot of God in Ezekiel's vision,[20] a topic also known as *ma'aseh merkavah*. Reading this vision in metaphorical terms, as discussed in Chapter 2, it can be understood as an account of God leaving his residence in the Jerusalem Temple prior to its destruction by the Babylonians. However, the richness of the metaphors and the Baroque detail of the vision make it fertile ground for all manner of esoteric interpretations.

---

[18] *Magick – with a final k is, in the broadest sense, any act designed to cause intentional change and refers to the system of Hermetic thought that strongly influenced Kabbalah.*
[19] *See Exodus 28:30. The urim and thummim were possibly a black and a white ball; drawing the white one meant 'yes', the black 'no'. They also 'gave' a guilty or innocent verdict when appropriate.*
[20] *Ezekiel 1:15-28*

At a later date, mystics turned to the Genesis creation story which they called *ma'aseh bereshit*. They were in conflict with normative Judaism from the start and the Talmud tried to curtail their activity:[21]

אין דורשין בעריות בשלשה ולא במעשה בראשית בשנים ולא
במרכבה ביחיד אלא אם כן היה חכם ומבין מדעתו כל המסתכל.

'One should not discuss illegal unions unless there were three besides him, nor the subject of creation without two, nor the chariot before one person, unless he is a sage and already has an independent understanding of the matter.'

In an argument that seems to have been directed against the Gnostic[22] and mystical ideas current when the Talmud was written, it continues:

בארבעה דברים רתוי לו כאילו לא בא לעולם מה למעלה מה למטה מה
לפנים ומה לאחור וכל שלא חס על כבוד קונו רתוי לו שלא בא לעולם

'Whoever ponders on four things, it would be better for him if he had not come into the world: what is above, what is below, what was before time, and what will be hereafter.'

In the same tractate of the Talmud is the story of another encounter with mysticism. This concerns the four sages who were able, while still alive, to enter *pardes* (paradise).[23] Their terrible fates were intended as a warning to show that only the greatest of sages can engage with such dangerous ideas and survive. 'Ordinary people' should avoid dabbling in the esoteric.

Despite these warnings, Jewish esotericism continued to develop with the *heikhalot*[24] literature, which is full of magic and Gnostic ideas. At this stage, the chariot (*merkavah*) and its world occupied the place in Jewish mysticism that for the fully Gnostic Jewish groups (as for Gnostics in general) was filled by the theory of the Aeons. The Aeons are the power and emanations of God which fill the *pleroma* – the divine fullness.

---

[21] *Tractate Hagigah 2:1 Mishnah*

[22] *Gnosticism is a dualistic belief system that was popular in Talmudic times. It posits that humans live in a material world created by a demiurge, an evil spirit often identified with the Judeo-Christian God. Gnostics also believe in the existence of another remote all good supreme being. In order to free themselves from the inferior material world they must obtain gnosis or secret esoteric knowledge, which a few wise teachers possess.*

[23] *Hagigah 14b. Entering pardes (paradise) was considered by the mystics as ascent to the heavens or descent to the Merkavah. The protagonists are clearly dealing with spiritual and ecstatic experiences, as is shown by their fates. Simeon ben Azzai looked into the pardes and died; ben Zoma was mentally incapacitated (looked and was smitten); Elisha ben Avuyah (also called Acher) forsook Rabbinic Judaism and 'cut the shoots', apparently becoming a dualistic Gnostic; Rabbi Akiva alone entered and left in peace.*

[24] *heikhalot – the halls of heaven through which one approaches the Divine*

Those who engaged in this chariot mysticism were called *yoredei merkavah* – literally 'those who go down in the chariot'. In English, they are more commonly known as 'riders of the chariot'.

Certain qualities of God, such as wisdom, understanding, knowledge, truth, faithfulness and righteousness had become personified as the Aeons by the Gnostics. This idea was utilised by those Jews engaged with *ma'aseh bereshit* (the subject of creation). The transformation of the Aeons of Gnosticism to the *sephirot* of Jewish esotericism was in process. The term *sephirot* first appears in the seminal work *Sefer Yezirah* (Book of Creation). Though this book's origins are obscure, it definitely existed by the 10th century but is thought to have been written some two centuries earlier. The *sephirot* in this book, while quite different from what they later became, were a clear stepping stone in the development of the concept. The early development of Kabbalah is shrouded in mystery, but we do know that by the 12th century it had emerged in Provence, France.

A major figure in this development was Isaac the Blind (c. 1160-1235), who lived near Narbonne. *Sefer ha'Bahir,* the first recognised work of kabbalistic literature, is sometimes attributed to him although it is generally considered to have been a compilation. It was written like a *Midrash* [25] and commented on the mystical and magical significance of the letters of the Hebrew alphabet. Its key idea was to develop the *sephirot* of the *Sefer Yezirah* into divine attributes, lights and powers, each of which had a function in the creation process.

The *Zohar* was the next important work, this being a series of documents covering a wide variety of subjects ranging from the nature of God to esoteric interpretation. It was written mainly by Moses ben Shem Tov (Moses de Leon) between 1280 and 1286 in Spain.[26]

Kabbalistic development continued to be strongly influenced by Gnosticism and magic. An example of a pure Gnostic idea taken into Kabbalah is the concept that, although God's creation is in a damaged and imperfect state, kabbalists can, by virtue of their state of consciousness, repair it. Another example is recording ideas in such a

---

[25] *Midrash - exegesis and interpretation of biblical texts by the use of stories that fill in the gaps*
[26] *By tradition, the Zohar was written by the 2nd century Rabbi Shimon bar Yochai. Scholars consider this most unlikely.*

way that only an initiate could understand them (secret arcane knowledge). This practice along with the reintroduction of the old idea that God had a consort, a female companion, led many at the time to consider Kabbalah heretical. Kabbalists believe the Torah to be divine and to have hidden meanings and divine power concealed within it. Two strands run through kabbalistic thought, one esoteric and the other more practical. By using both together, they claim to offer a coherent method of healing the world.

Kabbalism is thought by its followers to be a set of precepts provided by the good creator God so that people can improve their lives and achieve fulfilment. Kabbalists believe that:

- by studying the texts and following certain principles they can unlock the secrets of creation
- it is impossible to think of God except through contemplation of his relationship to creation
- direct experience of God is feasible and Kabbalism teaches practical methods that claim to achieve this.

This search for a direct experience of God, as we have seen, is more typical of eastern religion. Those claiming to have achieved contact with the Divine in different cultures often also report the perception of a variety of spiritual beings and angels, and indeed Kabbalah has an entire cosmology of angels and archangels.

Isaac ben Luria (the Ari) 1534-1572 was the most important individual in the development of Kabbalah. From Safed in the Galilee, he significantly developed the creation story with the introduction of three main doctrines; *tsimtsum* (contraction), *shevirah* (breaking of the vessels) and *tikkun* (repair or healing). He was so influential that Kabbalah after his time generally carries his name. Lurianic Kabbalah became a Jewish mass movement with special rituals, meditations and ethical disciplines devised by the Ari. It has significantly influenced the practice of many of the orthodox groups until today.

The kabbalistic creation story of Isaac ben Luria

Much simplified and minus much of the mythology, this goes as follows:

- God withdrew or compressed himself (*tsimtsum*), in a process of self limitation, so as to create a space to accommodate his new creation.

- This event occurred inside the *Ein Sof* – the infinite, unknown and unknowable God.
- The light (perhaps best considered as a kind of supercharged lightning flash) entered this space in a stream and caused the emanations of the *sephirot* (vessels of power).
- All except the first three *sephirot* were shattered by the power of the light (*shevirah*). These broken vessels represent evil.
- The shards of the broken vessels fell into the abyss formed by the contraction and became the *kelipot* (shells or husks) – a kind of negative mirror of the *sephirot*.
- Most of the light (or divine sparks – *nitzotzot*) returned to the *Ein Sof f* but some remained trapped in the vessels and fell with the *kelipot*.

A way of looking at *shevirah* is as a possible corrective action in which the broken vessels were ejected into the abyss because evil was present to such a degree that it was the only way that the balance could be restored. Whether a catharsis or a blunder, *shevirah* was cataclysmic – nothing was as it should have been. The four interlocking worlds of Kabbalah slipped when they should have been held stable, and the lowest world descended into the realm of the *kelipot*.

Much of the teaching of Isaac ben Luria concerns the corrective actions or repair (*tikkun*) needed to free the sparks of light trapped in the *kelipot* in order that creation can be perfected.

Other kabbalistic concepts:

Unity of God
This is stressed by kabbalists even though the different powers of the godhead exemplified in the *Sephirot* could be easily misinterpreted as separate divine agents. A favourite metaphor is that of water poured into different coloured bottles. The water assumes, for the time being, a particular colour.

Evil
Kabbalists give a great deal of consideration to this issue and have come up with a variety of responses. The most important ones are:
- *Sitra achra* (the other side). This is the domain of dark emanations and demonic powers. Though it emerged from one of the emanations of God, it cannot be an essential part of him.

According to the Zohar, there is a divine spark of holiness even in the *sitra achra*. The realms of good and evil are to an extent commingled and man's mission is to separate them. There is more than a suspicion of dualism here.

- The domain of evil is characterised as a natural **waste product** from an organic process. Analogies such as the dregs left behind when making wine or the dross remaining after refining pure gold are cited. Creation was as perfect as it could have been but, as in other processes, some inevitable waste by-product was formed - in this case, evil.

- Evil is an entity which is not in its **right place**. Every act of God, when it is in the place allotted to it in creation, is good. If it turns and leaves its place, it becomes evil.

- *Gilgul* (reincarnation). Innocent suffering is a punishment for sin in a previous incarnation, infant death particularly so. This is a widely held kabbalistic explanation for evil, and once more is recognisable as a standard component of eastern religions.

Marriage

Marriage is considered to be the crossing of threads in the fabric of life. The intertwining of two people's fate is part of a destiny designed in heaven with a specific purpose. On some occasions this purpose is to prepare the way for particular children to be born of the union.

Death and reincarnation

On death, the human being separates into distinct parts. The body disintegrates while the vital soul hovers for a while around the grave. The soul is taken into the world of *yezirah* (formation) where it contemplates its earthly performance and experiences either paradise or purgatory. If it is sufficiently developed, it is possible for it to ascend to the world of creation. From here it can descend into a new body (*gilgul*). Speedy burial is a condition for *gilgul*, hence its importance for believers. It is interesting to see how this concept came into Judaism. Josephus wrote that the Pharisees believed that, 'the souls of good men only are removed into other bodies, - but that the souls of bad men are subject to eternal punishment'. The Talmud does not discuss the matter, despite it being a concept common to Gnostics, Manichæans and some Christians during the second century CE. Only in the 8th-10th centuries, were some Jews influenced by the *Mu'tazila* Islamic sect and the Sufis who believed in reincarnation. This belief was rejected by the main medieval Jewish philosophers, such as Saadiah Gaon and Abraham ibn Daud (Maimonides does not discuss it at all).

From the very beginning, all the kabbalistic writing we have (starting with *Sefer ha'Bahir*) takes reincarnation for granted. It must, therefore, already have been an accepted belief in kabbalistic circles. Incidentally, there is a possible connection between these circles in southern France and their neighbours and contemporaries the Cathars. (The Cathars also believed in transmigration of souls between man and animals, the kabbalists only between men. The Cathars were later exterminated for their heretical views in the Albigensian Crusade of the Catholic Church).[27] After this period, ideas about *gilgul* developed in several directions and became a major doctrine of Kabbalah.

Hell
Kabbalistic ideas on hell are a matter of serious dispute between different groups and there is no consensus. Because the concepts of hell and reincarnation are in many ways mutually exclusive, attempts to achieve a compromise between these different views have failed.

The Golem
The Golem – an artificial man made by magic, particularly by the use of magic names. This concept seems to have two main sources:
- the idea (thought to originate in 10th century Italy) of resurrecting the dead by putting the name of God in the mouth or on the arm.
- the idea (and goal) of alchemy, which contrary to the common misconception of this being to transmute base metal into gold, is actually no less than the search to create life (for example, the homunculus [little man or dwarf] of Paracelsus[28]).

Madness
In certain cases, madness is believed to be caused by the *ibbur* (impregnation) of another soul into a living person. This requires to be treated by exorcism which must be performed by a kabbalistic master.

The sephirot (singular *sephira*) – can be translated as vessels of power or may be thought of as Divine attributes. These mirror human

---

[27] *Albigensian Crusade 1209-1229 – ordered by our old friend Pope Innocent III, who was also responsible for ordering Jews to wear badges as a sign of their religion.*
[28] *The popular view of alchemy was a smokescreen encouraged by the alchemists to disguise their real goals. Paracelsus 1493-1541 was a physician and alchemist.*

attributes as humans are created in the image of God. The sephirot are also considered to be progressive manifestations of the Names of God, emanations that represent the process by which *Ein Sof*[29] (the infinite One) descended from its isolation and made itself known to humanity.

The last *sephira* (*malchut* – מלכות) has the divine name *Shechina*, the presence of God on Earth. The *Shechina* is often considered to be the female aspect of God. In some forms of Kabbalah, she wanders the world, a bride in exile, lost and alienated from the godhead, and yearning to return. By careful observance of divine law, it is believed to be possible to end this exile, and restore the world to God.

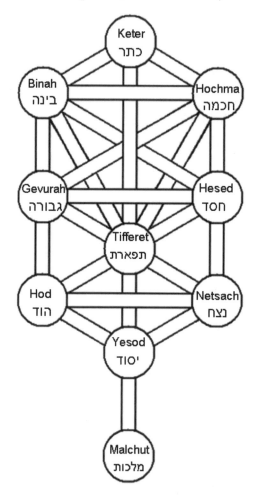

The tree of life showing the 10 Sephirot

This idea can be recognised as a retelling of the pagan myth of the goddess that was anathema to earlier Jews but which has been reinterpreted and made respectable for a Jewish audience. It brought back into Judaism what many considered to be the missing feminine aspect of God.

The following chart gives more details of the various properties that have been attributed to the *Sephirot.*

---

[29] *The kabbalistic God – Ein Sof – is neither male or female. The name means – no end or infinite. It is in many ways similar to the Hindu Brahman (see Chapter 6)*

Sephira in descending order	Psychological attributes	Traditional attributes	Linked Divine name	Male or Female
Keter כתר	Humility Nothingness	Humility Will Consciousness	Ehyeh	Male
Hochma חכמה	Wisdom	Intuitive knowledge	Yah	Male
Binah בינה	Understanding	Cognitive knowledge	Yahweh	Female
Hesed חסד	Altruism	Loving-kindness Mercy	El	Male
Gevurah גבורה	Power Self control	Judgement Power Authority	Elohim	Female
Tifferet תפארת	Harmony	Beauty Emotion Passion Grace	Yahweh	The male principle
Netsach נצח	Focus Integration Building	Endurance Eternity Patience (Victory)	Yahweh Tsevaot	Male
Hod הוד	Empathy	Majesty Splendour	Elohim Tsevaot	Female
Yesod יסוד	Mutuality Sexual relationship	Foundation Creativity Essence Stability	El Hai *or* Shaddai	Female
Malchut מלכות	Female radiance Deep inwardness	Sovereignty Kingdom Shechina	Shechina *or* Adonai	The female principle

For kabbalists, a main aim of worshipping God is to bring about sexual union between the sixth and tenth sephirot - the male and female principles, *Tiferet* and *Shechina*. They symbolise this desired union as they pray by assuming a rocking motion (known as *shockling*), which has become one of the characteristics of the orthodox.

This much simplified overview of Kabbalah and kabbalistic ideas shows it to be a fascinating edifice, with many complexities and subtleties. It also demonstrates it to be a man made construct, based on deep knowledge of Jewish texts and syncretic influences (eastern philosophy, Gnosticism and Hermetic[30] thought) combined with a good measure of imagination. It can be seen to intelligently incorporate many of the aspects of world religion that are absent from normative Judaism. It considers God as apophatic rather than cataphatic. It reintegrates the

---

[30] *Hermeticism is a complex system of thought – one of the main principles of which is, 'as above – so below' (or what happens in the macrocosm [the universe] is replicated in the microcosm [the individual]). This relationship runs in both directions, so by study of one it is considered possible to gain information about the other.*

feminine principle into the godhead. It has tendencies to monism rather than theism – although it is coy about this, because monism is considered heretical. In the mould of eastern religion, a kabbalist ultimately seeks *to receive*[31] a direct experience of God. In this spirit of religious inclusiveness, it also encourages a form of ancestor worship, for the *Zohar* claims that if one prays at the graves of sages their spirits can intercede with God on your behalf.

Kabbalistic Judaism, as practiced by the Hassidic followers of the Baal Shem Tov, is quite different from mainstream Judaism but there is no doubt that many of its followers are spiritually fulfilled by its esoteric practices. Looked at another way, however, Kabbalah is a man made, highly speculative set of ideas, full of magic and superstition, based neither on evidence nor claiming (direct) divine revelation. Like astrology, it can seduce intelligent people into studying its arcane, complex, fascinating and frankly eccentric and spurious ideas.

Its use can lead into dangerous areas. As was mentioned earlier, Lubavitch theology contains what appear to be racist ideas[32] which were derived from an interpretation of Kabbalah. This is another example of one of the main themes of this book, the misinterpretation of texts. If, despite these warnings, the reader wishes to know more there is a huge literature on Kabbalah, much of it wildly spinning off in directions far from its Jewish origins. Kabbalah has been hugely influential on esoteric thought in general and such derivatives as Christian Cabbala,[33] Hermetic Kabbalah and Practical Kabbalah each have their own literature. For a sensible, clear introduction to Jewish Kabbalah, Gershom Scholem's book simply titled 'Kabbalah' would be a good place to start.

---

[31] *The Hebrew root* - ק ב ל - *of the word Kabbalah is from to receive* - לקבל

[32] *For more details on this topic see the appendix p.242*

[33] *It was usual to distinguish between Christian Cabbala and Jewish Kabbalah by the difference of spelling, but recently this seems to be less used. In general though, if spelled with an initial C the reference is to the Christian Cabbala. The occultists sometimes use the spelling Qabalah to distinguish their development of these ideas.*

Afterword

*It's better to debate a question without settling it than to settle a
question without debating it*

Joseph Joubert

It is my hope that before reaching this point, the reader will
have paused to consider her or his own ideas on some of the
topics discussed. If so, then the purpose of the book has been
achieved. This purpose is not necessarily to change the reader's
mind, but to increase awareness that there are alternative opinions,
equally valid for those who hold them.

Some may consider that I have been disloyal to Judaism with several
of the opinions I have expressed in this book. They may consider
that certain basic tenets of the religion, perhaps the unity of God or
the evil of idolatry should not be questioned in the way I have. My
response to this was expressed on page 83, when I explained why a
closed minded or fundamentalist viewpoint cannot be allowed to
limit free debate.

I contend that we must continuously be on our guard against
anyone claiming to know the truth for other people. We cannot
accept arguments along the lines of, 'It is so, because it is the word

of God,' unless accompanied by rational supporting argument as to the morality of the position being advocated. Anyone relying on the 'word of God' argument alone is abdicating making an evaluation of the moral position and is arbitrarily selecting a course to follow. Such a course is only valid for themselves; for anyone else to accept it requires them to take the same leap of faith. Accordingly, it is totally unacceptable for the 'word of God' to be imposed on others.

I would also claim that I am keeping within authentic Jewish tradition. There is a long established Jewish tradition both of asking questions and of not accepting an instruction without due consideration, even if the instruction is from God himself. There is also the ethical tradition of *tikkun*. (The word simply means repair, but must be understood in the broadest possible sense.) *Tikkun* is a practice that starts with each individual, then spreads out to include the Jewish people and finally (and of the greatest importance) spreads out further to affect the whole world. This ultimate ideal of *tikkun olam*, of repairing, fixing and improving the world, is one of the greatest and most important ideas of ethical Judaism.

This sequence is important. The repair starts of necessity with oneself, it next must deal with one's own people and then finally it reaches the target of improving the world. There is no doubt that historically the Jewish people have done a disproportionate amount in working towards this goal, especially after they (for the most part) embraced the freedoms brought about by the Enlightenment.

Whether one looks at Nobel prizes or humanitarian work worldwide, Jews consistently punch above their weight. It is instructive to observe that the Jews who achieve such things are not generally those who look inwards and do not question. They are certainly not those who eschew a secular education for themselves and their children. Those who help humanity to progress are prepared to enter fully into the world and use their rational facilities to try and resolve problems.

It is the important intermediate step of *tikkun Yisrael*, repair of the Jewish world, which I have tried to address in this book. I consider that in today's world, the dangers of closed mindedness and fundamentalism are all too real, and I believe that it is the primary responsibility of those from within each religious tradition to challenge any bigoted and fundamentalist individuals found within their own faith.

It has been argued, and I believe with some validity, that only those with a shared background can successfully challenge their co-religionists with fundamentalist views. It is only moderate Muslims, for example, if they are brave enough to do so, that can challenge the excesses of some of their brethren in their rigid interpretation of the Koran, their shared sacred text.

Similarly, only moderate Christians can challenge the biblical literalists and evangelicals within their communities in order to moderate their dangerous influence. The more extreme evangelical Christians, who are among the greatest lobbyists for Israel in the USA, represent a danger to the world that is not always recognised. They are seen as Zionist, as they encourage Jews to return to Israel but their aim, their hidden agenda, is eschatological. They want to bring about Armageddon,[1] the last battle in which the Earth is destroyed. Accordingly, as examination of their record will show, they are strongly against any movement that may lead to Middle East peace.

It seems they will be (briefly) happy if they can foment a cataclysmic final battle – presumably a nuclear holocaust – for they are confident that they will be among the 'saved'. The vast majority of moderate Christians are rightly appalled by such ideas, but I contend that they have a responsibility to try and reduce their influence.

Similarly, it is the responsibility of moderate Jews to challenge the mistaken and dangerous ideas of our extremists. We must challenge, for example, those in the settler movement who read sacred text literally and know exactly how much real estate God has given them. We also have to deal with those who contend that violence in God's name is sometimes justified and claim to find support for such a position in their interpretation of texts

---

[1] *Armageddon, the place rather than the symbol or myth, is Megiddo, in Northern Israel*

While it is too much to hope that the ideas I have discussed will influence the followers of Baruch Goldstein[2] and Yigal Amir,[3] my hope is that the wider dissemination of these ideas might allow potential future zealots to stop and question their actions rather than take the path of violence and hate. Most importantly, one must try and open the minds of those young people who have never been exposed to these sorts of arguments and this type of evidence. They should be allowed the freedom to evaluate these issues for themselves rather than having no opportunity to do so. It is a truism that the price of freedom is eternal vigilance, and freedom is under as much, if not more, threat now than at any time.

I have no wish to proselytize the secular way among the religious. As has been discussed, the benign practice of religion can be a very positive influence in the lives of many. It all comes back in the end to being aware that what one believes is personal. Because one believes something, it does not make it true for anyone else. None of us is in possession of The Truth for other people, much less for all humanity. There are no final answers. We should all keep asking the questions.

As for my own provisional answer, I agree with Umberto Eco when he wrote:

> *I have come to believe that the whole world is an enigma, a harmless enigma that is made terrible by our own mad attempt to interpret it as though it had an underlying truth.*

This brings me back to another enigma, that of personal spirituality, which has been in the background throughout the book as an alternative to organised religion. This emerges in different ways for all of us, as it is not bound by the straightjacket of dogma or politics. Personally, I understand it as a curiosity about the world, a

---

2 *Baruch Goldstein, an American born physician and member of the settler movement, carried out the Hebron massacre in 1999, when dressed in his Israeli army uniform he murdered 29 Moslems who were at prayer in the Cave of the Patriarchs. His gravesite has become a shrine for those of similar views. A plaque was erected near his grave reading:* 'The holy Baruch Goldstein, who gave his life for the Jewish people, the Torah and the nation of Israel'. *The plaque was later removed, but the grave remains a place of pilgrimage for zealots.*

3 *Yigal Amir, an Israeli-born law student, assassinated Yitzchak Rabin in 1995. Now serving a life sentence in prison, he has attracted a following especially among haredi women, one of whom has married him and had his child, having been allowed conjugal visits.*

willingness in the Buddhist sense to reduce ego and be open to new ideas and to alternative ways of doing things. It is an awareness both that there are things unknown and of the numinous, of nature, love, God or of whatever particular name each of us chooses to give to mystery and beauty. In the end, it is this spirituality that for each of us can light the fire which makes us human.

Appendix

More details and evidence for ideas discussed in the text

The Many Names of God in Judaism (see Chapter 6)

Rabbi Elliott Kleinman compiled the following list of 'names, appellations and descriptions of God' found in our tradition. His list is gathered from the *Siddur*, Torah, Jewish texts and the writings of Jewish theologians.

1. Adonai
2. My Lord
3. The Divinity
4. Mighty One of Jacob
5. Most High
6. God Almighty
7. God of the Covenant
8. Everlasting Rock
9. YHVH
10. Lard of Hosts
11. YAH
12. Holy One
13. Shepherd of Israel
14. King of Israel
15. Creator of All
16. Ruler
17. Guardian of Israel
18. Rock of Israel
19. True God
20. Fear of Isaac
21. Everlasting God
22. God of Vision
23. El
24. Everlasting Ruler
25. Eternal
26. Ancient God
27. I am that I am
28. Creator of Heaven and Earth
29. Holy One of Israel
30. Rock
31. God of Truth
32. Praiseworthy One
33. Shield of Abraham
34. One
35. King of Kings
36. Eternal Father
37. Parent
38. The Name
39. The Place
40. Source
41. Awesome One
42. Eternal One of Israel
43. Lover of God's people Israel
44. Redeemer
45. God of our Ancestors
46. God of Isaac
47. Mighty One
48. Rescuer
49. Merciful
50. Faithful One
51. One who spoke and the world came into being
52. Lord of Hosts
53. Infinite
54. Rock of our Lives
55. Father of Mercy
56. God Who is Merciful
57. Master of All
58. Healer
59. God of Majesty
60. Living God
61. Compassionate One
62. Master of the Universe

63. Bountiful One
64. Generous One
65. Hidden of Hiddens
66. First Cause
67. Power that makes for Salvation
68. God of War
69. Peace
70. Judge of the Earth
71. My Rock
72. Ever-living God
73. Guide
74. God of Abraham
75. God of Jacob
76. Heroic One
77. Living Lord
78. Reviver of the Dead
79. Merciful One
80. Might
81. Possessor of Will
82. Good One
83. Maker of Peace
84. Giver of Knowledge
85. Mighty One of Israel
86. Sovereign
87. Ever-Patient One

This is still only a partial list. I would add the following to Rabbi Kleinman's list, and the reader may know of others:

YHWH-Yireh	The Lord will provide	(Genesis 22:14)
YHWH-Rapha	The Lord that heals	(Exodus 15:26)
YHWH-Niss'i	The Lord our Banner	(Exodus 17:8-15)
YHWH-Shalom	The Lord our Peace	(Judges 6:24).
YHWH-Ra-ah	The Lord my Shepherd	(Psalms 23:1)
YHWH-Tsidkenu	The Lord our Righteousness	(Jeremiah 23:6)
YHWH-Shammah	The Lord is present	(Ezekiel 48:35)
Atik yomav	Ancient of days	(Daniel 7:9)

In early tradition, it would seem that the patriarchs had their own individual personal God. Abraham's God, El, is also referred to separately as the shield (*magen* מגן) of Abraham.[1] Isaac's God is (*Pachad* פחד) fear[2], and Jacob's Mighty One (*Avir* אביר)[3]. Prayers still refer to the God of Abraham, the God of Isaac and the God of Jacob even though later tradition has combined them into the same godhead.

---

[1] *Genesis 15:1*
[2] *Genesis 31:42*
[3] *Genesis 49:24*

The ubiquity of the <u>Golden Rule</u> in world religions and thought

Confucianism

Surely it is the maxim of loving-kindness. Do not unto others that you would not have them do to you.

Analects 12.2 C6 BCE

Zoroastrianism

That nature alone is good which refrains from doing unto another whatsoever is not good for itself.

Dadistan-i-dinik 94,5 ? C6 BCE

Greek thought

How should one behave? We should refrain from doing that which we condemn in others.

Thales of Miletus C6 BCE

Judaism

Love your neighbour as yourself.

Leviticus 19:18 ? C5 BCE (P source)

What is hateful to you do not do to your fellowman. That is the entire Torah, all the rest is commentary. Go study.

Talmud Shabbat 31a [Hillel (30BCE-10CE)]

Buddhism

Hurt not others in ways that you yourself would find hurtful.

Uda-Navarga 5,18 C4 BCE

Hinduism

This is the sum of duty; do naught unto others which would cause pain if done to you.

Mahabharata 5:151 C4 BCE

Taoism

Regard your neighbour's gain as your own gain, and your neighbour's loss as your own loss.

T'ai Shang Kan Ying P'ien C3 BCE

Jainism

In happiness and suffering, in joy and grief, we should regard all creatures as we regard our own self, and should therefore refrain from inflicting upon others such injury as would appear undesirable to us if inflicted upon ourselves.

Yogashastra 2:20 ?C5 BCE

Christianity

Therefore all things whatsoever ye would that man shall do to you, do ye even so unto them, for this is the law of the prophets.

Matthew 7:12 C1 CE

Islam

No one of you is a believer until he desires for his brother that which he desires for himself.

Sahih Muslim bk.1 chap.mm18 C8 CE

Sikhism

As you deem yourself so deem others. Then shall you become a partner in heaven.

Kabir   1500 CE

Immanuel Kant

What you want to be applied to you, you must apply to others.

Groundwork of the Metaphysic of Morals C18 CE

Baha'i

Lay not on any soul a load which you would not wish to be laid upon you, and desire not for anyone the things you would not desire for yourselves. This is my only counsel to you, did you but observe it.

Baha'u'llah gleanings no.66 127-8   C19 CE

The dates given are educated guesswork, as almost all early dates are subjects of debate. Current thinking suggests that Confucius was the earliest, and that they are in approximate chronological order. The ubiquity of this concept is presumably because it attempts to regulate the relations of man and his fellow man, not man and his god.

Older stories 'recycled' by the Bible's authors

The Flood

This is the most famous story we have which is based on known antecedents. The table below compares the two flood stories found in Genesis with their probable Sumerian source.

Flood story detail	Genesis J story	Genesis P story	Gilgamesh / Enuma Elish
Extent of flood	Global	Global	Global
Cause	Human evil	The Earth was corrupted and filled with violence	Man's noise and sins
Intended for whom?	All mankind and animals	Mankind and the Earth	One city and all mankind
Instigator	Yahweh	Elohim	Assembly of Gods
Character of divine instigator	Anthropomorphic	Transcendent controller	Irresponsible
Hero's name	Noah	Noah	Utnapishtim[1]
Hero's character	Righteous	Righteous	Righteous

---

[1] *The protagonist's name changes in different versions of the story. It was Atrahasis in the Akkadian flood story the Enuma Elish (1900-1600 BCE); Ziusudra in a different version; and Utnapishtin (he who found life) in the final version of Gilgamesh from about 700 BCE.*

Detail	Genesis J story	Genesis P story	Gilgamesh / Enuma Elish
Means of announcement	Direct from God	Direct from God	In a dream
Hero ordered to build boat?	Yes	Yes	Yes
Height of boat	Not stated	3 stories (30 cubits)	6 decks below, 7 in all
Compartments inside	Not stated	Many	Many
Doors	Not stated	One	One
Windows	At least one	At least one	At least one
Outside coating	Pitch	Pitch	Pitch
Shape of boat	Not stated	300 x 50 cubits	Square
Human passengers	Noah, 3 sons and 4 wives	Noah, 3 sons and 4 wives	Family, kin and 'craftsmen'
Animal passengers	All species; one pair of unclean, 7 pairs of clean	All species, one pair of each	One pair of each (the seed of all living creatures)
Means of flood	Heavy rain	Ground water and heavy rain	Heavy rain
Duration of flood	Medium (40 days rain, 40 more until dry land)	Long (rain 150 days, one year until dry land)	Short (6 days flood, 7 more until land)
Test to find land	Release of birds	Release of bird	Release of birds
Types of birds	Three doves	Raven	Dove, swallow and raven
Ark landed at	Not stated: 'face of the Earth had dried'	Mountain – Mt Ararat	Mountain – Mt Nisir
Sacrifice after flood	Yes, by Noah	Not stated	Yes, by Utnapishtim
God/s bless the protagonist	Yes	Not stated	Yes, and grant him immortality as a reward
God's sign of good faith	Not stated	I (Elohim) have set My bow in the clouds (rainbow)	Marduk sets his bow in the sky (the star Sirius)
Theological result	Covenant with Noah	God promises never to disturb Earth's climate again	Gods are appalled by the devastation and withdraw from human affairs
Dating of text (approx.)	C9 BCE	C6 BCE	Earliest source 2100 BCE

The J flood story seems firmly based on the Gilgamesh flood myth, while the P story also reflects the worldview of the Mesopotamian creation epic – the Enuma Elish. This is noticeable in P's concept of the windows of heaven opening and the fountains of the great deep being broken up, which mimics the Enuma Elish story of Tiamat's body holding back the forces of chaos, the firmament above and the water's below (great deep).

Creation

P's story of creation (Genesis 1) also closely parallels the Enuma Elish creation story, particularly in the order of creation, as can be seen from the following table:

Enuma Elish creation story order	Genesis 1 (P creation story) order of events
Gods and universe coexist before creation.	God exists before creation; He creates the heavens and Earth.
Initially there is primeval chaos. (Tiamat)	Initially there is primeval chaos. תהו ובהו וחשך על פני תהום
Light emanates from the gods.	God creates light.
Marduk creates the firmament.	God creates the firmament.
Marduk creates land.	God creates land.
Marduk and Aruru create humans from clay.	God creates human beings in his image.
Gods rest and celebrate.	God rests on the seventh day.

Other stories, texts and traditions current in the region in pre-biblical times which appear to be utilised in writing the Bible

Extra-biblical tradition	Bible story
The vassal treaty between Assyria and her subject people	Deuteronomic covenant between Yahweh and Israel is strikingly similar in form and layout.
King Sargon 1st of Akkad (2371-2316 BCE) was said to have been placed in a basket of rushes coated with pitch by his mother (a priestess whose children were destined for sacrifice) and placed in the river, to be found by a princess and brought up in a royal palace.	The identical story is told of Moses. A significant detail is that the pitch coating is retained in the story. Pitch (tar) was common in the Tigris Euphrates region where the Sargon story is set but not in the Nile area of Moses' story. (The Egyptians had to import pitch from the Dead Sea area and there is no evidence that this occurred before Ptolemaic times.)
Early Ugarit literature has stories of local gods granting fertility to kings who have difficulty producing heirs, e.g. the mythical kings Akhat & Kerit.	Bible has several similar stories of God intervening to grant fertility to wives of important figures who are unable to conceive.

Extra-biblical tradition	Bible story
Hammurabi law code (c. 1700 BCE)	Many striking similarities with biblical law code[2] both in wording and content
Widespread custom of first born son being dedicated to local god (often to serve in the temples)	Custom continued (Exodus 13) Redemption of the first born procedure introduced to get around it (Numbers 18:15-16)

Political 'spin' in the *Tanach*.

Issue & reference	Known history	Biblical story
Hezekiah against Assyria ---------- 2 Kings 19:32-37	Hezekiah's revolt against Assyria was a disaster. Sennacherib conquered all cities of Judah except Jerusalem. He withdrew only after receiving tribute. About 20 years later, he was killed by his sons in a palace coup.	Implies that Hezekiah effectively defied the Assyrians, and further that Sennacherib retreated to Nineveh, and while there was immediately assassinated (as an implied punishment).
Pharaoh Shoshenk in Canaan ---------- 1 Kings 14:25-26	Shishak left full records of his campaign in Canaan (c. 925 BCE) in which he lists battles at Megiddo & other places, but not Jerusalem. If (as the Bible states) he was victorious and carried off such a treasure, it would certainly be recorded there as his triumph.	Shishak (Shoshenk) is mentioned in the Bible as successfully invading Jerusalem, and carrying off treasure from the temple and King Reheboam's palace. (This 'accounts' for the loss of the 'great treasures' of Solomon's Temple.)

J, E, D and P, the Biblical spin doctors (see Chapters 3 & 5)

This table summarises the traits and political biases that can be found influencing the texts of the four main biblical schools of writers.

	J	E	D	P
Kingdom	Judea (Southern)	Israel (Northern)	Judea - after North destroyed	Judea - most likely after North destroyed
Name for God	Yahweh	Elohim before epiphany at Horeb, then Yahweh	Yahweh your/our God.	Elohim before epiphany at Sinai, then Yahweh
Holy mountain	Sinai	Horeb	Horeb	Sinai
Favoured patriarch / matriarch	Abraham / Leah	Jacob / Rebekka	------------	------------

---

[2] *See 'The Ancient Near East - Volume 1. An Anthology of Texts and Pictures. James B. Pritchard. Princeton Univ. Press 1958' for details of Hammurabi's code and a detailed comparison with biblical laws.*

	J	**E**	**D**	**P**
Favoured tribe or group	Judah	Ephraim (tribe of King Jereboam)	Levites	Priests
Holiness or holy symbol in desert	Ark of the Covenant (associated with the Temple)	Tabernacle (associated with Shiloh)	You are a holy people (Deuteronomy 7:6)	Must aspire to holiness, - 'You shall be holy.' Leviticus 19:2
Priestly group	Aaron (temple)	Moses (Shiloh)	Moses (Shiloh)	Aaron
Treatment of Levites	Dispersed for massacre at Shechem	Favourable to	Favourable to	Separate them and make inferior to Aaronid family.
Treatment of Moses	Yahweh is the protagonist of the Exodus, Moses is a hero, but not highly promoted.	Personality highly developed, and story includes mythological elements (birth etc.) Miracles with Moses' staff.	Personality highly developed	Acknowledged but denigrated to a degree e.g. in striking rock incident, & Aaron developed as priestly hero.
Treatment of Aaron	Does not appear	Denigrated (Golden calf & snow white Miriam). Aaron is a Levite brother with only a minor role.	Denigrated	Important role. Frequent use of 'Yahweh said to Moses and Aaron,' Aaron a full brother & the firstborn. Miracles with Aaron's staff.
Role of Joshua	No role	Moses' faithful assistant, and the only Israelite not involved with the golden calf.	No role	No role
Covenant with	Abraham	Moses	Moses and David	No covenant at all. ארון העדות is often translated Ark of the Covenant but עדות is different to ברית- its meaning is more like a pact or treaty.
Creation order	Earth - Heaven - Man - Plants – Animals – Woman	------------	-----------	Heaven - Earth - Plants - Animals - Man and Woman
Surety for Benjamin and Joseph saved by	Judah	Reuven (the firstborn)	------------	------------
Receiver of Jacob's birthright	Judah (4th born) Reuben, Simeon & Levi disqualified. (Genesis 49)	Grandson Ephraim [Jereboam's tribe] via Joseph. (Genesis 48)	------------	------------
Wording of prohibition against idols.	Molten Gods (so painted Temple Cherubim are acceptable)	Gods of silver and Gods of gold (doubt cast on Cherubim)	------------	------------

	J	E	D	P
Treatment of Shechem (Northern Capital)	Negative. [Gen. 34] Obtained by massacre of inhabitants.	Positive. Land bought by Jacob [Gen 33:19]	Only one place acceptable for worship. (Jerusalem). (Deut 12)	------------
Name for Jacob	Jacob	Israel	------------	------------
Type of Deity	Highly anthropomorphic God with close relationship with humans. Other gods are acknowledged.	Distant God, speaks to man through dreams or via angels or prophets. Other gods are acknowledged.	Invisible. Eliminates anthropomorphic representation of God	No anthropomorphic qualities, His only action / function is to command.
Literary habits	Draws richly on place names & etymologies. God seen in strongly anthropomorphic terms.	Promotion of the second son (Isaac, Jacob, Abel, and Ephraim).	Text purged of polytheistic and henotheistic traces.	Centralisation is assumed as the status quo. Strong interest in order, boundaries & quantifying (measurements ages dates etc.)
Other items appearing primarily in this text (Political spin)	Strong bias to the Davidic line of Kings	Tribe of Ephraim particularly favoured.	Law of the King. Pro-Josiah reforms. Centralisation of the religion and of the temple. Social welfare & human rights laws.	Tabernacle stressed. Temple based religious system a priority. Stresses a separate and holy people so that Yahweh can live among them (in exile.)
Linguistic & dating	**Earliest stage biblical Hebrew.** Probably E composed in the early 8th century BCE, with J following after the destruction of the Northern Kingdom in 722 BCE. Some earlier poems are incorporated in these texts.		**Later stage Hebrew** (though earlier than Ezekiel which is exilic) Composed in the 7th century BCE	**Still later stage Hebrew.** Some older sources, but took its final form during and after the Exiles.
Sacrifice	Passim	Passim	Passim	Only by Aaron and his direct descendants. Very important as this is the only way to obtain forgiveness.

Charts showing evidence for issues referred to in Chapter 3

i. Examples of anachronisms in the text of the *Tanach*

Text states	Reference(s)	Detail
Money	Genesis 42:35(E), Genesis 44:1(J)	The first coins were introduced by the Lydian King Croesus c. 680 BCE, so money could not have been 'put in the mouth of the bag' by Joseph.

Text states	Reference(s)	Detail
Ur of the Chaldees	Genesis 11:28 (R) Genesis 11:31 (R)	The earliest Chaldean (Persian) influence in the area around Ur was around 1100 BCE, much too late for Terach and Abraham. When this text was composed it showed (anachronistically) the patriarch coming from a place which was of high status at the time of writing, but not at the time described.
Kiriat Arba now Hebron	Genesis 23:2 (P)	Kiryat Arba became Hebron after the time ascribed to Moses (See also Joshua 14:15)
Land of the Philistines	Genesis 21:34 (E) Genesis 26:1 (J) Exodus 13:17 (E) passim	The Philistines earliest date of settlement in the Levant was around 1200 BCE, so they could not have interacted with the patriarchs, nor could the Exodus be routed through their territory, nor be written of by Moses. The authors of the J and E texts, writing later, probably assumed that the Philistines had always been in the land.
Nebuchadnezzar *or* Nebuchadrezzar	with **r** or **ר** Ezekiel 26:7, Jeremiah 21:7 with **n** or **נ** Jeremiah 27:6 19,29:3, 2 Kings 24:1, 10,11, 25:1,8	The actual King's name was Nabu-kudurri-usur, which is written in Hebrew נבוכדראצר – Nebuchadrezzar. Contemporary writings would use this spelling. The Greeks later called him Nabuchodonosor, which became נבוכדנאצר – Nebuchadnezzar in Hebrew. In this form it shows Greek influence (so must date after 331 BCE). At the very least, this confirms later editing.
Camels	Widespread from the time of patriarchs on	Camels were not domesticated until 1100 BCE, and uncommon until about 800 BCE. The patriarchs would not have used them.
before any King ruled over the Israelites	Genesis 36:31	*These are the Kings who reigned in the land of Edom before any King ruled over the Israelites.* Logically, this had to be written after at least one King reigned in Israel, giving an earliest date of about 900 BCE, or 150 years earlier if the United Monarchy is accepted.
In those days there was no King in Israel	Judges 17:6, 18:1, 19:1, 21:25	Similarly, this only makes sense when there already is (or had been) a King. (The spin being to promote Kingship as the ideal).
Solomon's horses	Deuteronomy 17:17-18	Strange anachronistic reference by Moses to Solomon's horses, probably intended as a diatribe against the contemporary (to the writer) Egyptian diaspora Jews
Dan	Genesis 14:14	Dan was known as Laish in Moses' time.

Text states	Reference(s)	Detail
Until this day עד היום הזה	Deuteronomy 34:6 Joshua 8:29;14:14 1 Kings 9:13 2 Kings 17:23 1 Samuel 27:5-6 passim.	This commonly used phrase that something occurred which is so *until today*, proves the text was written after the event. If it then later ceased to be correct, then we have a window of time when this logically must have been written. For example, if we read, *'the city became known as Leningrad, as it is to this day'*, we can date this writing to the 20th Century.[3]
No record in the *Tanach* of the Egyptian occupation of Canaan	Silence	Not even a 'background noise' to give any impression that Canaan was under Egyptian control between the 16th and 12th centuries BCE. This silence is evidence of the non-historical nature of the stories.
King of Edom	Numbers 20:14-21	Edom did not have a King (and was not a state) until 7th C BCE.
Place names mentioned during Exodus and conquest		Many, such as Migdol and Kadesh-Barnea, which have been positively identified, did not exist until much later. (See also chart p.237)
Canaanites were *then* in the land	Genesis 12:26	Logically this must have been written at a time when the Canaanites were no longer in the land (therefore not by Moses).
Attribution of authorship to Moses	Silence in the Torah	The first reference citing Moses is post exilic (Ezra 7:6 and Nehemiah 8:1). The Babylonian Talmud (BB 14b) is the first to explicitly attribute the authorship of the entire Torah to Moses as the Divine's scribe.

ii. Duplications, contradictions & inconsistencies in *Tanach*

Example	Reference/s	Details
Capture of Jerusalem: Before Joshua's death	Joshua 12:8 Joshua 12:10	Jebus (Jerusalem) is given with other land to the Israelites; the King of Jerusalem listed among the defeated.
After Joshua's death	Joshua 15:63 Judges 1:8	*Joshua*: Tribe of Judah could not drive out the Jebusites, who remain there 'to this day'. *Judges*: Men of Judah took Jerusalem after Joshua's death.
By King David	2 Samuel 5:5-7	Jebus is still a Canaanite city until captured by David and made capital.
Naming of Beersheba	Genesis 21:31 (E) Genesis 26:33 (J)	Abraham and Abimelech swear a treaty. (E) or, Isaac's servants dig a well. (J)

---

[3] *See Finkelstein – David and Solomon pp193-194 for his explanation how this phrase is used to date 7th century BCE writing about earlier 9th century events.*

Example	Reference/s	Details
Plague of blood	Exodus 7:14-24	Two stories (J & P) are intertwined. In J Moses is the protagonist and blood only affects the Nile, in P Aaron also appears and all of Egypt's water is affected.
Who killed Goliath?	1 Samuel 17 vs. 2 Samuel 21:19	The famous story gives David the credit, but 2 Samuel 21:19 says it was Elchanan ben Yair. In the David story note that Goliath is only named at the beginning. During the fight he is only referred to as *the Philistine*. See the author's comments on p.52
Abimelech and the matriarchs. Stories of a patriarch passing his wife off as his sister.	Genesis 20 (E) Genesis 26:6-11(J)	In E's story Abraham passes off Sarah to Abimelech as his sister, for J it is Isaac passing off Rebecca. Abimelech would hardly fall for the same trick twice! (n.b. In Genesis 12 (J) Sarah is also passed off to Pharaoh as Abraham's sister, and Pharaoh takes Sarah for a time as a wife. Would Sarah allow this to happen to her once, much less twice?)
Benjamin and sons	Genesis 43:8, 44:32-34 (J) as boy; Genesis 46:21 (P) as father	In the J story when Benjamin is taken to Egypt by his brothers at Joseph's bidding he is clearly a youth - נער. By the time he returns with Jacob, he has (in the P story) fathered 10 sons (daughters are not mentioned in this list). This all supposedly occurred within the remaining 5 years of the famine.
Moses' death	Deuteronomy 34:5-12 (D)	Could Moses write of *this*? Same style as rest of D's writing. 'His burial place is unknown *to this day*'. Could anyone write that of himself!?
Moses- a very humble man	Numbers 12:3	Could he write this?
Contradictory laws	Exodus12:9 vs. Deuteronomy 16:7.\n\nExodus 21:1-11 vs. Leviticus 25:39-41 vs. Deut. 15:12-18.	These are two examples of laws that differ in significant details as to how they should be observed. The first relates to how the Passover sacrifice should be cooked, the second to treatment of slaves. (The differences include how slaves should be released, and while Exodus differentiates between treatment of male and female, Deuteronomy treats them the same.[4]) The different laws clearly come from different sources and the existence of many such detailed differences made the Oral Law essential as a code for practical observance.
Capture of Hazor and other cities	Joshua 11:1-11 Judges 4:23-24	Hazor; Captured by Joshua, or in the time of Deborah and Barak? Other examples; Gezer; Joshua 12:12 vs. Judges 1:29; Taanach and Megiddo; Joshua 12:21 vs. Judges 1:27; Dor; Joshua 12:23 vs. Judges 1:27
Pathogens	Genesis 1 & 2	On which day did God create bacteria, viruses, parasites etc.?

---

[4] see *Jewish Study Bible p.4 for more detail*

Example	Reference/s	Details
Egyptian cattle have three lives	Exodus 9:6 Exodus 9:19, Exodus 9:25 Exodus 11:5	All of Egypt's livestock were killed by the 5th plague. The 7th plague then killed (again) all livestock not taken to a place of shelter and finally the 10th plague killed (once more) the firstborn of all the cattle. A clear case of overkill!
Sun stands still	Joshua 10:13	This uses the flat Earth cosmology of the author's time. This cosmology is also apparent in Genesis 1:14-18 where the sun is put in the sky after the Earth already exists and also in Ecclesiastes 1:5 where the sun appears to go round the Earth.
Shabbat (not observed)	Numbers 7	Puzzling.
Who rescues Joseph?	Genesis 37:20-24, 28a, 29-30 vs. Genesis 37:25-27,28b	Reuben, who threw him into a pit to be rescued by Midianites, *or* Judah, who sold him to Ishmaelites.
Number of tribes	Song of Deborah (Judges 5:2-31)	This poem is a very early text and lists only 10 tribes, of which only 8 match the 12 found elsewhere in the text and generally accepted.
Iron chariots	Exodus 14:25 vs. Judges 1:19	God could make the wheels fall off the Egyptian chariots but surprisingly those of the Canaanites of the plain defeated him.
Two flights of Hagar	Genesis 16:6-16 vs. Genesis 21:9-21	Did Sarah send Hagar away twice?
Jacob acquires wealth	Genesis 31:25-43 vs. Genesis 31:9,11ff	By his own cunning *or* by advice of an angel in a dream?
Benjamin's benefactor	Genesis 42:37 vs. Genesis 43:9	Reuben offers a surety *or* perhaps it was Judah?
The Torah was written down in the time of Moses and has remained unchanged until today	This is not claimed in the text, but has become a matter of dogma in post-Talmudic times. Linguistically this is not possible as some of the language used did not exist in Moses' time, and with what characters was it written down?	At the time ascribed to Moses, the Phoenician alphabet (from about 1800) BCE was the first true consonantal alphabet in which the Torah could have been written. However, this developed far from Egypt, and given Moses' background (if literate) he would have been more likely to have known Egyptian hieroglyphic writing. Proto-Hebrew, which dates from about 900 BCE, is the earliest form of Hebrew in which it could possibly have been recorded but this is too late for Moses. The alphabet the *Tanach* is now written in only dates from around 400 BCE. The language and vocabulary of the Torah varies according to the source, but is invariably that of the time the source was writing. Many of the words and usages of the *Tanach* are much later than those of Moses' time.

Chart showing details and references for issues raising moral problems in the Bible (see pp. 97-100)

	Details	Comment	Reference(s)
a.	Genocide, arrogance and cruelty	Jericho, Lachish, Gibea, Makkedah, Libnah, Gezer, Ai, Eglon, Hebron, Debir, Hazor and land of Negeb - all the population put to the sword	Deuteronomy 7:17-24 The entire book of Joshua
	Morality of war and treatment of civilians	The text says it all	Joshua 8:18-29 (6:21, 10:6, 11:20 et seq.) Numbers 31:9-54
b.	Punishment of children for parent's crimes	Clearly a widespread concept in biblical times	Exodus 20:5,34:7 Numbers 14:8 Zephaniah 1:8
	Levirate marriage & *Halitzah*	Levirate marriage followed Iron Age inheritance traditions The *halitzah* ceremony is demeaning and cruel towards all concerned	Deuteronomy 25:5-10
c.	Slavery	Slavery was normal and acceptable in biblical times. In Numbers 31:29 some of the slaves being distributed were given to Eliezer the high priest. The fate of these 32 virgins is not recorded but there is a clear implication of human sacrifice, for the Midianite women would not have been allowed to serve near the holy cult objects	Exodus 21:2-11, 20-21, 26-27 Deuteronomy 15:12-18 (Hebrew slaves) Leviticus 25:44-46 Numbers 31:25-30
d.	Er and Onan	Spilling of seed, is this a capital offence?	Genesis 38:7-10
e.	Homosexuality	A capital offence? Times and attitudes have changed	Leviticus 18:22, 20:13
f.	Trial by ordeal	Justice systems have moved on	Numbers 5:11-31 Exodus 32:20
g.	Infertility as punishment	If Israelites are blessed with no infertility, logically this must be used to punish others	2 Samuel 6:23 Deuteronomy 7:14-15
	Treatment of leprosy	Priest as dermatologist! Can this 'treatment' of Leviticus 13:45 be considered morally acceptable, much less valid for all time?	Leviticus 13 – entire chapter
	Treatment of disabled	There are civil laws against this type of discrimination today	Leviticus 21:17-23

	Details	Comment	Reference(s)
h.	Women's role	Women's roles are those of ancient Middle Eastern societies	Genesis 3:16 Leviticus 6:11, 12:1-5, 27:3-7 Numbers 5:31
i	Mistreatment of children		
i(1)	Killing of children	Collective punishment: Aachen's children were stoned to death with him, after he was guilty of looting	Joshua 7:24-26
		Job's children were killed to test Job	Job 1:18-19
i(2)	Babies killed	Psalmist encourages the murder of Babylonian babies as reprisal	Psalm 137:9
i(3)	Non-virgin brides	An offence? A capital offence!!!	Deuteronomy 22:20-21
i(4)	Human sacrifice	Jephthah's daughter accepted by God as a sacrifice	Judges 11:39
		The King of Moab's sacrifice of his first born son is apparently accepted	2 Kings 3:27
		See also Midianite women (c above)	
i(5)	Elisha's curse	Excessive punishment for teenager's high jinks	2 Kings 2:23-24
i(6)	Rebellious son	Stoned to death - excessive (see Chapter 10 for discussion)	Deuteronomy 21:18-21
j.	Other examples of dubious morality		
j(1)	Rape of Dinah & aftermath	Indefensible	Genesis 34
j(2)	Elijah	Slaughter of Baal's priests	1 Kings 18:40
j(3)	Saul	Murder for foreskins	1 Samuel 18:25-27
j(4)	David	Treatment of Uriah	2 Samuel 11:5-27
j(5)	Male rape avoided	Unspeakable, especially the treatment of the unnamed concubine	Genesis 19:4-8, Judges 19:22-30
j(6)	Amalek	Genocide is morally unacceptable, however evil the people.[5] We have to judge people individually, not according to ethnicity	Exodus 17:14 1 Samuel 15

---

[5] *As stated in the main text, I would read Amalek as a metaphor for evil, rather than as a real people. With this reading it is more acceptable.*

Timeline of historical events in the Levant most relevant to Jewish History from 2000 BCE to 135 CE

Age	Dominant power	BCE	Event
Middle bronze	Canaanites	2000	
		1750-1540	Canaanites became Hyksos Kings in Egypt
Late bronze	Egypt	1480	Tuthmoses 3rd expelled Hyksos and Egyptians occupy Canaan. Battle of Megiddo 1483
		14th C.	Amarna letters – first record of the *Habiru*
	Egypt / Hittites	1289	Battle of Kadesh. Egypt vs. Hittites. No victor, treaty signed 1275
		1210	Merneptah Stele – the first record of the name *Israel* This name refers to a people not a land
Iron	Philistines on coast	1200	Invasion of sea peoples (Philistines and others)
		1150-950	Egyptians withdraw from Canaan (1150) leading to a 200 year recession in hill country
	Philistines	1080-1030	Philistines expand East, and begin fighting with hill people
	Egypt / Philistines	926	Pharaoh Shishak (Shoshenk)'s campaign in Canaan
Middle iron	Assyria	885	King Omri (885-874) sets up the first Kingdom of Israel.
		853	Battle of Qarqar King Ahab (874-853) and allies hold off Assyria's Shalmanasar III
	Assyria / Arameans	835	Arameans under King Hazael invade, occupy and destroy the north-east of Israel
	Assyria	820	Assyrians take Damascus, end Aramean power; this leads to a resurgence in Israel
		760	Severe earthquake in Judah Jerusalem left relatively unscathed
		747	Tiglath-Piliser 3rd gains power in coup in Assyria and in 738 starts campaign to conquer and annex Assyria's vassal states.
		743-729	King Ahaz of Judah In the first external reference to Judah he is recorded as paying tribute to Assyria
		737	Military coup in Israel, Pekah usurps throne. Unsuccessfully attacks Assyria
		730	Hoshea assassinates Pekah, becomes vassal King of Israel, then rebels against Assyria
		722	In response Shalmaneser 5th of Assyria conquers Shechem. Israel ceases to exist
		729-686	Hezekiah King of Judah. Judah prospers initially with influx of refugees from Israel

		705	Sennacherib comes to power in Assyria. Hezekiah rebels against him and in 701 loses Lachish and much of his territory to Assyria. Only Jerusalem and Judean hills to the south remain under Hezekiah's control
	Babylon and Egypt	696-642	Manasseh King of Judah (first 10 years as co-regent) His reign was a peaceful one, and time of recovery. Judah expands and trade increases. Despite this he gets a terrible 'review' in the *Tanach* for restoring religious pluralism
	Babylon	639-608	Josiah King of Judah Purges religious shrines, centres the religion in Jerusalem. Killed in Battle of Megiddo by Necho leaving Judah briefly under Egyptian control
		605	Nebuchadnezzar of Babylon crushes the Egyptians at the battle of Carcamesh (Syria). Egyptians withdraw
Late iron		597	Jerusalem besieged and captured
	Persia	586	Judah's vassal king Zedakiah rebels against Babylon. Jerusalem destroyed Babylonian exile begins
		539	Cyrus of Persia conquers Babylon. Some exiles return to the (now) Persian province of Yehud
		458	Ezra (on behalf of Artaxerxes I) promulgates the Torah as the authoritative civil law in Yehud
Classical	Greece	332	Alexander's conquest starts the Classical Age
		323	Death of Alexander leads to power struggle between his generals
	Ptolemies (Greeks from Egypt)	312	Ptolemy I wins Battle of Gaza and takes control of Judea
		301	Ptolemy I defeats Antigonus at Battle of Ipsus consolidating power in Judea for 100 years (Ptolemies win 5 more wars during this century)
		c. 280-260	Translation of the Torah into Greek (Septuagint) Other books of the *Tanach* were later added
	Seleucids (Greeks from Asia)	200	Antiochus I defeats Ptolemies at battle of Panion, and Judea moves to Seleucid control
		173	Maccabean revolt begins with political assassination by Matthias Hasmon
		167	Jerusalem sacked and the temple defiled by Antiochus Epiphanes
		164	Maccabees victorious Temple rededicated Judas ha'Macabee King
	Greece waning / Rome rising	142	Simon ha'Maccabee obtains independence (complete freedom from tribute)
		134-104	Yehohanan (John) Hyrcanus King expands Jewish territory with military campaigns and the forced conversion of conquered peoples

		128	Campaign against Samaritans by John Hyrcanus He destroys their temple on Mt. Gerizim, and tries to eliminate these 'heretics' who would not accept the centrality of Jerusalem or any sacred text other than the Torah
		104-76	Alexander Jannaeus King Jewish proselytising and expansion continues
	Rome	63 BCE	End of independence as Romans arrive in Jerusalem, Judea becomes a vassal kingdom again
		66-73 CE	(First) Jewish Revolt against Rome. Temple destroyed in 70 CE
		115-117 CE	Kitos War (Second Jewish Revolt)
		135 CE	Bar Kochba revolt In the aftermath of this third rebellion, Hadrian tried to expunge Judaism. Jerusalem was renamed Aelia Capotolina, and crucially Iudaea (Judea) was wiped off maps (to remove the memory) and replaced by the name Syria Palestina

Summary of the archæological evidence concerning the biblical account of the Exodus and conquest[6]   (all dates BCE)

Site	Biblical account	Archæological evidence	Agree-ment
Jericho (Tel-es-Sultan)	Major, strongly fortified city captured and burnt by Joshua (Joshua 12:9; 6; 24:11)	Destroyed around 1500 Neither walls nor evidence of significant settlement in the Late Bronze Age[7]	No
Ai (et-Tel?)	Major, strongly fortified city captured, burnt and permanently ruined (Joshua 7:2-8:29)	No evidence of fortification or of any occupation in the second millennium Abandoned before 2000	No
Bethel (Beitin?)	Captured by the tribe of Joseph; inhabitants slaughtered (Judges 1:22-26)	At Beitin is evidence of a tremendous conflagration at Late Bronze Age level. (dated to late 13th century)	Possible
Hazor (Tel-el Qedah)	A royal city captured and burnt by Joshua, but subsequently reoccupied by Canaanites (Joshua 11:10-12; Judges 4-5)	A Late Bronze Age destruction level found, but no evidence of subsequent reoccupation	Partially possible

---

[6] Based on 'The Exodus Enigma, Ian Wilson, Weidenfeld & Nicolson 1985', and updated by data from 'Who were the early Israelites and where did they come from? William G. Dever, Erdmans 2003.'
[7] Late Bronze Age – 1500-1200 BCE

Site	Biblical account	Archæological evidence	Agreement
Debir (Tel-el -Rabud	A royal city captured and inhabitants slaughtered (Joshua 10:39, Judges 1:11)	No destruction at the end of the Late Bronze Age	No
Gibeon	Population enslaved, but city apparently saved (Joshua 9: 10)	No evidence of significant Late Bronze Age occupation	No
Arad (Tel Malhata)	Arad's king defeated in battle shortly before main Israelite invasion (Joshua 12:14; Numbers 21:2-3)	No evidence of existence in Late Bronze Age	No
Lachish (Tel ed-Duweir)	Captured and the inhabitants slaughtered (Joshua 10:31-32)	City VII destruction was accompanied by a great conflagration dated to reign of Ramses II (late 13th century) City VI was destroyed c. 1150)	Faintly possible
Hebron	An Anakim city Captured and inhabitants slaughtered (Joshua 10:36-37)	No evidence of Late Bronze Age occupation	No
Hormah (Tel Masos or Khirbet el Meshiah)	A Canaanite city (Zephath) captured and renamed by the tribe of Judah (Judges 1:17; Numbers 14:21)	No evidence of existence in Late Bronze Age	No
Dan (Tel Dan)	Formerly known as Laish captured and burnt by Danite tribe, inhabitants killed, then town rebuilt for Danite occupation (Judges 18:27)	Evidence of slight cultural change in Late Bronze Age, but no fire	No

Alternative Texts of the Torah & Tanach

1. **Septuagint** - a Greek translation from the Hebrew of the Pentateuch made in the third century BCE. It is so named because it was (supposedly) made by 70 (or by some accounts 72 men, 6 from each tribe). According to legend, these scholars worked independently and produced translations that miraculously agreed word for word. It was universally regarded by Christians and Jews as *the* Old Testament until several centuries after Christ. The writers of the New Testament relied on it and often quoted it verbatim, and chronologists based their ancient dates upon it. Then the Jews, disliking its association with Christianity, retranslated it to be less favourable to Christianity and gradually abandoned it. Western Christians began using the Latin Vulgate, based on Hebrew rather

than Greek texts, as variations began to creep into the copies of the Septuagint but Eastern Christians, who spoke Greek for many centuries, continued using the Septuagint. It was supposedly commissioned by Ptolemy II Philadelphus of Egypt (285-247 BCE). Other books of the Hebrew Bible were later added to the translation.

2. **Samaritan** - an obscure and relatively uninfluential Hebrew text of the Pentateuch (Torah) preserved quite independently by descendents of the Israelites of the Northern Kingdom (Samaria). After a schism caused by the Southerners centring the religion on Jerusalem (rather than the Samaritans' Mount Gerizim), the Samaritans rejected the authority of the kingdom of Judah and of all the scriptures after Joshua and followed their separate version. This is written in their own Hebrew script which is much older than the one we are familiar with, having evolved directly from Phoenician around the 9th century BCE and is very similar to ancient

A page of Samaritan Torah

Hebrew. Our familiar square script developed much later, evolving via Aramaic and first being used around 400 BCE. The Samaritan text differs from the Masoretic text in about 6000 details. Many are orthographic (different ways of writing the same word). In 1900 cases, the Samaritan agrees with the Septuagint while the Masoretic text differs. This proves the antiquity of the Samaritan version.

3. **Masoretic** - a Hebrew text meticulously compiled by Jewish scholars between the sixth and tenth centuries CE, with numerous devices to ensure that no error in transcription could go undetected. These scholars introduced the *nekudot* (vowel pointing), paragraphs, and *parashot* (divisions in the text). Most Western Bibles, including the King James, were translated from the Masoretic text or from St. Jerome's Latin Vulgate, which in turn drew mainly from it. Jews consider this text to be the true, original Old Testament, and most modern scholars are strongly biased in its favour, despite the

millennium of precedence of the Septuagint. It is said that these Hebrew Scriptures were smuggled out of Jerusalem during the Roman siege of AD 70 by a priest hiding in a coffin. When he escaped, they were copied and compiled for the first time into the modern Old Testament, with the apocrypha rejected as non-canonical and removed. The earliest extant Hebrew text is from the 10th century CE and is in St. Petersburg.

Development of the Talmud

After the failed Bar Kochba revolt (135 CE) the **Tannaim**[8] began compiling the materials of the *Mishnah* (the Oral Law). This was redacted by Hillel's descendent Rabbi Judah ha-Nassi around 200 CE. The *Mishnah* consists of six *sedarim* (orders) which together contain sixty three tractates. The *sedarim* are:

- Zeraim – deals with the holiness of the land and agricultural practice
- Mo'ed – festival observance
- Nashim – women (and men's rights over them!)
- Nezekim – damages, tort and contract (*pirke avot* [sayings of the fathers] is rather oddly included here).
- Kedoshim – holy ritual in the Temple
- Toharot – deals with holiness of the people and laws of ritual purity

Around 250 CE *pirke avot* gave the *Mishnah* a pedigree by creating a (mythic) lineage from Moses at Sinai all the way down to the Tannaim along which the Oral Law had been transmitted. This gave it equal weight with the Torah.

In the third to fifth centuries the **Amoraim** produced two versions of the *Gemarra* (an elaboration of and a commentary on the *Mishnah*) in Palestine the *Yerushalmi*[9] and Babylon (the *Bavli*). The *Yerushalmi* was closed around 425, the *Bavli* after 500. Nothing is known of the individuals responsible for the editing involved in these works. The *Gemarra* made more reference to *Tanach* (especially the *Yerushalmi*) but this was still not by any means central.

---

[8] *Tannaim, Amoraim, Savoraim and Gaonim were all schools of Rabbis who contributed to the Talmud. Tannaim means 'repeaters' for they originally recited the Mishnah orally, before committing it to writing.*
[9] *Yerushalmi - the Palestinian Talmud was named for Jerusalem but was composed in the Galilee.*

The 'basic' Talmud consists of *Mishnah* and *Gemarra*. Commentaries continued to be added. In the sixth century, the **Savoraim** in Babylon completed the ordering of the Talmud and added additional material. From the seventh century, the **Gaonim** took over.

The Talmud did not start by taking the Torah text and interpreting how it should be applied. It worked from the *Mishnah*, which by then had been accepted as the Oral Law. It has a definite bias towards temple practice, so presumably it was hoped to reinstitute this at some stage.

Lubavitch theology of the soul

(see Chapter 7 – Chosen People and Chapter 12 - Superstition)

Rabbi Shneur Zalman of Liady, the founder of Chabad and Lubavitch, expounded the kabbalistic doctrine of two souls in the opening two chapters of *Tanya* (Chabad's central text – first published 1797). This states that every Jew possesses two souls.

One is the godly or divine, soul – an actual portion of God above. This is the seat of spiritual and self sacrificing impulses. This soul strives ever upward towards its divine source. Only Jews possess this and so are capable of such striving. The second is the animal soul or life force. This is the seat of our natural and baser impulses and life preserving instincts. All human beings have an animal soul, which originates in the realm of the *kelipot* (see Kabbalah section) the shells or husks which can be considered as the source of evil. Not all animal souls are equal, however. For a Jew they originate in *kelipat nogah* in which good and evil are mixed, while a gentile's animal soul derives from three impure *kelipot* which are totally evil.

As a result, non-Jews (according to the *Tanya*) are incapable of truly doing good deeds. Any good they do is for their own sake, their self-glorification. This racist theology would imply that non-Jews are essentially born impure.

Examples of superstition in the *Tanach* (see Chapter 12)

Superstition and folklore.	Reference	Detail
Nephilim	Genesis 6:4	These are a mythological remnant - supernatural beings that have sex with women. They are sometimes considered as giants - the aboriginal people of Canaan.
Old folk tale recycled	Genesis 37:37-42	Contemporary folk belief that if sheep see spots when copulating their offspring will be spotted
Mandrakes	Genesis 30:15	Mandrakes were thought (as they are shaped like mini-humans) to be aphrodisiac and to enhance fertility.
Household gods - Teraphim	Genesis 31:19-35	Rachel stole her father's (Laban's) household gods. As well as being symbols of luck, possession of these artefacts had significance for inheritance in ancient society.
Idolatry/folk medicine - Nehushtan	Numbers 21:9 \n\n 2 Kings 18:4	This idol (bronze serpent) made by Moses at Yahweh's instruction, was destroyed by Hezekiah. It could cure snake-bite. This is an ancient symbol of healing, the caduceus being found from 4000 BCE. Many bronze serpents have been excavated from Middle and Late Bronze Age digs in Israel
Urim and Thummim	Exodus 28:30	A form of divination \n Used in the casting of lots by the high priest
Trial by ordeal	Numbers 5:11-31; Exodus 32:20	The suspect woman is to drink the water of bitterness (containing a curse) and if guilty will be magically affected by it[10]
Disease and infertility as punishment	passim	Disease (especially leprosy) and infertility (among women only) is implied to be divine retribution for not keeping the law

---

[10] *For comment on trial by ordeal see Chapter 10*

Glossary

Agunah (plural **Agunot**) – so called chained women, whose husbands either refuse to give a divorce, or have disappeared.

Akedah – the Binding of Isaac – Genesis 22.

Anthropomorphic - having human characteristics, e.g. anger, jealousy.

Apikoros – A Jewish term for an unbeliever, a heretic, usually used pejoratively. Derives from the Greek philosopher Epicurus.

Apocalyptic theology – the theology, probably starting in the 2nd century BCE book of Daniel that cosmic forces of evil are loose in the world, and a battle must be fought against them at the end of time. This strongly influenced Christianity.

Apophatic theology - describes God by saying what (s)he is not, e.g. God is unknowable, beyond the realm of speech or description.

Avidya – Hindu concept that suffering is a result of human failure to see things as they really are.

Bavli – The Babylonian Talmud. This is also the version referred to if no distinction is made.

Beth Din (plural **Batei Din**) –Rabbinical Jewish Court(s) usually with three judges enforcing religious law.

Brahman – The absolute reality behind all things. The Hindu equivalent of god, which can be wearing any one of an infinite number of masks.

Brit – a covenant.

Brit Milah – Circumcision.

Bronze Age – From 3200 BCE to 1200 BCE.

Cataphatic theology – describes God by saying what he is like (by analogy), e.g. God is a shepherd.

Dayan (plural **dayanim**) – Rabbinic judge in a Beth Din. *(q.v.)*

Deism – Belief in a God that is not that of revealed religion, and that does not intervene in human affairs.

Deontological – Philosophy that the moral content of an action is independent of its consequences.

Doxology – prayers praising God, flattering and complimenting him.

Dualism – belief in the existence of both good and evil supernatural beings

Enuma Elish – the Mesopotamian creation epic poem.

Eschatology – dealing with the end of days; how the world will end.

Eruv – an artificial boundary, encircling an area that allows religious Jews exemption from certain commandments.

Gemarra – Commentary (via discussion and debate) on the *Mishnah*, the work of the Amoraim in the 3rd to 5th centuries CE.

Gematria – numerology. The practice of assigning numerical values to words (derived from the fact that every Hebrew letter also has a numerical value) and finding 'meanings' from the resulting numbers.

Get – a Jewish bill of divorce.

Gilgamesh – A real king of Uruk, approx. 2600 BCE, about whom an epic tale developed.

Gilgul – reincarnation.

Gnostic – a religious philosophy that stressed the importance of *gnosis* or (usually secret) redeeming knowledge, and distinguished between the wholly spiritual supreme God and the so called demiurge (i.e. the Jewish and Christian God) who is responsible for matter and evil.

Halitzah – a ceremony performed as a symbolic act to declare unwillingness to perform Yibbum *(q.v.)* or levirate marriage.

Halachah – Jewish law. A rabbinical legal rule.

Haredi (plural **Haredim**) – ultra-Orthodox Jew (literally one who 'trembles' before God).

Hasidism - Jewish mystical movement founded in 18th century Eastern Europe by Baal Shem Tov. Against Talmudic learning, he maintained that God's presence was in all of one's surroundings and one should serve God in every word and deed.

Hermeneutics – the study and interpretation of sacred texts.

Immanent – (of God). Present in all things. cf. *transcendent (q.v.)*

Iron Age – From 1200 BCE to the Classical Age beginning 332 BCE.

Kaddish – A doxology *(q.v.)* Prayer in the synagogue service and in a different version the prayer said by the bereaved.

Kelipot – Kabbalistic concept. Shells or husks left after creation containing waste products and evil.

Khisab al Jumal – The Islamic equivalent of Gematria *(q.v.)*

Kiddush ha'Shem - Sanctification of God's name by becoming a martyr rather than compromising on one's beliefs.

Levirate marriage – where a man marries his brother's childless widow, in order to continue his brother's line.

Logos – the rational, analytic and scientific thought that enables human beings to function well practically in the world cf. myth(os) p.32

Ma'aseh Bereshit – mystical speculation on the creation story.

Ma'aseh merkavah – mystical speculation on Ezekiel's throne chariot.

Mamzer (plural **mamzerim**) – Colloquially a *bastard*, born of a forbidden relationship. A mamzer cannot marry freely within the Jewish Community. Descendents of a *mamzer* remain *mamzerim* forever.

Masorti – Conservative (Judaism)

Matzah – Unleavened bread eaten by Jews during the Passover festival.

Maya – (Sanskrit) In Hinduism an illusion that one must see through in order to achieve liberation from the endless cycle of reincarnation.

Mechitza – A partition or division separating the genders in orthodox synagogues etc.

Messiah – (in Judaism) an anointed king who will lead the Jews back to the land of Israel and establish justice in the world.

Mezuzah (plural **mezuzot**)– A capsule containing a scroll with various writings affixed to the doorposts of Jewish houses.

Midrash – exegesis and interpretation of biblical texts by means of stories that fill in the gaps.

Minyan – a quorum of 10 men necessary to perform certain rituals.

Mishnah – The Oral Law, the first part of the Talmud, compiled by rabbis known as the Tannaim up to around 200 CE.

Mitzvah (plural **mitzvot**) – A Jewish religious commandment. Also has the connotation of a good deed.

Monism – considers that all is one 'substance'. There is no fundamental separation between the physical universe and god/s.

Monolatry – the worship of and exclusive loyalty to one chief god, while acknowledging the existence of other gods

Pietism – a devotion (often excessive) to a deity or deities and the observance of religious rules and principles in everyday life

Pilpul – traditional method of Talmud study in *yeshivot*. Uses intense textual analysis and debate.

Pirke avot – A *mishnah* tractate. Ethical sayings of the early rabbis.

Rebbe – the spiritual leader of a Hassidic community.

Sanhedrin – an assembly of judges, effectively a High or Supreme Jewish Court.

Sefer Torah – the scroll of the law (Five books of Moses).

Shabbat – the Sabbath.

Sheol – the underworld. The lowest tier of the 3 tiered biblical cosmology. Traditionally a land of destruction, forgetfulness and silence

Shiva – A Hindu God, combining the Creator and destroyer.

Shiva Nataraja – Lord of the Dance, symbol of the cycle of life.

Shivah – the (Jewish) week of mourning after someone dies.

Shoah – the term most acceptable among Jews for the Nazi Holocaust.

Siddur – the Jewish prayer book.

Stele – An ancient upright stone erected for a purpose and usually inscribed.

Syncretism - the development of one religious practice on the back of another. The copying of ideas between religions.

Talmud – *Mishnah (q.v.)* and *Gemarra (q.v.)* together make up the Talmud, along with later commentaries.

Tanach – The Hebrew Bible, equivalent to (but not exactly the same as) the Christian Old Testament. The word is an acronym for Torah, *Nevi'im, Ketuvim* – the three sections of Torah (Pentateuch), Prophets and other Writings.

Tannaim – The rabbis who compiled the *Mishnah (q.v.)* up to around 200 CE.

Tanya – (also known as *Likutei Amarim*). The central text of Chabad (Lubavitch) Hasidism.

Tao – (Chinese religion / philosophy): the way and order of the universe.

Teraphim – household gods.

Theism – posits that a god or gods exist separately from the universe.

Theodicy – The reconciliation of the existence of a just powerful God and the presence of evil.

Tiamat – In Babylonian mythology, the sea - a monstrous embodiment of primordial chaos.

Tikkun olam – literally 'repairing the world' – the Jewish concept of helping other people (of all backgrounds) and improving their lives.

Torah min hashamayim – literally Torah from the heavens – the concept that the entire Torah was dictated verbatim by God to Moses at Sinai.

Transcendent – (of God) Remote, above and outside our daily world. cf. *immanent (q.v.)*

Trefe – Ritually unclean – forbidden

Yerushalmi – The Jerusalem Talmud.

Yeshiva (plural **yeshivot**) – Jewish religious seminary usually for boys.

Yibbum – Levirate marriage - marrying one's brother's widow.

Bibliography

Albright, W.F. *The Archæology of Palestine.* Pelican 1949

Alter, Robert & Kermode, Frank. *A Literary Guide to the Bible.* William Collins 1987

Anderson, R.T. & Giles, T. *The Keepers.* Hendrickson 2002

Armstrong, Karen. *Muhammed.* Victor Gollancz 1991
  A History of God. Heinemann 1993
  A Short History of Myth. Canongate 2005
  The Great Transformation. Atlantic Books 2006
  The Bible: The Biography. Atlantic Books 2007

Baigent, Michael & Leigh, Richard. *The Elixir & the Stone.* Random House 1997
  The Inquisition. Viking 1999

Baring & Cashford. *The Myth of the Goddess.* Arkana 1991

Bickerman, Elias J. *The Maccabees.* Schocken Books 1947
  The Jews in the Greek Age. Harvard U.P. 1988

Blackburn, Simon. *Plato's Republic – A Biography.* Atlantic Books 2006

Bloom, Howard. *The Lucifer Principle.* Atlantic Monthly Press 1999

Boyer, Pascal. *Religion Explained.* Heinemann 2001

Buber, Martin. *Tales of the Hasidim.* Schocken 1947

Campbell, Joseph. *The Power of Myth.* Doubleday 1988
  The Hero with a Thousand Faces. Princeton 1949
  Myths to Live By. Penguin 1972
  The Masks of God. Viking Penguin 1959

Ceram, C.W. *The Secret of the Hittites.* Alfred A Knopf 1955

Cohen, A A & Mendes-Flohr, P. *Contemporary Jewish Religious Thought.* Free Press 1988

Cohn, Norman. *The Pursuit of the Millenium.* Harper Torchbooks 1961
  Cosmos, Chaos and the World to Come. Yale U. P. 1993

Cornfeld, Gaalyah & Freedman, David Noel. *Archæology of the Bible: Book by Book.* Harper & Row 1976

Cross, Frank Moore. *Canaanite Myth and Hebrew Epic.* Harvard U.P. 1973

Dawkins, Richard. *The Blind Watchmaker.* Longman 1986
  The God Delusion. Bantam Press 2006

Dennett, Daniel C. *Breaking the Spell.* Penguin 2006

Dever, William G. *Who Were the Early Israelites and Where Did They Come From.* Erdmans 2003

Dostoevsky, Fyodor. *The Brothers Karamazov*

Durkheim, Émile. *The Elementary Forms of Religious Life* (1912) Translation Carol Cosman. Oxford 2001

Eliade, Mircea. *The Sacred and the Profane.* Harvest, San Diego 1957

Ehrman, Bart D. *God's problem.* Harper One 2008

Faber, M.D. *The Psychological Roots of Religious Belief.* Prometheus 2004

Festinger, L& Riecken, H & Schachter, S. *When Prophecy Fails.* Harper Torchbooks 1964

Fishof, Iris. *Written in the Stars. Art and Symbolism of the Zodiac.* Israel Museum 2001

Finkelstein, Israel & Neil Asher Silberman. *The Bible Unearthed.* Free Press 2001 *David and Solomon.* Free Press 2006

Fox, Robin Lane. *Pagans and Christians.* Viking 1986

Friedman, Andrew N. & Eugene d'Aquili. *Why God won't go away: Brain Science & the Biology of Belief.* Ballantine 2001

Friedman, Richard Elliott. *Who Wrote the Bible?* Jonathan Cape 1988 *The Bible with Sources Revealed.* Harper 2003

Frankl, Viktor. *Man's Search for Meaning.* Beacon Press 1959

Glatzer, Nahum N. *The Dimensions of Job.* Schocken Books 1969

Goodenough, E. R. *Jewish Symbols in the Greco-Roman Period.* Princeton U.P. 1953

Harbour, Daniel. *An Intelligent person's guide to Atheism.* Duckworth 2001

Harris, Sam. *The End of Faith.* Norton 2004

Harris, Solomon N., *From Judaism to Jewishness.* Kavim, Tel Aviv. 2007

Heschel, Abraham Joshua. *Man is not Alone. A Philosophy of Religion.* Harper Torchbooks 1951

Hitchens, Christopher. *The Portable Atheist.* Da Capo Press 2007

Holloway, Richard. *Godless Morality.* Canongate 1999

Hopkins, Keith. *A World full of Gods.* Weidenfeld & Nicholson 1999

Hume, David. *The Natural History of Religion.* 1757. Available online at http://www.philosophyofreligion.info/humedcnr.html

Ingersoll, Robert G. *The Gods.* 1872. Available online at http://www.infidels.org/library/historical/robert_ingersoll/gods.html

Insoll, Timothy. *Archæology, Ritual, Religion.* Routledge 2004

Jacobs, Rabbi Louis. *A Tree of Life.* Littman Library 1984

Jewish Study Bible, The. Oxford University Press 2004

Johnson, Paul. *The History of the Jews.* Weidenfeld & Nicolson 1987

Josephus. *The Antiquities of the Jews.* *The Jewish War.*

Josipovici, Gabriel. *The Book of God.* Yale U.P. 1988

Jung, Carl. *Man and his Symbols.* Aldus Books 1964

Kant, Immanuel. *On the failure of all Attempted Philosophical Theodicies.* 1791

Kaplan, Aryeh. *Sefer Yezirah: The Book of Creation.* Jason Aronson 1995

Karpin, Michael & Friedman, Ina. *Murder in the Name of God* Metropolitan Books, New York 1998

Kenyon, Kathleen M. *Digging up Jerusalem.* Ernest Benn 1974

Khayyam, Omar. *The Ruba'iyat of Omar Khayyam.* 1120. Available online at http://classics.mit.edu/Khayyam/rubaiyat.html

Knohl, Israel. *The Divine Symphony.* JPS 200

Kriwaczek, Paul. *In Search of Zarathustra.* Weidenfeld & Nicolson 2002

Kugel, James L. *How to Read the Bible: A Guide to Scripture, Then and Now.* Free Press 2007

Leigh, Richard. *Mythic Logic* in *Erceldoune & other stories*. Egoetia Press 2006

Levi, Primo *If this is a Man?* Orion Press 1960
  The Drowned and the Saved. Michael Joseph 1988

Levy, Thomas E. *The Archæology of Society in the Holy Land*. Leicester U.P. 1995

Lincoln, Bruce. *Theorising Myth*. University of Chicago Press 1999

Maccoby, Hyam. *Revolution in Judea*. Ocean Books 1973
  Judaism in the First Century. Sheldon Press 1989
  Paul and Hellenism. SCM Press 1991

Maimonides, Moses. *Dalalat al-Hairin - Guide for the Perplexed* 1186

Mallowan, M.E.L. *Early Mesopotamia and Iran*. Thames & Hudson 1965

Markoe, Glenn E. *The Phoenicians*. British Museum Press 2000

Maringer, Johannes. *Gods of Prehistoric Man*. Weidenfeld & Nicolson 1960

Meek, Theophilus. *Hebrew origins*. Harper Torchbooks 1960

Mehr, Farhang. *The Zoroastrian Tradition*. Element 1991

Miles, Jack. *God: A Biography*. Simon & Schuster 1995

Milgram, Stanley. *Obedience to Authority*. Harper Collins 1974

Murdoch, Iris. *Metaphysics as a Guide to Morals*. Chatto and Windus 1992

Otto, Rudolf. *The Idea of the Holy*. 1923

Park, David. *The Grand Contraption*. Princeton 2005

Patai, Rafael. *The Hebrew Goddess*. Wayne State Univ. Press 1990

Pritchard, James B. *The Ancient Near East. Volume 1* Princeton U P. 1958

Rosenthal, Gilbert S. *What can a Modern Jew Believe?* Wipf & Stock 2007

Roux, George. *Ancient Iraq*. George Allen & Unwin 1964

Rushdie, Salman. *Is Nothing Sacred?* 1990 in *Imaginary Homelands* Granta Press 1991

Russell, Jeffrey Burton. *The Devil*. Cornell Univ. Press 1977

Scheindlin, Raymond P. *The Book of Job*. W. W. Norton 1998

Scholem, Gershom. *Kabbalah*. Keter, Jerusalem 1974

Schneur Zalman, Rabbi of Liady. *Tanya (Likutei Amarim)*. available online at:
  http://www.chabad.org/library/article_cdo/aid/6239/ jewish/Likutei-Amarim.htm

Stark, Rodney. *One True God*. Princeton Univ. Press 2001

Stoyanov, Yuri. *The Hidden Tradition in Europe*. Arkana 1994

Thomas, D. Winton. *Documents from Old Testament Times*. Thomas Nelson 1962

Thompson, Thomas. *The Mythic Past*. Jonathan Cape 1999

Watts, Alan. *Myth and Religion*. Eden Grove Editions, London 1995

Wilson, Ian. *The Exodus Enigma*. Weidenfeld & Nicolson 1985

Yamauchi, Edwin M. *Persia and the Bible*. Baker 1990

Young, Dudley. *Origins of the Sacred*. Harper 1992

Zimbardo, Philip G. *Stanford Prison Experiment*. Zimbardo Inc. 1972

Index